HELL AND HAZARD

Also by Henry Blyth

THE POCKET VENUS

OLD Q
The Rake of Piccadilly

HELL AND HAZARD

or

William Crockford
versus
the Gentlemen of England

HENRY BLYTH

WEIDENFELD AND NICOLSON
5 Winsley Street London W1

For N, Jonquil and Michael

SBN 297 17769 9

Printed in Great Britain
by Ebenezer Baylis & Son, Ltd.
The Trinity Press, Worcester, and London

Contents

Illustrations

[*Between pages* 80 *and* 81]

Foreword

Hell and Hazard completes a trilogy on the subject of gambling and dissipation in the 18th and 19th centuries which I began with *The Pocket Venus* and followed with *Old Q*. Gambling and dissipation are social evils from which those who enjoy wealth and privilege are particularly prone to suffer; they are evils born out of idleness, and the young and temperamentally unstable can be destroyed by them.

The Pocket Venus described the mid-Victorian world of the turf, and told the story of Harry Hastings, the 4th and last Marquis of Hastings, who was ruined by Hermit's Derby in 1867 and died a year later, a broken old man of 26. William Douglas, 4th and last Duke of Queensbury, whose story I told in *Old Q*, lived in the Georgian and not the Victorian age and was an altogether different personality. He was a dedicated gambler, but on the whole a shrewd and calculating one, and although he was a dedicated seducer, he was also calculating in his many amours. His background was that of wild extravagance and foolhardy wagering amongst the young bucks of Society, but he himself remained aloof and scornful of all such foolish excesses. His life was dedicated both to self-indulgence and to self-preservation.

Now, in *Hell and Hazard*, I have set out to look at Georgian and early Victorian Society from the other side of the fence – that is to say from the professional bookmaker's angle; and I have chosen as my central character William Crockford, who founded Crockford's Club in St James's Street in 1828 and was given the title of 'The Father of Hell and Hazard'. Crockford enjoyed none of the advantages of Harry Hastings or William Douglas. He was the son of a fishmonger in Temple Bar, and was reared on the fringes of some of the worst slums in London (and London slums in the 18th and 19th centuries were as bad as any in Europe). He was a confirmed gambler, but he was also a professional; and he chose the career of bookmaker and gambling club proprietor because it was for him the only road to great wealth and a position in Society. When he resigned from the management of his club in 1840 it was said of him that he retired 'much as an Indian Chief retires from a hunting country where there is not game enough left for his tribe'. He had by then ruined a generation of upper-class young Englishmen.

Uncontrolled gambling is a vice of which historians have been well aware, but which for the most part they have not examined in much detail. They have seen it as a disease – which of course it is – but they have not fully understood either the causes or the symptoms, and this is because gambling is not a subject which is easily comprehended by those who are not them-selves gamblers. Many of the young aristocrats who destroyed themselves in the 18th and 19th centuries – and Harry Hastings was a typical example – were compulsive gamblers. This is a subject which has now come within the province of the profes-sional psychiatrist, and it is best that a layman such as myself should not venture too far into this very complicated field of mental instability. But one must yet be aware of its existence, and for those of my readers who know little about gambling, I would like to outline briefly my own views on the compulsive urge towards self-destruction which it can arouse.

I myself believe that the gambling mania, and much of the wild and dissolute behaviour of the Restoration, Regency and early Victorian rakes, were the outcome of lack of purpose in the lives of young men who suffered from too much leisure and too much wealth, with too little opportunity to prove their manhood. These young men – some of them gifted with intelli-gence, wit and even brilliance – were usually bored, often restless, frequently antisocial in their outlook, and sometimes disillusioned. Moreover feminine influences in general, and maternal ones in particular, were often excessive in their lives, especially during the 18th century, an era in which women played a prominent part. I accept the psychiatrists' view that gambling and sex are often related, and that excessive participation in either is often the outcome of frustration rather than of avarice or sensuality. And here I would like to emphasise a point that is not always understood by non-gamblers; this is that the compulsive gambler is not in search of gain, but only of stimulation. The thrill comes from the moment of uncertainty, not from the moment of success.

I have been handicapped in my biography of William Crockford, as I was in that of Harry Hastings and William Douglas, by knowing too little about the early, formative years. Character is usually formed in childhood, and certainly during youth, and it is important to any biographer to know something of what these early influences were, especially the parental influences and the influences of the background in early life. But where one knows little, one must seek to make deductions, and it is an interesting point that each of the three – Harry Hastings, William Douglas and William Crockford – lost his father at an early age.

'Solitary trees, if they grow at all, grow strong; and a boy deprived of a father's care often develops, if he escapes the perils of youth, an independence and vigour of thought.' The words are those of the young Winston Churchill, and the point is well made. Harry Hastings did not escape 'the perils of youth', and they brought about his downfall; but both William Douglas and William Crockford survived them and developed independence and vigour of thought, and it enabled each of them to survive into a prosperous old age. This is not to say that the character of either was improved by this solitariness in youth. It is merely to record that as the result of it each became determined, cynical and ambitious. Otherwise they had little in common, for one was born with a ready entry into London Society and the other had to fight his way up the ladder in order to achieve a comparable status. But for both, the end was the same. One died, immensely rich, in Piccadilly; the other died, immensely rich, in Carlton House Terrace; and few enough tears were shed about either at his passing, for hedonists are seldom mourned.

Now that my trilogy is completed, I am left with mixed feelings about the Georgian and Victorian eras – feelings which I did not expect to experience when I set out on my task. It is the custom today to belittle the Victorians, and to laugh at their rigid codes of behaviour. There can be no doubt that much of this criticism is justified, but in the world of sport, and above all in the sphere of sportsmanship, I learnt that there is something to be said for this Victorian code of gentlemanly behaviour. Gentlemen of the Georgian era were not sportsmen; they lied and cheated outrageously, and they complained bitterly when they lost. Certainly the celebrated English *sang froid* was a product of Victorianism, and so was Victorian class consciousness and snobbishness. But the Georgian upper classes were not only quite happy to fraternise with the riff-raff of the gambling world, they were also quite happy to behave as they did, and even an aristocrat would stoop to the lowest forms of trickery and downright dishonesty such as were practised by the rogues who infested Newmarket Heath.

Thus the world of William Crockford became the world of deceit and 'the double-dodge', and the depths which this criminality finally reached were revealed by the events of the Derby of 1844 and by the legal enquiry which followed it. After this, leaders of turf and gambling reform such as Admiral Rous and Lord George Bentinck succeeded in giving the word 'sportsmanship' an honourable meaning. The Victorian sportsmen who followed still bet heavily, but they ceased to associate with rogues, and they learnt to win with dignity and to lose without resentment or complaint.

The gentleman-sportsman now became a figure who was universally admired, and, for a time, the Victorian era created the myth of the all-conquering amateur, and of the gifted aristocrat who could out-ride, out-box and out-stay the seasoned professionals. For a time this myth became a reality. An Earl of Lonsdale could boast – or rather could casually concede – that he had beaten the champion heavyweight boxer of the world; an Indian prince batted more successfully and infinitely more gracefully than any professional cricketer in England or Australia; and at Aintree the rider of the Grand National winner was one year a Balkan count and the next an English lord, who was not only an officer in the Grenadier Guards but also an M.F.H.

Those days have gone, but even during this golden era of amateurism there was one sphere in which the ruthless professional always triumphed over the gay Corinthian, and this was the sphere of gambling. William Crockford, the father of modern bookmaking, proved this conclusively during his career, and it has been proved again and again since Crockford's Club closed its doors and ceased to be the very centre of the fashionable world of gentlemen and sportsmen of the early-Victorian period. The bookmakers and the club proprietors of today all trace their professional ancestry, whether they realise it or not, from the man who opened this famous club in St James's Street in 1828. It was Crockford who hunted the coroneted game as they browsed in their natural habitat, and it was Crockford who destroyed them against a background of gilded splendour and elegant luxury. Seldom has the hunted gone more willingly to the slaughter, or the hunter prosecuted a more bloodless, yet more inevitable, attack. But at least it can be argued that 'Crocky' was humane, for the prey were never brought down until their stomachs had been filled with the choicest foods and the very best champagne, and all at the hunter's expense.

The Victorian turf was not reformed overnight, nor were the young gamesters quickly weaned from their follies and extravagances. Indeed the most alarming aspect of the mid-Victorian turf was not that it was corrupt but rather that it continued to encourage the most extravagant wagering. Gamblers of today have no conception of how heavy the betting was in the Hastings era. The Queen was appalled by it, and she had every reason to be. At a time when the poor were existing on wages that could be counted in shillings per week rather than pounds, and women could be employed at a penny an hour in the Welsh coal-mines, Harry Hastings lost more than one hundred thousand pounds in the two-and-a-half minutes in which it took to run the Derby. This was a shocking state of inequality; and it was shocking, too, that young men should remain so unconscious of it. No such inequality exists today; and the era of wagering 'deep' has long since past. The pound, in Harry Hastings' day, was worth at least ten times what it is today, and yet there is scarcely a backer on the turf now who would dare risk ten thousand on a single bet. That, by Harry's standards, would be a modest wager; and was it not said of the dashing Colonel Mellish in the Crockford era that he never opened his mouth under £500.

A further aspect of the gambling which took place during the Crockford era and the early Victorian period was the manner in which the gaming laws were flouted. Quite stringent gaming laws existed, but they could be easily circumvented, and the rich could always get round them. Similar problems exist today, but here again the time has passed when the rich man could bet with impunity on credit, whilst the poor man – betting with ready money with his street bookmaker – was breaking the law.

No doubt 'Crocky' and his cronies would smile indulgently on our modest bets, our careful, middle-class way of life and our stereotyped vices. How respectable is St James's Street today! The gambling hells have long since disappeared and so have the brothels. The quiet of the night is no longer destroyed 'by the rattling of dice and jingling of money, intermingled with the most horrible imprecations'.

We live in an age when gambling is less obsessive, and dissipation less ruinous (and, I suspect, less imaginative). More important still is the fact that we live in an age that is less destructive and less cruel. The age of Georgian brutality is dead – that era of the cudgel and the whip. Criminals are no longer hanged in public, as they were in Crockford's time, bulls and bears are no longer baited as a form of sport, and lunatics are no longer jeered at as a form of sabbath entertainment for the family. But many of the best things still survive. There is still racing across the flat expanse of Newmarket Heath, as there has been since Roman times, and the Derby is still run at Epsom, its outcome dependent on courage and artistry.

'Betting,' wrote 'The Druid' in his obituary notice on Harry Hastings, 'is said to be the touchstone of the Englishman's sincerity.' There has never been a better sporting writer than 'The Druid', and if the phrase seems fulsome to modern ears, it yet contains some truth. Life itself is a gamble, in which a man is dealt either a good or bad hand, and character is strengthened by resolution in the face of adversity. Antipathy to all forms of gambling is the outcome of caution, a quality that is not altogether admirable, least of all in the young. I am not therefore unduly depressed by the fact that Englishmen still continue to back horses, or even to play roulette, for gambling is like drinking: it only becomes an evil when is it uncontrolled.

With this observation I am happy to close my trilogy, and the reader is left to form his own opinions.

TWO WORLDS
Piccadilly and Temple Bar

In this country all is contrast – contrast between wealth the most enormous and poverty the most wretched.

Thus wrote Greville in his diary. The truth of this observation provides one of the keys to a full understanding of the social history of England during the 18th and 19th centuries.

Man is a product of his environment. To understand something of *why* an adult behaves, the way he does, it is necessary to know something of his parentage, his childhood and his environment. The sins of the fathers are not inherited by the offspring. This, at least, we know. But if a child is born into a way of life that gives him either too much of everything, whether it be of wealth or adoration, or else too little of everything, whether this takes the form of physical or moral starvation, then his character will usually suffer. The damage done in childhood and youth may not be irreparable, but it is likely to be considerable.

William Crockford was born amidst poverty at Temple Bar. He died in luxury at Carlton House Terrace, surrounded by wealth. His education was negligible. That of his children was excellent. He sent his sons to Harrow and to Oxford or to Cambridge. One of them became a vicar in Cornwall. The contrast in *their* lives was not great. They were born into wealth, and only achieved the transformation from notoriety to respectability. But William Crockford himself rose from the gutter and understood the exact meaning of the contrast to which Greville referred. He was a cockney, born within the sound of Bow Bells. But since so little is known about his childhood and upbringing, his biographer can only assess the man as he is to be seen in the full opulence of his later life, and then work backwards from the character of the man that is thus apparent. It is not an attractive character, for he was a hard man of business, and his business was that of exploiting the rich. To understand *why* he was what he was, the contrast that existed in his life must be understood.

The contrast between the rich and the poor in 18th- and 19th-century England was generally accepted as inevitable. The Englishman lived in an era that was harsh and cruel, and he had become harsh and cruel himself. Disease often made life intolerable for him whether he was rich or poor, crime was on his doorstep whether he was rich or poor, and so was the retribution visited upon the criminal. Piccadilly might become the heart of the fashionable world, Mayfair the most desirable of residential centres, but for most of the 18th century the gallows still stood close to them, at the top of Park Lane, and he could not travel any distance by coach or on horseback without seeing the bodies of highwaymen swinging from gallows erected on the public heaths or at cross-roads along his path.

There were those who tried to arouse the Englishman's conscience about the squalor and suffering that existed side by side with luxury and wealth, and about the terrible injustices of life, but this lesson took long to comprehend. Hogarth depicted the ugliness of 18th-century life with a savage, yet almost detached, assessment. But even he did not condemn the state of affairs so much as present it as something that existed. Man, rich or poor, young or old, was a cruel, vain and heartless creature; puffed up with pride and avarice when rich and influential, made foul by vice and dishonesty when poor. He was either fat, gross and coarse, or lean, filthy and cringing. How Hogarth seemed to despise humanity!

During the Industrial Revolution the contrast between rich and poor was at its worst in the industrial north, but always, throughout both the 18th and 19th centuries, it was evident in London. The distance between St James's Street and Temple Bar, at the entrance to Fleet Street, is less than two miles; from Piccadilly Circus to Drury Lane not very much over a mile. These distances were all that separated grandeur from degradation, and a life of elegance and luxury from a life that was not living, but just existing, and homes that were not houses but merely hovels.

A feature of London's West End in the 18th century, and particularly of Piccadilly, was that it was all so bright and clean and new. The houses were new, the paintwork was bright and gay, the gardens with their flowers were magnificent, and the inhabitants of these homes – the elegant men and beautiful animated women – matched their surroundings and added further colour to the scene. All around, too, were the pleasant fields and meadows and streams of London's green belt, so that the inhabitant of Mayfair could enjoy as much peace and rural solitude as he could at his country seat. The young rake, lounging in his club in St James's Street, rightly felt himself in the heart of sophisticated Society and a sophisticated town; yet a quarter-of-an-hour's brisk stroll could bring him to the delights of rural England. 'Along the north and west,' Hugh Phillips has written in his history of Mid-Georgian London, 'gentlemen's mansions overlooked the country. Grazing meadows ended at their back doors.'

And what mansions they were! How proud, how stately and even – in the case of Devonshire House – how remote, set back in lordly aloofness from the Mayfair streets and half-hidden behind high walls. The pride of Mayfair was its three squares – Grosvenor Square, Hanover Square and Berkeley Square; and a roll-call of those who had lived in these squares during the 18th and 19th centuries would have included many of the most illustrious names in the English peerage and in London Society.

The move westwards into the rural atmosphere of Hyde Park gained a steady impetus during the latter part of the 18th century, and Mayfair became truly magnificent once its amenities had been improved. By the end of the century the public executions at Tyburn had been transferred to Newgate, the dreadful processions down Oxford Street on hanging days were ended, and Oxford Street itself was gradually changed from a narrow, muddy cart-track pitted with holes and smelling evilly from its open drains into what was instead a reasonable (though still by no means fashionable) thoroughfare.

It had been Lord Chesterfield who had pioneered the 'West End' by building 'a most superb and magnificent edifice' on open land to the north-west of Shepherd Market in the middle of the century. At much the same time Crewe House sprang up in Curzon Street, opposite the Market, and although it was only a modest affair in comparison, having but a paltry eighteen bedrooms (which made entertaining on any scale impracticable), it also lent tone to the district. It was certainly the smallest of the eight great mansions that so richly adorned 18th-century Mayfair. The others were Chesterfield House, Devonshire House, Londonderry House, Dorchester House, Grosvenor House, Lansdowne House and Apsley House. The last named, which was built by Lord Apsley, became famous later by its designation of 'No. 1 London' when the great Duke of Wellington took up residence there.

Apsley House was at the south-western extremity of Piccadilly, hard by the turnpike which marked the end of the street. From his windows Lord Apsley had a magnificent view up Piccadilly to the walls which surrounded Devonshire House, which flanked the western side of Berkeley Street. Here it was that Charles Fox's Duchess, the exquisite Georgiana, had her famous boudoir draped in blue and silver – a room so sacred to her memory that long after her death, and long after the whole house had been altered and redecorated, it remained exactly as it had been in her prime, when all fashionable London had been at her dainty feet.

Further eastwards up Piccadilly, and virtually on the fringes of it, was Burlington House, a hundred yards or so beyond the entrance to St James's Street, which in its turn had St James's Palace at its southern extremity. St James's Street was the home of London's two most select clubs – White's on the south-eastern side and Brooks's opposite – together with several well-appointed shops which were much patronised by the young rakes.

Eastwards from St James's Palace ran Pall Mall, which housed many of the wealthiest, if not necessarily the most high-born, of the members of Society. The Palace itself was not imposing. It was a very modest affair compared with the immense and highly ornate homes of the Bourbons at Versailles and the Hapsburgs at Schönbrunn. Indeed it was even put somewhat in the shade by the magnificence of some of the mansions in Pall Mall. There had been a time, during the reign of Charles I, when this street had been used by the well-to-do as a court for playing the popular

4

French game of *paille-maille*, which was a kind of croquet and very fashionable as a sport, although it was to be noted that some of the players, less able to get their tongues round the French pronunciation than they should have been, were in the habit of referring to it rather vulgarly as 'Pell Mell'. (Today this same pronunciation is taken as evidence of good breeding.)

Adjacent to the Palace, and standing at the corner of Pall Mall, was Marlborough House, which Wren had designed at vast cost for the Duchess of Marlborough. It, too, had a beautiful garden, which gave on to the Mall. The Mall itself was a noble double avenue of splendid trees which led from Buckingham House at its western extremity to Whitehall at its eastern, and it also owed its name to *paille-maille*, for the 'Mall' as it came to be known was called after the mallet used in the game. The Mall was the great meeting place for London Society in the 18th century, just as 'The Ladies' Mile' in Hyde Park was for Victorian Society a hundred years later. On a fine summer evening everyone who was anyone in Society paraded slowly up and down, the women eyeing each other's dresses and the men eyeing the women's figures which these dresses only partially concealed. It was a great exchange for gossip, and here, as a contemporary writer noted, 'we see the ministers, the courtiers, the *petits maitres*, and the coquettes; here we learn the news of the day, and make our parties until it is time to dress for the Court or for dinner.'

Buckingham House, at the western end of the Mall, was another imposing mansion, which had been built by the Duke of Buckingham at the beginning of the 18th century and was later sold to George III as a future residence for Dowager Queens. (It did not become the sovereign's royal palace until 1837.)

The view from the windows of Buckingham House was as fine as any in London, down the long double avenue towards Whitehall and the Horse Guards' Parade, and with perhaps the finest London house of all, Carlton House, at its furthest extremity. Carlton House had been built by the first Lord Carlton at much the same time as Buckingham House, because it, too, enjoyed such a splendid view from its windows, up the Mall and over St James's Park. Towards the end of the century the Prince of Wales took up residence there, and made it into one of the most fashionable meeting-places of the day, where not only his intimate friends but also the leading politicians were able to congregate and discuss the affairs of State and ponder on the vexed problem of whether or not the King was incurably mad.

This, then, was the magic circle of fashionable London, embracing the cream of Society and including within it some of the most imposing mansions in any town in Europe. Here the rich and titled lived in luxury, elegance and ease. Their country houses were vast, and their town houses almost as large. Their retinues of servants were impressive, and included not only indoor staff but outdoor as well, since their town houses had large gardens and extensive stabling. Thus one of the great London mansions would be staffed by a small army of male servants consisting of up to a dozen liveried footmen, as well as butlers, chefs, valets, grooms, ostlers, gardeners, coachmen, chaisemen, postilions, page-boys, stable boys and often a negro slave or two, kept almost as a pet; whilst the female staff consisted of nearly as large a company of ladies' maids, housekeepers, cooks, kitchenmaids, dairy-maids, scullery-maids, housemaids, washerwomen, cleaners and seamstresses. One aristocrat kept three full-time pastry-cooks on his kitchen staff because he argued that a gentleman enjoyed nibbling a biscuit from time to time.

This was the way of life in Mayfair Society, and the great householders could not envisage any other. At a time when – as Johnson once observed to Boswell – a man could exist on six pounds a year, and live in comparative comfort on less than a pound a week, an aristocrat such as Lord Durham could remark that a gentleman might 'jog along' on an income of £40,000 a year, although the inference was that even this did not really amount to exceptional wealth. Yet a simple calculation reveals that this income of £40,000 could have supported more than six and a half thousand members of the poor each year, and could have saved more than twice that number from the threat of starvation.

The rich in their Mayfair mansions were surrounded by every form of luxury and elegance: their Adam staircases were broad and magnificent, their libraries filled with rare books, their walls hung with splendid paintings, and their furniture was made by

Chippendale, Sheraton and Hepplewhite. Their women-folk wore fabulous jewels. If, as collectors of valuable antiques, and the rare and the unusual, they developed some expensive hobby, then the cost of it was of small consideration, so that when the Duke of Devonshire took up botany, he was happy to send a special expedition to the East Indies to search for rare plants.

They were a convivial and hospitable clan, and they loved entertaining on a lavish scale. They could admire Lord Crewe's neat little house in Curzon Street, but although they found it delightful they were forced to ask themselves how he proposed to manage with only eighteen bedrooms, for they considered something nearer sixty to be essential.

They were rarely parsimonious and seldom ungenerous – indeed their acts of generosity were on the same liberal and expansive scale as the rest of their activities; but poverty they accepted as part of the universal pattern of life, and although they pitied the poor, the ardour of reformers such as Fielding and Coram often struck them as being unwise and unpractical.

Curiously enough they did not go out of their way to avoid contact with the poor, and it was fear of footpads and highwaymen which kept them off the meaner streets rather than the fear of the London mob. When their carriages had to be driven through the slums on the way to Covent Garden, or were brought to a halt in the mud and filth of some narrow side street (and such side streets were to be encountered in Mayfair as well as in the East End) they looked out on the ragged creatures which surrounded it with genuine sympathy and commiseration. This to them was but the way of Nature and of Life; for the poor would always be with them.

The London mob, although boisterous, bawdy and often uncontrolled, lacked the undercurrent of vicious resentment which was so soon to become apparent in the Paris mob across the Channel. But then, of course, the very rich and the very poor in England had certain things in common. They both loved gambling and they both loved sex, and this curious affinity existed into the Victorian era, when it was the middle classes who made enemies of both rich and poor.

Because they were neither disdainful nor inhumane, but

merely apathetic and unimaginative, the rich in London gave freely to charity and were often at pains to distribute *largesse* at appropriate seasons of the year; and they were also in the habit of rewarding faithful servants liberally, for they believed in *noblesse oblige*. Thus their consciences were eased, and indeed it has been for ever thus. Decent and humane people shut their eyes to the existence of human misery, and when they encounter it in their own walk of life they administer only a palliative, by giving money to charity; but not their minds and their efforts to tackling the problems of eliminating want.

This was the way of life in Mayfair, where Society lived in luxury. This was also the way of life among the rich City merchants who lived a quite separate existence in the City itself, east of the Strand, in their large houses in the shadow of St Paul's, around Cheapside, the Royal Exchange, at Charing Cross and Covent Garden.

What, in contrast, was the way of life in the slums which existed down by the stinking, dung-congested Thames? What was life along the Fleet River which led into it, which was also known as the Fleet Ditch because of the offal which filled it, so that the dead dogs and cats – and the occasional dead child or prostitute as well – brought its slimy flow to a standstill except when the winds and tides were high? What was the way of life in the darkened alleyways round Temple Bar, where the homeless slept huddled up in dank corners or lay in empty drain-pipes for shelter, and even those with homes had often no more than a freezing garret in which to lie, with the rain pouring in from the leaking roof; or a dank and evil-smelling cellar without sunlight and indeed without light of any sort, and certainly without fresh air, a commodity to which many of them remained unaccustomed, as they lived and worked in buildings which were without any form of ventilation?

What of the poor who clustered together in the infamous 'rookeries' at Whitechapel, around St Giles's Circus and off the Grays Inn Road – so called because these areas were hopelessly overcrowded and the inhabitants lived a fighting, noisy existence like rooks in a tree?

What of those who lived in the shadow of Newgate Prison, and who were constant witnesses of public executions, when men were hanged as a public spectacle, some screaming for mercy, some drunk and some insensible, while the crowd howled out imprecations and were stirred by some hideous blood-lust that often expressed itself in violence or sexual excess? And what of the inmates of this prison, rotting away in gaol until the day of their release, their bodies festering from the conditions under which they were housed, and their minds festering with misery and bitterness? Here human beings were incarcerated like animals in a cage, old lags with youthful first offenders, young men with vicious perverts and young girls with women who had been reduced to the final stages of degradation; dirty, half-naked and emaciated, some manacled by chains around ankles, waist and wrists. Some of them were half-starved, and others half-mad from the poison of gin, with children clinging to their tattered skirts and these same children in danger from all those about them, who would corrupt them whilst they were alive and tear the rags from off their skinny backs the moment that they were dead.

For the most part those who lived in poverty were without hope. They suffered their misery with astonishing stoicism, believed, as the rich believed, that poverty was all part of the order of things, and only tried to better their wretched conditions by acts of crime and violence – living for the day and un-mindful of the morrow, in the knowledge that for them life was indeed destined to be nasty, brutish and short.

This was the majority. But there were always a resolute few who were determined to extricate themselves from their place in the bottom of the pit by struggling upwards with unrelenting determination. They despised the weak and envied only the strong. They were often illiterate but they were always cunning, and they learnt to study human weaknesses and human stupidities, so that they could profit from the ignorance of others. On the whole they did not hate the rich, for this is one of the oddities of human nature; they only envied them, and determined to reach their level. But if they did not hate the rich, they certainly had no pity for them. This was the eternal rat race, in which the cleverest reached the top by climbing over others. And in their way they showed a certain consistency in their outlook, for they despised *all* who were weak, and so they pitied neither the rich whom they destroyed nor the poor from whose ranks they had risen.

The cleverest of them amassed wealth and some died happy in the knowledge that they had beaten the field. Their motto was a traditional one of success – 'there is no place for sentiment in business'. To this they added a private corollary of their own, that there is no place for it in human relationships either. This religion of hedonism had many disciples, but the high priest of them all was William Crockford.

It is frustrating for a biographer to be able to record no more than the year of his subject's birth, but this is the case with William Crockford. The year was 1775. That is all that is known for certain. But in view of the fact that when he died on 24 May 1844, his age was officially recorded as 69, he must have been born *before* 24 May 1775. No official record exists of his birth, and none was necessary at this period, for infants were coming into the world and leaving it again with too much frequency for any such records to be attempted. However there is a record in the Church of St Clement Danes, which was a few hundred yards from his birth-place, that he was baptised there on 12 February 1776, and was registered as the son of William Crockford and his wife, Mary Ann. One may hazard a guess that perhaps he was baptised on his first birthday, in which case he was born on 12 February 1775, but this is only a surmise.

Fortunately there is no doubt about the place of his birth, for he retained an affection for it throughout his life (it was one of the few affections that he revealed for anyone or anything); and by chance there are at least two pictures in existence of his birth-place. William Crockford was born, probably in the bedroom on the second storey, above his father's fish-shop, which stood hard against the north-west buttress of Temple Bar – that is to say he was born just outside the boundary of the City of London to which Temple Bar was the main gateway from the west.

The shop is clearly shown by the coloured drawing made of it by John Wykeham Archer to illustrate his book, *Vestiges of Old*

London, and is revealed as a sizeable three-storey building, obviously very old, with a frame of timber filled up with lath and plaster, and surmounted by a single gable. On its façade there was the inscription:

SHORT & SON
Late Creed
FISHMONGERS
ESTABLISHED in the
REIGN of KING HENRY the VIII

Clearly the name of Short and Son had some prestige, for otherwise William's father might have preferred the use of Crockford and Son; and no doubt the claim that the business had been founded in the reign of Henry VIII was genuine, which would make the building of Tudor origin and therefore more than 200 years old.

It was a bulk shop. This term was of Flemish origin, and referred not only to the open stall which stood in front of the shop, on which the merchandise was displayed, but also to the general stoutness, solidarity and indeed bulk of the premises, implying that this was a substantial business housed in a substantial building. Bulk shops were common in the district, and were remarkable for only one thing – the curious local tradition whereby the stall could be used as a bed by passers-by after the shop had been closed for the night and the merchandise cleared from it. The heavy canopy which stretched out from the front of the shop provided an excellent shelter from the rain, and the stall itself – although hard and very smelly – was preferable to a bench, and was well raised above the predatory nose of any stray dog or rat that might be searching the gutters for offal, and might be tempted to take a nip at any protruding finger or toe.

The local tradition went even further, however, for at Temple Bar not only were the beggars, vagrants, drunken roisterers or worn-out trollops permitted to sleep there, but also indigent poets and authors, who used to roost there in small literary swarms, not unlike the starlings and pigeons that roosted under the eaves of nearby St Paul's. Perhaps this literary flavour was imparted to the district by the nearness of Fleet Street, to which the Temple Bar gave access. Whatever the reason, the result was the same. Poets and writers dreamt away the summer nights on the stall beneath William's bedroom window, a reminder to him that those who lacked a hard, practical outlook to life were doomed to poverty and discomfort.

William Crockford was a materialist, and no doubt so was his father – a shadowy figure about whom almost nothing is known – and it seems unlikely that either of them looked upon Temple Bar as an historic place at which to be born or to live. Yet Temple Bar itself *was* an historic spot, and the gateway itself was haunted by the memories of those who had passed through it – and the memories, too, of those traitors whose heads had been impaled on long spikes above it, to spin in the wind and to rot away until they fell and were lost amongst the garbage and mud in the streets below. Some were retrieved by the children as playthings, and some by the more astute members of the community who realised that a famous head had a market value for wealthy collectors of *objets d'art*, if that be the right term to use.

Indeed the counterfeiting of heads, and the robbing of local graveyards for skulls which could later be passed off as genuine examples of aristocratic crania, had become quite a thriving little trade in the district at one time. But the trade had declined after the middle of the century, for the last head to be exhibited on the top of Temple Bar had been that of Simon, Lord Lovat, who had been executed along with other rebel lords on Tower Hill in 1747. Lord Lovat was also the last person to have been beheaded in England, and thereafter capital punishment in England consisted of being hanged by the neck at Tyburn or elsewhere until the criminal was dead – which was frequently quite a long time in view of the inefficiency of a length of rope and a gallows as compared with a wooden block and an axe.

William Crockford did not live to see any skulls rattling above his bedroom window on stormy nights, but he did not miss them by very much. They were still to be seen revolving in the wind only three years before his birth in 1775, when a good business was being carried out by those who hired out spy-glasses at a halfpenny a look; but the violent spring gales of 1772 blew the last skull down from the top of Temple Bar, leaving only the long, sharply pointed rods which stuck from the top of it as reminders of a traditional spectacle of old London.

What, one might ask, would have been the effect on the impressionable mind of a child who could look out of his nursery window and see such a grim sight? And the answer, in the 18th century, would have been that it had very little effect, for the gallows at Newgate and Tyburn provided an everyday glimpse of tortured bodies and rotting corpses, and the children of the period were all well accustomed to such sights as part of their daily life.

One writes of these things in an attempt to create the world into which Crockford was born and the surroundings in which he grew up; and it is not surprising that he grew up to be a person of harsh insensitivity and without sentiment. A study of his world suggests that it would have been remarkable had he grown up in any other way, for if he had been gentle, sensitive and considerate his surroundings would probably have destroyed him, since pity for the plight of others was not a quality that was developed in the young who lived around Temple Bar. They fought for survival, and the majority of them were beaten in this unequal struggle.

The place was sordid and ugly, and the people who passed back and forth through Temple Bar were coarse and ugly themselves. One of the most famous of them, and a man who bore a physical resemblance to William Crockford, was Boswell's Samuel Johnson, who died when William was a boy. Indeed Boswell's description of his mentor might well have applied to Crockford in later life. 'He is a man of dreadful appearance ... He is very slovenly in his dress and speaks with a most uncouth mouth.' This was the type the City bred. Men who lived in a tough and brutal age and were able to face up to it.

It must be understood that until the 18th century, and still to a certain extent today, the City of London was a quite separate entity from greater London to the west, which embraced Westminster, Whitehall, the royal palaces and the seat of government. This ancient City of London had for centuries been surrounded by its ancient walls, with access to it through its equally ancient gateways – at Aldgate, Moorgate, Ludgate, and Bishopsgate –

and even in the 18th century these gateways were closed at sunset, so that the old City seemed then to resume its seclusion, when it had sheltered from attack behind its walls – walls that the Romans had built more than a thousand years before.

Temple Bar itself divided the City from the West, and it divided Fleet Street from the Strand. It had been largely destroyed by the Great Fire of London and was rebuilt after it by Wren between 1669 and 1673, so when William Crockford was born it was little more than a hundred years old. The City of London, lying as it did on the banks of the Thames, had always been of great importance to the commerce and trade of England, which was increasing steadily throughout the 18th century. Westminster, too, and the social world outside the City walls, were also becoming increasingly important. And these two worlds – of trade and of fashion; of poverty and of elegance; of finance and of government – were separated from each other by Temple Bar. The world of Westminster ended with the Strand. The world of the City of London began with the start of Fleet Street.

Although both Westminster and the City of London lay along the banks of the Thames, their very attitude to this great 18th-century thoroughfare – a thoroughfare far more important to London's prosperity than any road – was markedly different. To those who lived in Mayfair the Thames provided a picturesque route to the rural delights of Chelsea and Richmond, but to those who lived in the City the Thames spelt only commerce and, stinking and dun-coloured though it was, it yet gave them their living and furnished the economic necessaries of their lives. Clerkenwell, Smithfield, Limehouse, and Whitechapel were thickly populated suburbs, just outside the City boundary. They were the homes of the working man and the breeding-ground of the London mob – that vociferous, violent and largely uncontrolled mass of humanity which lived in dirty, narrow and unlit alleyways beside the river and answered to no law, benefited by no charities, were untamed by any religion because they had no churches in their midst, and were mostly illiterate because they had no schools. Here was the home of the pickpocket, the thief, the footpad and the highwayman. Only those who were well-armed with weapons as well as courage ever ventured into this human jungle – unless, of course, they themselves belonged to the same breed of ruffian and cut-throat and were instantly recognisable as such, and this applied to William Crockford, who had been born almost amongst them.

Temple Bar joined Fleet Street to the Strand. Neither of them was a particularly salubrious thoroughfare, least of all after nightfall, but whereas the Strand ran westwards to the open spaces and wide streets of Whitehall, St Martin's-in-the-fields and St James's Park, Fleet Street ran eastwards to the Fleet Ditch, to St Paul's and on to Cheapside, the Royal Exchange and Whitechapel. Only the major streets in the City were cleaned or had any form of oil lighting, and the numberless minor streets and alleyways which led off them were narrow, dirty and dark even in daylight and formed a depository for every form of household refuse and rubbish. Sheds and shacks abounded, blocking the way, and half-starved mongrel dogs, mostly vicious and some mad, roamed about in search of food. Live bullocks were driven along by herdsmen and were a constant danger. Beggars were to be encountered everywhere, scavenging for scraps in the piles of rubbish and offal with eyes as sharp and stomachs as empty as the mongrel dogs with whom they were in competition.

The smell was appalling, especially in summer, and above all near the Thames or the Fleet Ditch, and to the stink from open drains, mud, filth, dead animals, horse and bullock manure was added that of the fish and meat which were exposed on open stalls along the length of the streets. Cattle were slaughtered on the premises of many a butcher's shop, so that rivers of blood flowed into the open drains and imparted a startling contrast to the otherwise unrelieved greyness of dirt and dung. And to the smell of blood was added the far worse smell from those traders engaged in side-lines to slaughtering – the gut-spinning, tripe-dressing, bone-boiling, tallow-melting and paunch-cooking in open vats.

But worst of all – and far more terrible than anything else – was the dreadful smell of putrefaction that rose from the graveyards of the poor. The wealthy City merchant was buried in his splendid lead-lined coffin, sunk deep into the ground, but the pauper's interment was in a wooden box or a sack in a shallow grave, often

after the body had been left waiting – and literally rotting, because of disease – in the tenement room in which he had died, and
surrounded still by the living, children as well as adults, who had
no means of rapid disposal of the corpse which lay in their midst.

The scene in slum churchyards of the 18th and 19th centuries
is almost too ghastly to contemplate, for the earth did actually
open up to reveal its dead; bloated and swollen limbs and faces
were to be glimpsed when coffins bulged and burst and the
nauseous gases of putrefaction were emitted. And always the
earth was impregnated with the decay of human remains, and
when the rains came yet more oozing, putrefying slime was
added to the Fleet Ditch and the waters of the Thames.

In St Paul's churchyard, under his splendid marble headstone
or in his spacious family vault, the City merchant slept undis-
turbed. But the paupers lay rotting side by side beneath the mud
and refuse in macabre confusion.

Westwards from Temple Bar ran the Strand, one of the most
famous and the most infamous of London's great thoroughfares.
At its eastern end, in Butcher's Row, it was little more than a slum,
where the meat was suspended for the flies to consume, and all
manner of villainy was plotted in the dingy upper rooms in the
rat-infested houses. At its western extremity, where it terminated
at Charing Cross, it was wide and respectable, giving plenty of
space for its great attraction, the pillory; but in the middle, the
Strand was a street to suit all comers and all purposes, with its
numerous coffee houses (including the Spread Eagle, where it
was said the clientele changed completely every six months due
to hangings and other forms of violent death), its shops, taverns and
frequent processions. A haunt of prostitutes, the prices they
charged were also graded according to which end of the Strand
they plied for hire, so that James Boswell, in his *London Diary*,
could note that whereas the cost of a high-class courtesan in the
West End might rise to fifty guineas, one might yet find satisfaction at the east end of the Strand with 'a low brimstone' whose
fee might not exceed sixpence.

But the most colourful area of the Strand, and the meeting-
place of rich and poor, as well as of the fashionable West End
with the literary-minded elements of Fleet Street, was where

London's two great theatres were situated, at Covent Garden and Drury Lane. Here a young man could truly see life, and mingle with the great, the illustrious and the notorious. The young James Boswell, visiting London in the 1760s, fell at once under the spell of the stage and its winsome actresses, and particularly the seductive Mrs Louisa Lewis. From her he contracted a highly unromantic dose of the pox after spending a night of 'supreme rapture' with her at The Black Lion Inn, in Water Lane, off Fleet Street, where he so excelled himself as to perform the sexual act five times, which he held to constitute a display of quite exceptional gallantry, most comforting to his ego.

Students of social history have noted the fact that in the great towns of Europe the areas which contained the theatres were also usually those which were notable for their brothels, their drinking-houses, their gambling dens and the bawdy behaviour of their local citizenry. This is not surprising. Theatres tend to arouse sexual desires; and being places of entertainment, they are naturally surrounded by other places of entertainment, such as taverns and brothels. Violence in the streets is also not surprising, for men who are in search of women tend to become quarrelsome and aggressive, in the same way that dogs become vicious when in pursuit of a bitch. Certainly the theatre area of London in the 18th century provided no exception to this social phenomenon, and the narrow streets surrounding Drury Lane and Covent Garden were filled with prostitutes each night, contained countless brothels, and also numerous taverns in which prostitutes either solicited or performed on the premises.

An inn such as The White Lion, close by Drury Lane, was famous for the concerts and dances which took place in its upper rooms and usually degenerated into orgies. Such festivities were often attended by ladies of fashion from the West End as well as by local harlots, and one of the oddities of London life was the fact that these fashionable ladies would arrive in their elegant carriages, which would be held up in the crush of the narrow streets. Poverty-stricken bystanders would then howl obscenities at them, whilst the men lewdly exposed themselves, but such conduct did not disturb the carriage folk at all – and indeed many of them seemed rather to enjoy it. Many of these alleged 'balls' were in fancy dress and the women wore masks so that they could not be recognised, and if their inclination was to behave with impropriety or complete abandon, their lovers of the evening would not know who they were. Which leads to a further aspect of the social life of the rich during the age of laxity – namely that the anonymity bestowed on a woman by her mask resulted in sexual indulgence which would never have been practised if masks had not been worn.

Attempts have been made to assess the number of prostitutes that must have been plying their trade in such areas as the Strand during the 18th and early 19th centuries, but accurate figures cannot be given. It is however possible to break them down into categories of age groups and types. As regards age, there were certainly children of both sexes to be encountered in the streets, some of them under ten. Quite a large percentage of female prostitutes – about one-sixth – were under fifteen. There was also a small percentage over sixty.

As regards types, there were those at the very bottom of the ladder – namely the poorest of street-walkers, Boswell's 'low brimstones', who could be bought for coppers but who had to be used in dark corners or alleyways since they had no homes to go to. Then there were the girls of a slightly higher status who actually possessed a room of their own, or were allowed to use one in a tavern. Then there were the brothels, some of which were primitive in the extreme and others well-appointed houses with comfortable beds and offering quite a high class of girl. Such girls seldom went on to the streets, and if they did would have the protection of professional bullies who would ensure that they were not molested. The women who kept these brothels went to remarkable lengths in order to procure for their customers just the type of fresh young girl who was most in demand (for it was an age much obsessed with defloration and the corruption of innocence) and the story is told of one brothel-keeper – a Mrs Nelson, of Wardour Street – who even went to the lengths of getting herself engaged as a French governess at a fashionable girls' boarding-school in order to entice two of its most attractive pupils.

Next in the list of prostitutes was the courtesan, who preferred to operate on her own, although she often graduated from a brothel in the first instance, and so bettered herself that she finally enjoyed the comfort of her own house and servants. Then there were the eternal ranks of the amateurs – the servants, seamstresses, children's nurses, and barmaids – who were not full-time prostitutes but who could be picked up without difficulty, all the more so by those men who had homes of their own to which these amateurs could be taken.

Finally, at the end of the century, the numbers of these prostitutes and their pimps and procurers were greatly swelled by an influx of low life from the Continent, for not only members of the aristocracy fled across the Channel during the French Revolution, but also some of the dregs of the Paris slums, and others whose way of life it had been to batten on the weaknesses of the upper classes – then in the process of being liquidated. They introduced a new and vicious element into the London underworld, and although it has been the custom in modern times to laugh at the British lower classes for their instinctive suspicion and even hatred of all foreigners, it can be said in defence of this outlook that during the French Revolution they were given good reason for hating this influx of members of the Parisian underworld.

Prostitution in London during the 18th and 19th centuries was the most highly organised in any city of the world. Not only were prostitutes to be encountered in large numbers in the streets – and also in the fashionable London parks after dark – but catalogues of girls available were distributed in the so-called Piazza of Covent Garden. This up-to-date list of practising harlots was issued annually, and gave not only the names and addresses of the women but also a detailed description of their appearance, and what variations or perversions they were willing to undertake. This catalogue was known variously as *The New Atlantis, Harris' List of Covent Garden Ladies*, or *Man of Pleasure's Kalander for the Year*.

Many of the brothels operated under the cloak of being a *bagnio*, or bathing-place for turkish baths, medical sweating and cupping. A few establishments were in fact used for this purpose and were highly respectable and used by many fastidious members of Society, but the majority were primarily brothels. The most flagrant type of brothel made no pretence to hiding its activities, and its girls were to be seen posturing naked at the windows, and making obscene gestures in their attempts to lure the passing gallant. Since so many of these young men visited the area first of all to get drunk, then to gamble and finally to fornicate, it often happened that their normal caution and judgement would be overcome, and despite their determination not to become involved with some cheap and pox-ridden harlot, they would end the night up some alleyway with just the type of woman they should have avoided – and often without the use of contraceptive sheaths of linen, fish-bladders or rubber which were widely in use at the time. One of the surprising aspects of these brothels was that most of them charged a fixed price, so that a client was not cheated in this respect, although he was in almost every other.

The affinity between sex and gambling – and indeed of excess of any one sort with another – has already been emphasised. Providing the necessary amenities were made available to him, it could be said of the 18th-century gallant that where he could drink to excess he would also wish to fornicate to excess. And where he could both drink and fornicate to excess, he would also wish to gamble to excess. (He also enjoyed being quarrelsome to excess, but amenities for duelling and stabbing were not provided by the saloons of the period, because on the whole these were bad for business, and might well result in the premises being broken up.)

It is not surprising therefore that the area of the Strand, Covent Garden and Drury Lane was filled with gambling hells of every description – those that catered for the lowest tastes and the lowest bets, and those that served a better type of client, and the big gambler, and gave him quite high-class food, wine and women. But in all these establishments cheating was commonplace, either in the direct form of loaded dice or marked cards, or the more indirect form of encouraging a client to drink heavily before playing, so that he was incapable of judgement or caution in his play. Women were used extensively – as decoys, to bring a client into the house, both as *agents provocateurs* to encourage him to gamble and as part of the amenities of the place, so as to bring him added stimulation when excited, and comfort when deflated after having been dispossessed of his money.

It is perhaps significant that one of the worst gambling hells in the Covent Garden district was Mordington's described by a jury giving a verdict on one of its inmates at the time as 'a place of debauchery, idleness and evil'. It was run as a gambling saloon, but in association with Molly King's brothel adjoining it, and the gamblers were encouraged to cease their play and to adjourn next door if their luck seemed to be out, and they were becoming discouraged. A short session with one of Molly King's gay and buxom girls usually had the effect of sending them back to the tables with renewed determination, if not necessarily with renewed vigour. Yet Mordington's, with its evil reputation, was but one of the gambling saloons inaugurated by Lady Mordington, who pleaded the privilege to run it on account of being a peeress, and to whom reference has already been made.

Emphasis has been repeatedly laid in this book on the prevalence during this period of male aggressiveness and the manner in which the male ego was expressed by acts of lawlessness, cruelty and violence. Such outbreaks of lawlessness amongst the young are common to all periods, and the youth of today frequently indulges in acts of senseless destruction, smashing up public property and assaulting innocent people in the street. Modern outbursts cannot be compared to the violence to be encountered in 18th-century London, in which the London mob often committed acts of violence from desperation whilst the idle rich committed acts of equal violence merely to satisfy their baser impulses, with young men often urged on by the young women. And their happy hunting ground, in most cases, was the neighbourhood of the Strand.

Vice, of course, goes hand in hand with crime, and the taverns, streets and alleyways were filled with petty criminals of every description who preyed on the gambler and the drinker, either by means of robbery with violence, or by housebreaking, by picking pockets, counterfeiting money, pilfering from shops, or working for the crooked gambling dens. Nor was the profession practised by Fagin ignored by the London underworld of the 18th century, and frequent use was made of children for

the purpose of pimping, picking pockets, begging or petty pilfering. These children were instructed in their work by experts,
who taught them how to steal and how to accost in the same way
that Fagin taught his pupils.

The criminals of London were like rabbits – that is to say,
they lived a largely subterranean existence, and made use of
numberless bolt-holes and underground passages and burrows
into which they disappeared with startling suddenness when
pursued. These underground passages were so numerous in the
slum areas, and the alleyways so labyrinthine that they almost
resembled the catacombs of Rome, and were certainly to be
compared to the smugglers' passages and caves which were in
use along the coast of England. The likeness is made even closer
because many of these passages did lead down to the river's banks,
and here also there was such a conglomeration of boats, wharves,
pierheads, 'stairs', outlets to drains and the stinking flotsam and
jetsam of the slum-lined Thames that criminals were able to
hide themselves in safety until the hue-and-cry was over.

No map of London of the period has ever attempted the carto-
graphy of this subterranean world – indeed it was probably never
mapped even by those who used it most; and nowhere was it more
intricate in its patterns than in the eight or so acres of land which
surrounded Temple Bar and included the old tenements of the
City and the exits leading to the north. Some of the old, timbered
houses, shacks and sheds dated back to the London of mediaeval
days; and some of the narrow passages and lanes went back even
further into the City's history.

Crockford had a passion for gambling, and he lived in an area
full of gambling-hells. He had a head for figures and a natural
business instinct, and everywhere he saw evidence of how the
unintelligent, the ignorant, the vain and the flamboyant were
being made to pay heavily for their weaknesses. He lived in an
era of cheating, and his wits were sharpened by many an encounter with those trying to cheat him. These rogues taught him
all the tricks of the trade and a great deal about human nature.
He had courage, and he soon realised that in order to make big
money it was necessary to bet heavily (whilst always ensuring as
far as possible that the odds were in his favour). And although his

'manor' was the Strand, he was given plenty of opportunities to study the habits and the characteristics of the fashionable world.

This world, he soon decided, must become his hunting ground of the future, for here were the ranks of the carefree, reckless amateurs, with vast resources at their command who were only interested in opposing themselves to backers as heavy as themselves for it was their ambition 'to bet deep'. He studied their attitude to life, and in his expeditions to the West End, to St James's Street and Piccadilly, he noted how they lived in their grand houses and their luxurious surroundings. Such gamblers must ultimately be challenged on their own ground and in their own lavish world if they were to be deprived of their wealth.

Finally Crockford's youth at Temple Bar taught him much about women. He soon developed a voracious appetite for sexual indulgence, which was easily satisfied as he was surrounded by women who were willing to offer themselves to any man – or boy. He was coarse in his habits, dirty in his person, fat, flabby and pallid, foul of mouth and without any sort of refinement, but he learnt that these attributes are no bar to sexual indulgence. His earthy virility and his ruthless determination to get what he wanted were each qualities which women could admire.

Thus, when all was said and done, if a man's ambition in the 18th century was to succeed in life by the cunning of his brain and his knowledge of human nature, then Temple Bar was as advantageous a place as any to begin his education. There was little about human nature that he would not have learnt by the time he had reached man's estate, for even to survive required no little determination.

William Crockford spent his childhood at first watching and later helping in the family business of selling fish. The shop itself was well-to-do compared with others in the vicinity, and so he cannot be said to have spent this childhood in poverty, as has sometimes been alleged. He was surrounded by poverty, however, and by every type of vice and crime.

A customer on leaving the shop could turn left and pass through the narrow entrance under Temple Bar into Fleet Street. But if he turned right on leaving the shop, and proceeded westwards, he was confronted by a fork which led to two narrow alleyways.

The right-hand alleyway was Butcher's Row, and was lined with butchers' shops. The left-hand, or lower alleyway, led into the Strand, and the area enclosed by these two alleyways formed a small island of slum property.

Beyond this island of small houses was one of London's most famous churches – St Clement Danes, so called because of the tradition that England's Danish King, Harold, and many of his followers, had been buried in its churchyard a thousand years before. Butcher's Row was a most evil street, of Tudor origin, decrepit, tumbledown and vile-smelling, 'a sort of nesting place for the plague and fevers', to quote a contemporary comment. It contained several dingy lodging-houses, which were occupied either by rogues or by penniless writers and poets, who when they were evicted on non-payment of their rent, which was frequently, went to roost instead on the stall outside the Crockford fish shop. The street had a bad name throughout London, partly because of its unsavoury history – it was in a chamber in Butcher's Row that Guy Fawkes and his accomplices met to plan the Gunpowder Plot in 1605.

If the customer decided to go northwards, and to follow the footpath which led up behind the fishmonger's shop in Lincoln's Inn Fields, he found himself in Shire Lane. This was one of the most notorious pathways in London, and for a long time it was better known by its nickname of Rogues' Lane. This was the centre of a thieves' kitchen, and it was from the houses in Shire Lane that the secret passages ran underground into the Strand. No one was safe in Shire Lane after dark, and even local residents avoided it. Adjoining it, on the left, was Ship Yard, which also housed a colony of thieves, and the old houses here were connected by a honeycomb of underground passages and escape routes known only to the inhabitants. A speciality of the Yard was the counterfeiting of coins, a very dangerous pastime in view of the savage sentences inflicted by the courts on counterfeiters.

Finally, to complete the geographical picture, there was situated to the north-east of Temple Bar, a distance of some half-mile as the crow flies, the fearful prison of Newgate, outside which public executions were regularly held, especially after 1784 when Tyburn ceased to be used as an execution centre because of overcrowding and the disorderliness shown by the 'Tyburn Procession' when it proceeded along Oxford Street. There was accommodation for 5,000 spectators in comfort outside Newgate, so that it had everything to recommend it.

A child brought up in the area could learn much about life and the pursuit of vice and crime. He could also learn much about death and the punishment of criminals if he lived near Newgate Gaol. Here, outside the high walls, with the crowd shrieking in fearful and orgiastic ecstasy, the bodies were flung down from the beam above, and wriggled and twisted in terrible suffering as they slowly strangled to death, while their faces turned black and their friends tugged desperately at their feet in order to shorten their agony.

Children were taken to witness these executions as a form of entertainment, rather than to learn the salutory lesson that crime did not pay, but to any child or youth with an inclination towards a life of crime, here certainly was food for thought. Children themselves could be hanged, and still were so, even for trifling offences. Not until 1790 was the burning alive of female traitors abolished. Not until 1814 was the act of public disembowelment discontinued. Not until 1832 was the practice discontinued of public dissection of the body and suspension in chains on a gibbet. Not until 1837 were such minor offences as rick-burning, robbery and burglary considered no longer worthy of capital punishment.

All these punishments were possible in the lifetime of William Crockford; and not until 1868, long after his death, was the last man hanged in public outside Newgate Gaol.

Today it seems unbelievable to think that a boy on his way to the market, or running to fulfil some errand, could stop to gaze upon a corpse hanging in chains from a gallows, or suspended from a gibbet on an open piece of land, or dangling from a pole in the river. But William Crockford, as a child, must often have seen such sights. They probably confirmed him in the belief that money was best made by keeping just on the right side of the law.

The lack of information concerning William Crockford's childhood and youth make his life at this time a matter of surmise.

B*

It is known that his father died when the boy was still quite young, and that his mother then took over the running of the shop, but the date of his father's death is uncertain. There is no record of it in the registers of the period at St Clement Danes nor is there any evidence that he was buried in the churchyard there. But it seems certain that the shop continued to operate successfully under the management of Mrs Crockford, and this suggests that she was probably a woman of strong character and of some business acumen, and it may well have been from her that Willian inherited his astuteness. She probably trained him from childhood with a view to his taking over the business when he reached maturity, and it is certain that even as a small boy he was helping in the shop and – acting on her instructions – was doing some of the buying of fish in the Billingsgate Fish Market.

This must have been a hard life, necessitating early rising and much hard bargaining. There were no tougher nor more knowledgeable sellers of merchandise in London than those who traded in the City's three great markets – Smithfield for meat, poultry and provisions and situated just north of Newgate; Leadenhall, also for meat and poultry, dating back to the 14th century, and situated off Leadenhall Street, in the heart of the City; and finally Billingsgate, situated on the banks of the Thames between London Bridge and the Tower of London, and dealing exclusively in fish.

What was it like, this Billingsgate Fish Market, where the young William Crockford spent so much of his time, often in the cold, dank hours before dawn, when the oil lamps spluttered and the stink of fish could turn even the most hardened stomach? If this was his school and college, what of its curriculum, its undergraduates and its teachers?

In the first place Billingsgate was a small harbour as well as a market, and was used not only by fishing-boats but also by travellers and those who wished to make excursions up the Thames. Because it was used by travellers its taverns remained open all night, and since the arrival and departure of ships might be delayed by storm or tide, these travellers – and the sailors of the ships – would often be left to carouse and curse until they could go aboard. This in part accounted for Billingsgate's reputation for drunkenness and foul language.

The market itself opened at 4 a.m. for the use of the regular wholesalers and 'bummarees', or middle-men, who brought fish in bulk for re-sale. (The derivation of the word 'bummaree' is obscure – possibly it came from the French, *bonne marée*, with its implication of good fresh fish.) The supply of fish was usually large and varied, including cod, eels, Yarmouth bloaters, haddock, lobsters, crabs, whelks, mussels, red herrings, sprats, turbot, oysters and salmon. Curiously enough the Thames itself was still full of fish at London despite its pollution (and perhaps because of it in the case of some fish with a preference for carrion) and even late in the 18th century it was still possible for the Londoner to take his rod and line and spend a quiet evening fishing off London Bridge.

The market was open six days a week and on Sunday for the sale of mackerel alone (and then only *before* the hours of divine service). The average Londoner had a liking for fish, and delicacies such as salmon were highly prized in Mayfair. In bad weather, when the gales made the work of the fishing fleets impossible, the price of fish rose to surprising heights in the market. Although the harbour itself was quite trim and well-ordered, and some of the buildings on the quay were large, the market was a dismal and evil place of 'dirty pent-houses, scaly sheds, and ill-savoured benches with flaming oil lamps and a screaming, fighting and rather tipsy crowd', to quote a contemporary description.

It was the women stall-holders of the market, 'the ladies of the British fishery' as Addison once referred to them, who really ruled the place and dominated it by their Amazon-like pugnacity and unquestioned authority. In the slang of the period 'a Billingsgate' was an evil-tongued and quarrelsome slut, and this definition certainly applied to many of the Billingsgate sellers.

William Crockford was not illiterate, and since his father was a tradesman of reasonable means it can be supposed that William did receive a certain amount of schooling. The children of the very poor in London at this time gained what little knowledge they ever had from the Sunday Schools and the charity religious teaching which was then beginning to be developed.

For the most part the children of the poor were sent out to earn their living at the earliest possible moment and there was no time for their education. Even in Victorian times children were still being employed in the coal-mines at 4 or 5 years of age, and the general attitude to the use of children in industry was that 9, at latest, was a suitable age for boys and girls to undertake a working day of 12–14 hours of hard manual labour. Chimney-sweeps in London – the wretched, bedraggled tribe of soot-covered 'climbing boys' and 'climbing girls' – were being forced up narrow flues almost from infancy once the use of coal fires on domestic hearths had become general during the 18th century (and the smaller and more under-nourished they were, the better their chances of employment). Not long after William Crockford was born, however, an Act of Parliament was passed which went so far as to forbid the use of boys and girls under 8 for climbing chimneys.

William Crockford did not have to climb chimneys as a child. His worst hardship was battling with the angry Billingsgate fishwives before dawn on a winter morning. There were a few schools in the district surrounding Temple Bar, and a *Report of the Commissioners on the Education of the Poor*, published in 1819, lists some eight of them, including the St Mary le Strand Charity School of 25 boys, which does not suggest that the education given locally was very extensive. There were also a number of single teachers who imparted a smattering of knowledge to children of poor but not impoverished parents for a small sum. To all of which one need only add that even the sons of the rich who were sent to Eton, Harrow or Winchester received an education that was of poor quality, and unless they were out-standingly bright they were taught for the most part by over-worked and underpaid ushers in cramped classrooms and from bad text books.

In this respect the children of both the rich and the poor gained their knowledge from life rather than from scholarship; and the poor held the advantage, for the lessons which they learnt from poverty sharpened their wits and stimulated their cunning.

No doubt William's mother considered that her son could start helping in the shop at about 8 or 9 a.m., and so he probably ceased his schooling as soon as he was old enough to buy for her at Billingsgate. In his leisure hours he must have played in the streets surrounding his home, watched the hangings outside Newgate Gaol and paddled in the mud of the Thames.

His manner of speech was broad cockney, and he used the vernacular of Sam Weller, mixing up his v's and w's. This habit he never lost, and even when he was rich and famous, and rubbing shoulders with the aristocracy, he still used the harsh, crude phraseology of the Temple Bar gutter. One significant item from his mysterious youth remains to prove the extent to which he could read and write. It is a bill which he laboriously produced for his mother when he was working in the shop, and it runs as follows:

			s.	d.
April	3.	To pair sowls	1	3
	5.	Sprats		3
	6.	3 Vitens		9
	12.	7 Red herrings		6
	19.	2 Makerils		8
			3	5

Thus one can record of William Crockford that he was literate – but only just!

He was educated in the Strand, but the price of such education was negligible, and when he began to gamble on his own it was only for coppers. Once his sexuality had developed, which it did at an early age, his fornication cost him little more. In a period when the young James Boswell, writing of his sex life in this same neighbourhood of the Strand, could note in his diary that he had enjoyed the pleasure of two prostitutes in one evening *and* three bowls of punch in a tavern at a total expenditure of 1s 9d, it was not necessary for the maturing youth to spend very much on his drinking and whoring.

But always before him was the spectacle of the idle rich, squandering their money at the gambling hells in the district because they had no brains and even less common sense. They gambled, but they had no knowledge of gambling; and they were happy enough to lose their money providing they could boast and swagger whilst they were doing so, and thus bolster up their self-esteem.

'Go west young man' was the advice given to the adventurous youth of America in the 19th century. William Crockford, whilst still a young man, must have been inspired by the same slogan. His aim was to bet on the same scale as they bet in the West End of London – and that was to 'bet deep'.

He was conscious, too, of the sharp contrast in the social life of the 18th century. In youth he learnt all that there was to learn about poverty the most wretched. In manhood his aim was to strive towards the goal of wealth the most enormous – a goal which he knew that he was one day destined to attain.

2

THE PRECEDENT
How to Enter Society by the Back Door

Night after night, when his work in his mother's bulk shop was ended, and the shutters outside it had been securely fastened, Crockford would walk slowly along the Strand, past the pillory at Charing Cross and up the Haymarket into Piccadilly or along Pall Mall to St James's Palace. Sometimes he would walk past the Horse Guards Parade behind Whitehall and then enter St James's Park, but this he would do only after dark, when the pimps and prostitutes had taken possession of the long avenues of trees, for during the daylight hours the Mall was the exclusive preserve of the Fancy, and no place for a fat and grubby lad from the East End who smelt of fish. But once he had reached St James's Street he could watch and spy, for this was the game reserve which he was one day destined to enter and despoil.

At the beginning of the 19th century, and during the Crockford era, St James's Street was at once a residential area and a shopping centre. Arlington Street, which adjoined it at its northern extremity, was, of course, a very fashionable locality either to be born in (as was Horace Walpole) or to live in (as Nelson had done for a time). Lord Sefton, who was destined to become one of the leaders of the Crockford 'set', lived at No. 21 Arlington Street, and the Cecils lived next door. Charles Fox lived at No. 9 for two years. But the same area had been ringed during the 18th century by some really high-class brothels, so it maintained its cosmopolitan atmosphere, as indeed did most of the St James's area. The northern end of St James's Street was under the command of a certain William Tomlins, who swept the crossing up to the entrance to Albemarle Street and behaved in a somewhat dictatorial manner to everyone, in contrast to dear old Betty, the apple woman whom Horace Walpole had so loved and who ruled the further end of the street for so long during the 18th century and indeed was said to have been born there, another example of its democratic atmosphere.

But although citizens of all ranks and classes did seem to live in and around St James's Street, it was primarily a shopping centre for the wealthy inhabitants of the great houses off Piccadilly, Park Lane and Pall Mall. They rarely went shopping themselves, of course, except perhaps when the women visited a milliner's in Bond Street, accompanied by a gallant escort who spent his time ogling the girls behind the counter, or when the dandies went to buy a hat or a cravat. But the prosperous tradesmen of St James's Street were called upon to supply the Court and the aristocracy with the essentials of life, including saddlery, oysters, Macassar oil, Chelsea china, wines and hats.

St James's Street, however, was unique in one way. It was the home of the most fashionable and select clubs in London, and above all of Brooks's and of White's. Both were exclusive to a degree, and each housed behind its rather sombre exterior the gilded youth of the era; idle, bored and elegant young men with wealthy parents and time lying heavily on their hands. They were dissolute; they were dissipated. They talked a great deal about sex, and explored its more curious byways in the local brothels or as members of the Hell-Fire Club or other such bizarre establishments, but gambling alone never failed to rouse them from their apathy, and it was at these rival institutions of White's and Brooks's that gambling was the ruling passion. To indulge in sexual activities required a certain physical exertion which Old Etonian idlers such as George Selwyn found exhausting, but one could gamble whilst seated at a table, or exchange extravagant and extraordinary wagers whilst stretched full length in an easy chair.

Thus the game which Crockford, the hunter, was destined to pursue throughout his life with such relentless determination were now to be seen browsing in their reserve and drinking at their water-holes, still unmindful of the dangers which were to overthrow them. Yet the problem seemed formidable. How could an uncouth fishmonger's son ever hope to invade this most affluent and most exclusive circle, where half the members were titled and a large percentage had been educated at Eton? The answer is that the young Crockford at first never envisaged such a step, even in his most optimistic daydreams. But he realised from the outset that he could operate on the outskirts of this hallowed circle by running a gambling hell of his own in one of the narrow side streets off St James's Street where the very rich were wont to wander when in search of *divertissement* and a change from the sombre surroundings of their clubs; and he knew that he could also take them on at Newmarket, mingling almost as one of them during the parade before a big race, always providing he had money enough to bet with them and perhaps a runner in the race as well.

But to prosper so greatly that he was in a position to open a club of his own in St James's Street, and to make it even more select than Brooks's or White's was more than he ever imagined when first he found himself drawn westwards from Temple Bar.

As the months and years went by, however, and he became an habitué of the hinterland to St James's Street in the taverns and hells of Jermyn Street and King Street, he heard stories of how men with origins as humble as his own had entered the elegant world of fashion by opening clubs of their own and then inviting the high-born to become members. It was a risky affair, as he soon learnt, for the fancy had to be lured with bait as carefully selected as that by any fly-fisherman, but it could be done and it had been done. For example, there was the case of White's itself, which had been the inspiration of a man who had not only risen from poverty and obscurity, but who had not even enjoyed the advantage of being born an Englishman.

The story of the Italian, Francesco Bianco, was a legend in the district, and William Crockford, all eyes and ears and with his imagination still on fire at the contemplation of this wealthy world of gamblers, had often listened to accounts – some accurate and some inflated – of how this poor immigrant had opened a small chocolate house in St James's Street a century before, and by some curious trick of salesmanship, aided by good luck, had attracted a number of wealthy patrons to it, so that it had not been long before he was able to take on bigger premises and to launch out in a more ambitious way. Francesco Bianco, or Francis White as he later called himself, had died in 1711, and they had buried him beside the gentry in the churchyard of St James; but his wife had then carried on the business and made a great deal of money out of it. A woman of enterprise, she had started a ticket agency in the club, so that members had been able to book tickets for the Opera through her, and she had also promoted a series of *ridottos*, masquerades and fancy-dress balls, which were all the rage in Society at the time and which had made her very popular with the wives and mistresses of the club members. She had finally retired to live and die in the country, a wealthy woman indeed, leaving her husband's former associate, John Arthur, to carry on the club. He, too, made a fortune out of it, hobnobbed with aristocracy and gentry and also retired in the fullness of time, a very rich man.

The young Crockford listened to this story of the foundation of White's and turned it over in his mind. He realised that the founder had shown foresight in his realisation that St James's Street, leading as it did from the great houses of Piccadilly down to the royal palace of St James's and to the Mall, was destined to become one of the most fashionable thoroughfares in London. White's wife, and later his partner, Arthur, had continued his policy; and his wife had been shrewd enough to make St James's Street popular also with the ladies, by organising fashionable entertainment for them, whilst keeping the club itself the exclusive preserve of the male. And Crockford pondered on these things.

The history of the rival institution, Brooks's, provided him with further indications as to how one might succeed. The club had originated in a gambling club in Pall Mall which had been opened by a certain William Almack some time during the 1760s. The antecedents of William Almack were wrapped in obscurity, only one fact being certain – that he was a Scot and a nobody. His real name was not Almack, but since to be a Scot was at that time to arouse a profound suspicion of being a Jacobite, the wise Scotsman, when travelling south to make his fortune out of the simple-minded and unbusiness-like Sassenach, either made many loud protestations of his dislike of the Jacobite cause or else pretended that he was not a Scot at all. This was a little difficult in

the case of the average man from across the border, with his
strange habits and uncouth accent.

But since no Scot of any worth alters his name without a pang,
this particular Scot – a man of some ingenuity and ambition, as
the incidents of his career were soon to prove – contrived to overcome the problem by making an anagram of his real name, and
called himself Almack. It seems reasonably certain, that he was in
fact born Macall or McCaul and that he was a Celt from Galloway
or Atholl. He was first brought to London as a young man by the
Duke of Hamilton, to whom he acted as valet, and in company
with many another ambitious young servant of the aristocracy
who learned how to ape the manner and customs of the aristocracy, he decided in middle age to launch out into business on his
own. Like White, shortly before him, he appreciated at once the
advantages of St James's Street, and he became proprietor of the
Thatched House Tavern; and later, also like White before him,
he decided to found a Club that should bear his name (or rather
an anagram of it) and that should be patronised by the wealthy
élite. No suitable premises were available in St James's Street at
the time, and perhaps he did not originally intend to throw down
the challenge so immediately to the select coterie at White's, and
so he opened Almack's Club at premises in Pall Mall, where it
was surrounded by mansions of fashion and was within a stone's
throw of St James's Street and the Palace.

From its outset Almack's was noted for its gambling, and for
the depth of its play. This was really inevitable (as no doubt the
founder intended it should be) because one of the founder-
members was Charles Fox; and it was not long before the depth
of the gambling at Almack's began to put even that at White's
into the shade, and the rivalry between the two clubs then became
acute.

Almack now grew far more ambitious. He determined to
become 'the leading caterer of the fashionable world' and to
this end bought a large site in King's Street, just off St James's
Street, and announced that here he would build a magnificent
set of Assembly Rooms, which – by their spaciousness and luxury
– could provide facilities for up to a dozen balls a week.

It was a risky project, for the building proved very costly, and it was still incomplete on the date of the great official opening, 12 February 1765, when the invitation cards which Almack sent out were specially designed by his famous architect, Robert Mylne. To make matters worse, the weather was terrible. 'The new Assembly Rooms at Almack's was opened the night before last,' noted Horace Walpole, 'and they say it is very magnificent, but it was empty; half of the town is ill with colds, and were afraid to go. They tell me the ceilings were dropping with water. The Duke of Cumberland was there . . . There is a vast flight of steps, and he was forced to rest two or three times.'

Almack had advertised that the building 'was built with hot bricks and boiling water', but this did not help him and the whole evening was a fiasco. Society was ready enough to be wooed by these upstarts, especially when the result was the provision of splendid places for their entertainment, but Society also enjoyed making caustic comments at these upstarts' expense. One of those who was absent, and nursing a cold, was George Selwyn, a lovable personality but a bit of an old woman, a snob and a man who loved to make witty remarks; so he was delighted to receive and later to recount the description of the opening given to him in a letter from his old friend, Gilly Williams, who wrote him the news that 'Almack's Scotch face in a bagwig waiting at supper would divert you, as would his lady in a sack, making tea and curtseying to the duchesses'.

But the duchesses and other high-born ladies, although they were fully alive to the way in which Almack was out to exploit them, were in no way averse to being exploited. As has already been remarked, the custom was growing of using the balls and dances held at these fashionable assemblies as a cover for gambling, in which the ladies took as active a part as the men, for they were limited in the number of public places where they could go to wager, whereas their menfolk had the choice of innumerable gambling hells as well as of their clubs. It was for this reason that they allowed themselves to be co-opted into serving on the organising committees of such festivities, knowing full well that in return for their labours, and for the invitations which they sent out to their wealthy friends, they would receive a discreet payment *and* be given a percentage of the bank's winnings.

Almack knew all this, and he at once formed a highly select committee of lady-patronesses, who undertook the sale and distribution of tickets at ten guineas each (the equivalent of more than a hundred pounds today). Indeed this committee was so select and so powerful that Grantley Berkeley described them as 'a feminine oligarchy less in number but equal in power to the Venetian Council of Ten'.

There was nothing unusual about this. Women of fashion even went so far as to run their own gambling hells during the 18th century, and Lady Mordington and Lady Cassillis not only operated a chain of them, but even had the audacity to claim exemption from the gambling laws because they were peeresses of the realm. 'The surest road into the graces of a fine lady was to be known as one who betted freely, and lost handsomely,' observed Trevelyan, who was sharply critical of the bad influences exerted by the women of the period. 'It was next to impossible for a lad still in his teens to keep himself from the clutch of these elegant harpies . . .'

Thus Society, as Trevelyan sourly noted, was one vast casino, in which gambling had become more important than sex.

Almack, who was fully alive to all this, and especially to the influence exerted on their menfolk by the ladies of Society, was therefore assured of success in his ventures. His Assembly Rooms became so fashionable that no one who was seeking to win a place in Society could dare to ignore them. He was recognised as 'the leading caterer for the amusement of the fashionable world' – and attained this recognition by making his clubs exclusive, and by using ladies of Society as his willing decoys.

As for his club in Pall Mall, its reputation for deep play was fostered by its chief founder-member, the young Charles James Fox. It might have been supposed that since Charles had been the proprietor's benefactor at the club's inception, by joining it at once himself and by encouraging all his wealthy gambling friends to follow suit, William Almack would have felt benevolent towards him and would have tried to prevent the wilful young man from losing quite so heavily and so repeatedly. There is, unfortunately, no evidence of this. Charles was not only a rash backer, he was also an unlucky one; and although he was worldly-wise in the matter of politics, he was but a child in the ways of gambling and an easy victim for the astute professional gambler. Almack realised this from the outset, and there is no doubt that Charles Fox contributed a great deal towards the fortune that the club's founder was able to amass before his death in 1781.

During his service as valet to the Duke of Hamilton, Almack had met and married the Duchess's lady's maid, Elizabeth Cullen, and by her had had two children – a son William, who became a barrister, and a daughter, Elizabeth, who married one of the doctors who attended the Prince of Wales. Thus he demonstrated that a man might rise from the gutter – or worse than the gutter in his case, since he had risen from poverty in, of all places, Scotland – and attain wealth for himself and respectability for his offspring.

Some three years before his death, William Almack sold his club in Pall Mall to a local wine-merchant and money-lender named Brooks, who gave it his name and moved its position from Pall Mall into a site nearly opposite White's and halfway down St James's Street, but the new proprietor did not long enjoy the fame accorded him by his ownership of the new premises, and he died in 1782, only a year after the death of Almack.

The point which interested William Crockford, when he came to study the careers of these famous club proprietors, was that only Brooks died poor; and the reason for his financial collapse was not hard to discover, for although he was a money-lender he was never a business-like member of his profession, and he incurred too many bad debts. He spent far too much money when setting up the new premises in St James's Street and throughout his short career he revealed the same attitude to his clients that he had formerly shown when serving them as their wine merchant: that is to say, he encouraged them to spend freely and assured them of his willingness to await payment until it was convenient for them to settle with him. Unlike Almack, he even seemed to have taken pity on some of them and to have befriended them when they found themselves in straitened circumstances. He was described by Tickell, in verse addressed to Sheridan, in the following lines:

Liberal Brookes, whose speculative skill
Is hasty credit and a distant bill;
Who, nursed in clubs, disdains a vulgar trade,
Exults to trust, and blushes to be paid.

The young William Crockford thought deeply upon these things, and he was not discouraged. It was not in his nature to make the same mistakes as the benevolent Brooks.

But William Crockford's excursions into the world of high life were not limited to the West End alone. He was a gambler himself, dedicated to the lifelong study of all forms of betting whereby the amateur who did not really know what he was doing might be deprived of his cash by the professional who did; and now, as the 18th century drew to its close, William Crockford became increasingly interested in another sphere of gambling, the turf.

The turf, as he well knew, was no arena for the faint-hearted or the foolish to enter, for on it was waged a war without mercy. Not a war of kill or be killed, but a war of ruin others or yourself be ruined. But this arena had one great advantage which gambling in the West End had not, for in it a man from the gutter might readily take on his social superiors and – if he were clever enough – might defeat them. And finally, if he prospered enough, he might even match their way of life, and might own carriages as ornate, servants as numerous, mansions as large and – best of all – race-horses as fast or even faster than any which they possessed.

'All men are equal on the turf and under it.' That was the high-sounding phrase in current use amongst sportsmen, and it was in part true. If a man had money enough, he could buy a horse that might win the Derby – and once he had won the Derby, then his name would be written for ever into the scrolls of this great race, alongside those of the kings and princes, dukes and earls who were destined to be inscribed there also. Thus Newmarket and Epsom had ceased during the 18th century to be the exclusive preserves of the aristocracy and gentry, and had become also the hunting-ground of optimists, crooks and upstarts who were in search of riches.

To be a nobody and yet win the Derby! It was the dream of every poor man on the turf, as it is to this day. It could be done – it *had* been done. All that was needed was courage, luck and resolution.

It could be done. It *had* been done. And one man above all others stood out as an example of what might be achieved on the turf with courage and good fortune. This was a man who had risen from a background more obscure and from a home life more poverty-stricken than that of almost any of the small-time operators in the minor London hells, but one who had yet become an intimate friend of the aristocracy, and whose name had become a household word throughout sporting England. This was the incomparable rogue, gambler and braggart who had owned that incomparable racehorse, Eclipse. This was the idol of the man in the street. This was 'Colonel' Dennis O'Kelly.

The legends surrounding his name were numberless. No one, it was said, had ever enjoyed a greater luck than he. No gambler had ever won more, no student of horseflesh had ever been more inspired in his judgement, and no connoisseur of woman-flesh had ever been more knowledgeable in his assessment or more virile and salacious in his sexual exploits than this amazing Irishman.

Francis White, the founder of White's Club, had died more than 60 years before William Crockford had been born. Almack had died when William was only a child. But O'Kelly had still been alive when William had first started to take an interest in gambling, and the exploits of the man were still very much alive in London at the time when William was ready to start out on his own career as a gambler. The O'Kelly story had contained every ingredient of sex, melodrama and astonishing good fortune. William listened to the details of this remarkable career as it was told, again and again, in the hells of London and the taverns of Newmarket. He could never hope to compete with O'Kelly, he realised that, for O'Kelly, as befitted an Irishman, had possessed charm in abundance, the ability to talk himself into any situation and to talk himself out of it again when things had become too hot for him, the actor's ability to ape the gentry so skilfully that they were tricked into believing that he was one of them, and the showman's flair for behaving with flamboyant extravagance in an age when flamboyance was a prerogative of the idle rich.

Nature, as William realised, may endow an Irish rogue with such gifts but she seldom bestows them on a stolid, overweight cockney with coarse habits and a flabby body. Even so, he realised that there was much to be learnt from a study of the career of Dennis O'Kelly.

As far as anyone could ascertain, Dennis O'Kelly had been born in poverty in Ireland in about 1720. His brother had been a cobbler by trade, but Dennis had been inspired with loftier ambitions from the moment when, as a young man, he had discovered that he could talk a businessman into a deal or a young girl into bed with equal facility. From this he concluded that his future lay in London, where the streets were paved with gold, the businessmen had more money and the women had more experience. He had been told in early manhood that he would either end up on the gallows or in a mansion; and his philosophy was that he would have to risk the former if he was to achieve the latter.

At the age of about 25 O'Kelly had kissed his many mistresses goodbye and had crossed the Irish Channel on money that he had either borrowed or stolen. He was a strong, sturdy young man with little to recommend him in business other than his blarney, or to a woman other than his gaiety, his self-assurance and his exuberant virility. He had a good calf, and he therefore pondered on the advisability of entering the aristocratic world as a footman, since he realised that livery would suit him, but on his arrival in London he was struck by the congestion of the traffic there, which he rightly assumed could only get worse, with the carriages of the rich, the cattle of the farmers and the waggons of the tradesmen making the muddy roads almost impassable. He therefore decided to become a chair-man, for a lusty young fellow could display his calves as effectively between the shafts of a sedan chair as he could whilst serving tea in a drawing-room; and the opportunities for escorting rich and attractive women home at night were unique.

He did not remain a chair-man for long, for as he had hoped and planned, a wealthy lady of fashion soon required him to serve her in another capacity; but it was not long before he was given his *congé* on account of his persistent infidelity, and so he became a billiards marker – a profession which has been graced by many a rogue and wastrel since the game first became fashionable at the court of Louis xiv. The next step in his career, and one which was really inevitable, was incarceration in the Fleet Prison for debt, but he was rescued from this unhappy plight by two fortuitous if wholly unconnected events in 1760 the one being the death of George ii, which resulted in some debtors being released, and the other being the interest which his obvious virility aroused in the body, if not the heart, of London's foremost brothel-keeper, the ambitious but rather over-sexed Charlotte Hayes. An astute and sophisticated businesswoman, she yet found his blarney irresistible, married him on an impulse and then lavished so much money on him that he was able to buy Clay Hill, a fashionable and capacious residence at Epsom.

Thus was O'Kelly's fortune made. And since his wife knew nearly all the wealthiest and well-born young men in Mayfair, most of whom were her clients, he was successfully launched as one of their number. It was soon after this that he felt that his position warranted a title or rank of some sort, and he toyed with the idea of becoming Count O'Kelly, but his wife suggested that some vague connection with an irregular unit of the Middlesex militia might be more in keeping, and having joined this body of men, he rapidly promoted himself to Major and finally to Colonel, which was as high as he deemed it prudent to go without actually being required to command a body of men.

Now he needed only a stroke of luck to launch him as one of the leading owners of the turf, and here his native instinct for a thoroughbred stood him in good stead. At the sale of the Duke of Cumberland's stud in 1765, one of the colts on offer was a little chestnut with a broad blaze and one white stocking which had been named Eclipse because he had been foaled in the year of the great eclipse of the sun. An astute cattle- and sheep-dealer from the Leadenhall Market named William Wildman had gone to the sale expressly to buy this colt, but the sale had started early and the lot had been knocked down before he arrived. But Wildman had conceived an obsession about the horse with the white blaze and the one white stocking, and he insisted on the animal being put up again, and then bought him. He then sent Eclipse to be trained at stables not far from Clay Hill.

Here O'Kelly saw him at exercise and came to the same conclusion as Wildman. This was a remarkable animal – a racehorse of unpredictable potential. But Eclipse was in every sense the high-mettled racer – wild, bad-tempered and at times almost uncontrollable. O'Kelly sent the manager of his stud over to the stables to advise on how such a tempestuous creature might best be handled; and it was not long before O'Kelly was able to talk Wildman into selling him a share in the horse.

As soon as Eclipse began to race (which was not until his 6th year) the promise of his earlier days was at once fulfilled. It was clear to all that he was of a different class to his opponents and the betting fraternity quickly grew hostile to him as he was never beaten. Threatening letters were sent to Wildman, who was astute but something of a coward; and so O'Kelly offered to buy Eclipse outright from him, for O'Kelly was even more astute than Wildman and was nothing if not courageous. And perhaps he had written some of those anonymous letters himself.

Eclipse soon proved to be the greatest racehorse of the century – 'a horse of incomparable mettle and abominable temper'; and it was not long before Epsom became famous throughout sporting England for two things: it was the home of the great new race, the Derby Stakes, and it was also the home of Eclipse. This dual fame it has never lost.

Eclipse never ran in the Derby, for he was too old to take part in it, but his son, Young Eclipse, won the race in its second year, when the winning owner's name was listed in the race-card as Major O'Kelly; and it was after O'Kelly had won the race again in 1784, with another of Eclipse's progeny named Sergeant, that he felt constrained to award himself the full rank of Colonel in honour of the occasion.

O'Kelly died in 1787, when William Crockford was a boy of 12. By this time he owned a magnificent estate at Edgeware which had previously been the property of the Duke of Chandos, and, like Francis White before him, he was able to leave his wife a considerable fortune. The sporting world went into mourning for him, and did so again two years later when Eclipse also died.

'Eclipse and O'Kelly'! The names have been synonymous with the supreme achievements on the turf from that day until now. There will never be a greater stallion than the horse, or a greater rogue and more fortunate gambler than the owner.

The pointer was clear for the young William Crockford. A man from the gutter might achieve fame and riches in the social world through charm and his ability to seduce wealthy women. He might achieve it by the sheer force of his personality and the persuasiveness of his tongue. But he might also achieve it by entering the racing world firstly as a gambler and a bookmaker and then – having acquired wealth – by owning a great racehorse with which his name would be for ever linked.

O'Kelly had been no Adonis, but he had possessed an earthy virility, and Crockford had the same coarse masculinity. Even so, the metamorphosis from fishmongering at Billingsgate to love-making in Mayfair was more than he could hope to achieve. He realised this also. On the whole, he felt it would be wiser to keep his sexual activities quite separate from his business ones. He had no hope of marrying a wealthy courtesan and thus entering Society via her bed. He felt that it would be wiser to marry unobtrusively, keep his wife in the background, and achieve his aims through wealth attained by gambling and a social position attained as a result of successes won on the turf. At heart he was of the same breed as Uriah Heep; outwardly servile and humble in the presence of the rich, but inwardly plotting their downfall. And in the years to come William Crockford, like Uriah Heep, was to spend much of his time rubbing his fat white hands together in the background whilst the young blades who despised him were losing their patrimony to him by their extravagance and senseless folly.

But if the turf was one road which an upstart might follow in search of wealth and fame, there were also others, and notably that of the prize-ring. Throughout the 18th century the aristocracy and gentry of England had been preening themselves under the title of 'sportsmen'. The craze for pugilism had swept the country, stimulated – as any craze will always be – by the appearance of outstanding personalities. A nobody could become rich by gambling over fighters. He could become as rich, and far more famous, by becoming a fighter.

The young Crockford was drawn to the ring by its potential as a medium for gambling, and he may even have come under the spell of its heroes. But never at any time did he contemplate the possibility of becoming a bruiser himself. At Billingsgate, and in the rookeries surrounding Temple Bar, he had learnt how to look after himself, but not with his fists. Cunning and sly, he preferred to hold his own through trickery, threats and the figurative, if not quite the actual, use of the knife in the back. Like all cowards he both resented and despised those who won the respect and admiration of their fellows by frequent displays of manly courage; and like all cowards he found that a rival who could achieve popularity through physical prowess was able to give him a sense of inferiority. In the years to come one such man in particular, the hero of England, John Gully, aroused in William Crockford a feeling of the deepest resentment. He never challenged Gully in the ring, but they fought many a battle on the turf and in the field of gambling, where hitting below the belt was an accepted form of attack and kicking a man when he was down was held to be the most advantageous way of disposing of him. In all such fights Crockford was well-matched with 'Honest' John; and each was destined to develop the most devious and dubious methods of assault upon the other.

To young Crockford, therefore, observing the habits of the rich from his expeditions to the West End, and listening to the stories that were told about their way of life as he drank his ale in one of the many taverns off St James's Street, the lessons to be learnt were becoming ever clearer. A man with sufficient ambition *could* rise from the gutter to become wealthy, and even a millionaire. He *could* make the acquaintance of the nobility, and he *could* attain a status almost equal to theirs. He could also bet with them, and he could lend them money, providing always that he did not make the mistake of the benevolent Brooks, who lent it without adequate security.

He could not become a gentleman, but – if so minded – he could probably ensure that his children and certainly his grandchildren might attain that much-desired status.

Thus gradually he came under the spell of the West End of London, and of St James's Street in particular; and gradually his ambitions increased. As he walked home in the early hours of the morning after a night spent in one or other of the gambling hells of King Street or Jermyn Street, he would turn over in his mind the possibilities of one day invading this territory which, to the gambler's eye, was so richly stocked with game. He could never hope to emulate O'Kelly; but there was no reason why he should not emulate White or Almack.

A Crockford Club in St James's Street! At first it was only a dream; but he was determined that if ever this dream materialised, it should result in the most splendid club that the West End had ever seen. He knew little enough of the inside of such buildings as White's, Brooks's or Boodle's, but he had watched the wealthy clubmen as they arrived outside these premises in their crested carriages and with their powdered flunkeys to hand them out; and there were always footmen, waiters and cook-boys from these clubs who could be cross-questioned in the dingy taprooms behind St James's Street and who were ready to describe just how their wealthy masters lived, with whom they slept and what they ate.

A fat and greedy young man, but one who yet had a sound knowledge of what constituted good food, and especially of all delicacies connected with fish, the young Crockford was interested to learn how unenterprising was the cooking in the majority of these fashionable clubs – and indeed in the homes of so many of the rich. One or two members of the aristocracy employed French chefs in their kitchens, and of the few hotels that existed in London there was the Clarendon, in New Bond Street, where French fare was served; but the average Englishman was still wedded to his eternal round of roast beef and boiled fowl, and as soon as the Napoleonic wars began, his habitual scorn of all 'froggy' food was redoubled.

And yet the evidence suggested to William Crockford that the young dandies of White's and Brooks's, so elaborate in their dress and so supercilious in their manner, were beginning to find that roast beef and soggy vegetables did not match up with their otherwise fastidious and disdainful way of life. Thus anyone with the ability to look beyond the end of his nose and to forecast the future, could realise that once the struggle with the French was over, English insularity must inevitably diminish, and English palates would then demand a change from beef and mutton and native sauces. 'Heaven preserve any Christian man,' wrote Heinrich Heine, 'from the English sauces! Heaven preserve everybody from their plain vegetables!'

To Crockford, with his shrewd observation of the Mayfair scene, it was becoming increasingly obvious that whereas the lower classes in the towns and *all* classes in the country would have to be dragged protesting into the ways of the 19th century, the fashionable world of Mayfair was growing increasingly critical of the nation's lack of culture, its lack of originality and its lack of taste in all things from food to clothing. To be outstandingly successful, a club of the future would have to abandon the insularity of the 18th-century clubs, and be ready – and indeed eager – to welcome into its midst the cream not only of London Society but also of European Society; and not only the idle and dissipated rich but also the leaders in politics, the arts – and even business.

William Crockford did not foresee all this in his youth; and and indeed he may not have foreseen much more than the simple fact that a man will gamble more freely and with less caution after he has enjoyed an excellent dinner, with the best of wine and in the best of company, than he will after a meal loaded with starch and taken in the company of dolts and morons. But even to appreciate this elementary fact is, for the professional gambler, the first step along the road to riches; for the secret is not to *invite* men to gamble, but rather to set the scene so skilfully that they will ultimately insist that they be permitted to do so. Thus money spent on providing a lavish background and offering lavish fare gratis, and seemingly out of the goodness of the proprietor's heart, is money well spent. A gambler who thinks in hundreds will be wagering in thousands after the second bottle of vintage champagne.

Young Crockford walked back to Temple Bar through the tree-shaded paths of the Mall, and there may well have been times when even the solicitations of the young prostitutes who took over this sylvan scene once darkness had fallen failed to penetrate his concentration. And at dawn, when he found himself amongst the foul-mouthed fishwives of Billingsgate, bargaining with them over coppers when his head was full of plans that would make him think only in terms of golden sovereigns, he may have been struck by the anomaly of his position, so that he became resolved to leave for ever the world of his upbringing.

3

THE GENTLEMEN VERSUS THE PLAYERS

The Triumph of Professionalism

England moved into the 19th century in a chastened mood. The French Revolution had come as a shock, with its terrible stories of cruelty and violence, and the war with France which followed had aroused the fearful thought of invasion, and of the possible spread of mob violence across the Channel. And suddenly England seemed to be no longer the snug and safe island where a rich man might live, love and gamble without taking any serious thought to the future.

The feeling in St James's Street was one of apprehension cloaked by an outward appearance of indifference. The male ego, that turbulent spirit which had made the gilded youth of the 18th century so truculent and defiant, so that it was for ever picking a quarrel and reaching for a sword, was made to look a little less impressive now that there was real fighting to be done. In the new mood in which Society found itself, there was a growing tendency to look with ever-diminishing tolerance on the wild escapades of the irresponsible young. To lose a fortune at Epsom or at hazard no longer seemed quite so dashing now that others were losing their lives fighting against the French.

At first the war had little effect on St James's Street. Beau Brummell and his circle of fellow-dandies remained indifferent to it, even though they could not ignore it; and Society scarcely became involved. Nelson's young officers were admittedly gentlemen, but for the most part they were only the sons of country squires of modest means. But with the advent of the Duke of Wellington, and the Peninsular War, things became different. The army did then include amongst its officers a number of members of the aristocracy. Nelson had never quite seemed a gentleman (after all he had only been the son of a parson and educated in local schools in Norfolk) but Arthur Wellesley was the son of the Earl of Mornington and an Old Etonian. Nelson was never a leader of Society, but Wellington, when he reached his prime, was as much the master of St James's Street as he was of his troops in the Peninsula. He was nothing if not the perfect gentleman, and a dandy as well, without any of the effeminacy of Brummell. And he did not approve of gambling.

Change was in the air, and already there were those who foresaw that the gambling mania which had obsessed Society throughout the 18th century might well be curbed before the 19th century had grown very much older. The women, for one thing, would see to this. They were gambling less themselves, and once they ceased to make heroes of the extravagant young fops of St James's Street who were seeking their favours, the aura of dare-devilry and panache which had surrounded these young gamesters for so long would rapidly lessen.

The turf remained the same, of course, and its aura was certainly in no danger of being diminished. The Duke of Grafton had won the Derby in 1802, and Lord Egremont had won it in 1804, 1805 and 1807. Lord Foley had won it in 1806, his colt Paris beating the topically-named Trafalgar belonging to Lord Egremont by inches (always assuming the judge's eyesight was as accurate as it should have been). Racing had therefore become the pastime of the aristocracry, but the memory of Colonel O'Kelly remained as a reminder that at Epsom a man from the gutter could yet rival a man from a palace.

Perhaps the young William Crockford was conscious of these social changes; and he may have realised that in his life-time he would see the passing of that age of suicidal betting which had been a feature of the social life in England and France during the 18th century. He was the ambitious hunter entering a country where the game was still plentiful, but where the supply was by no means inexhaustible. He had only just been born into the right age. Indeed had he been born 50 years later Society would not have tolerated the way in which he exploited and ruined the aristocracy.

There is ample evidence that at this period he had already become obsessed by gambling, and by the prospect which it held out to him of enrichment. Sometimes he wagered unwisely; and sometimes he used the money which had been entrusted to him for buying in the market to play hazard or to back a prize-fighter, and lost it all; but for all that, a contemporary chronicler was able to record that 'misfortune never affected the stability of his mother's credit in business'.

And all the time he was learning. He lived in a world of gamblers, and when he was not gambling himself he was watching the ways of others who were. He soon discovered that his own temperament was well suited to gambling, because he was bold without ever being rash, and systematic without being over-cautious. He understood the psychology of those who opposed him, his patience was inexhaustible and he realised from the outset that the successful gambler always seeks to bet when the odds are in his favour, and never does so when they are against him. It is true that he was still scarcely literate, and that when it came to preparing a bill for the fishmongering business he would list 'sowls' instead of soles, and write 'makerils' instead of mac-kerel, but there was never anything wrong with his mathematics. He had never heard of Pascal, and he could not speak a work of French, but he would have understood the implication of Pascal's argument when considering the losses of French aristo-crats at the gaming tables, which was in essence, '*C'est magnifique, mais ce n'est pas géomètre.*'

But theory of probabilities or no, William Crockford's agile brain soon appreciated the fact, as Galileo had discovered many years before him, that when three dice are in use in a game of hazard, the total of 10 comes up more often than the total of 9, for out of 216 possible combinations of the three dice, there are 27 combinations which can total 10 and only 25 combinations which can total 9. It is with this sort of knowledge that fortunes amongst gamblers are made.

Night after night was he to be seen, regular as the hour, at the place of rendezvous, *setting the castor, taking on the nick, the doublets and the imperial plan*, and receiving deposits to return large amounts (but considerably short of the real calculated odds) on all the remote and complicated chances of the dice . . .

The quotation is from the biography of William Crockford which appeared soon after his death in *Bentley's Miscellany*, which goes on to comment on the fact that the average player of the day had no knowledge whatever of assessing the correct odds which should be taken, and was invariably dazzled by what seemed an astronomical figure but which was in fact well *below* the figure which should have been quoted. This was a style of betting which Crockford was to exploit to great effect in the years to come, when he would lay ante-post doubles and trebles over future events, and against horses that might easily go amiss long before the race in which they were entered ever took place.

William Crockford also displayed his knowledge of human nature in another way. When laying the odds, he would often produce a bank-note of a size far greater than any other in use at the table, and announce his willingness to lose it to anyone with courage enough to back against him. The lure of big money is an infallible bait; and the small-time gamblers of his East End world would gaze fascinated at this bank-note and would dream of the riches which it implied. Thus they would be lured into trying to deprive the fishmonger of it, either in one of the many long-priced eventualities on which there was virtually no prospect of their collecting, or else by allowing themselves to get out of their depth and to back in sums far higher than they intended.

Thus William Crockford learnt his trade as a professional gambler amongst the small-time operators in the gambling hells near his home – in the Strand, around Covent Garden and in the Billingsgate Fish Market. Then, when he had amassed a small bank, and had learnt all that the East End of London could teach him, he migrated to the West in search of the second world – the fashionable world – and began to haunt the bigger gambling hells around St James's Street, where the play was 'deep' and the players were of substance: wealthy tradesmen of the locality who were accustomed to serving the rich and even the rich themselves, the young bucks from White's and Brooks's who had strolled round the corner to idle away a few hours in plebeian company.

Here, in these surroundings, there was but one rule for survival amongst the under-privileged. The rich might default and get away with it, but if a member of the lower classes ventured into a gambling game, especially if he came from the other end of London, then it was necessary for him to show the colour of his money; for if he lost he was expected to pay immediately. There was no place in this second world for the upstart *without* money. But the upstart *with* money was made welcome, for a golden sovereign was a golden sovereign and worth 20 shillings of an Englishman's money no matter whether it came from the silk purse of a duke or the greasy pocket of a still greasier fishmonger.

Nowhere could a young man with ambition learn better about the hard facts of life, and learn more quickly, than in the gambling hells of London, and especially those which by their situation could attract 'the pigeons' and were therefore the lair of 'the rooks', for 'the pigeons' were the simpletons and 'the rooks' the shrewd and cunning operators who deprived them of their money.

Did they ever emerge the winners, these simpletons from Mayfair or up from the country, when they swaggered into these hells and shouted for ale? They won their simple Pyrrhic victories, of course, bedding the big-bosomed, buxom and accommodating wenches of the establishment in the straw of the stables or in the frowsty bedrooms upstairs, winning a little before they lost, and perhaps thrashing some drunken bully or elderly watchman whom they might encounter whilst relieving themselves in the stable yard, but their purses were empty when they left. Consider, in passing, a contemporary list of the staff employed at the sort of gambling hell which the young Crockford would have patronised (but with his eyes open, for he was no 'pigeon') – a staff whose single purpose was to entice gamblers with money into the establishment and to ensure that they left it without any:

A *Director* to superintend the play. An *Operator* to deal the cards and, as an expert in sleight-of-hand, to cheat the players. Two *Crowpees* [croupiers] to watch the play and see that the players do not cheat the *Operator*. Two *Puffs* to act as decoys, by playing and winning with high stakes. A *Clerk* to see that the two *Puffs* cheat only the customers and not the bank. A *Squib*, who is a trainee *Puff* under tuition. A *Flasher*, whose function is to talk loudly of the bank's heavy losses.

A *Dunner* to collect debts owing to the bank. A *Waiter*, to serve the players and see that they have more than enough to drink, and when necessary to distract their attention when cheating is in progress. An *Attorney*, to advise the bank in long-winded latin terms when the legality of the play is ever questioned. A *Captain* to spring to the defence of the bank if any player should draw his sword. An *Usher*, to light the player upstairs when he desires to relieve himself, or to spend a few moments in dalliance with one of the house wenches. A *Porter*, usually an ex-service man, to stand on duty outside the premises, and who has made it his business to be on good terms with the night-watchman and local soldiery. An *Orderly Man*, to serve as a look-out and to warn the *Porter* when trouble with the law is afoot. A *Runner*, to ply between the house and the courts when cases involving gambling are being heard. And finally, numerous part-time employees of the house who work on its behalf, including sundry link-boys, watchmen, chair men, affidavit men, ruffians of all sorts, bailees, street urchins, pimps, prostitutes, touts and beggars.

The total might therefore number nearly twenty full-time servants of the house, with as many again receiving payment from it but not on the permanent staff, their combined efforts directed against the wealthy young gamester who entered the establishment.

What chance had he got against such an organisation? He would have his small moments, for his hopes had to be elevated and his conceits pandered to; and the prostitutes in the pay of the house would make it their business to gaze on him in admiration, so that he convinced himself that he was indeed a hell of a fellow, win or lose, and a true gallant and rake. And perhaps, in a round-about way, his ego *did* benefit in the end and he was not altogether a loser, for when he left the establishment in the early hours of the morning he would be bowed on his way, and the *crowpees* and the *puffs*, the *squibs*, the *flashers* and the *dunners* would treat him with exaggerated deference, so that he swaggered out into the London night convinced of his own daring and manliness.

Although he was an expert with dice, and was later to make his fortune over hazard, the young Crockford, at the start of his career, tended to specialise in card games, and above all in whist, piquet and cribbage; and it was cribbage which was instrumental in bringing him the capital that he so urgently needed and thus launching him on his adventurous career into the second world of London – the world of great wealth and great opportunity.

Cribbage is a game which is at its best when played by only two players. It is a game of skill, the skill lying in the ability of the players to memorise the cards played; and it is a game pre-eminently suitable for those who have a flair for cards. It is a game calling for judgement, so that losses deliberately incurred can be offset against successes that are to come. The purpose of the game is to collect various combinations of cards and then to discard those that may be less advantageous when the hand is played and there is a show. In short it is a game – like poker – in which the good player will usually beat the bad. It is also a game in which a bad player will often pride himself on his skill without ever realising that he has none.

Two of the most popular taverns and gambling houses in the St James's area were The Tun Tavern, in Jermyn Street, which was kept by a bookmaker named Jerry Waters who was supported by his two pretty daughters; and The Grapes, in King Street. The Tun Tavern was the haunt of racing men, where turf intelligence was discussed and owners, jockeys and trainers were often to be encountered. The Grapes, on the other hand, was the drinking place of the well-to-do tradesmen of the district, and especially those from St James's Street, which was just round the corner.

One of the 'regulars' who patronised The Grapes was a butcher whose shop was in King Street. He supplied many of the large houses in the district, and since his meat was good and his service reliable, the business had thrived and he had prospered. He was a 'warm' man.

Much has already been written in this book about the male ego – its importance and its influence in a man's life. It has been seen as one of the motivating forces behind the wealthy young rake's urge to gamble. But the male ego is not only to be encountered in the young and the well-born. It is to be encountered in almost every male who smarts under some secret sense of inferiority, and whom it encourages in acts of flamboyance and self-assertion.

The butcher was just such a man. Large and florid, as is customary in his trade, successful and richer by far than most of the tradespeople who patronised The Grapes, he was much given to boastfulness, and he prided himself on his astuteness and knowledge of the world. He was a gambler, and he loved to demonstrate his importance by making flamboyant wagers in larger sums than was customary in The Grapes. Here the small fry – the hangers-on, the minor tradespeople, the footmen, coachmen and other male domestics from the big houses of the district – were content to risk in an evening about five shillings (which for some might amount to a week's wages). The bigger fry would bet in sovereigns; and occasionally a hundred-pound note would be flourished, which was considered a very big bet indeed.

The butcher bolstered his ego by betting 'deep'. He loved to advertise his prosperity and to draw forth exclamations of admiration from the other inhabitants of The Grapes by making the biggest bet of the evening. His speciality was cribbage, at which he considered himself an expert. He was a braggart, a fool and a rich man; exactly the type of gambler for whom William Crockford was searching in order to make the one big killing that would give him capital enough to start on his career as a professional gambler.

Crockford watched his man for several nights, noted his manner of play, assessed his ability and then set about laying a trap in which to ensnare him.

It was not very difficult. The butcher was encouraged to boast of his prowess, and was encouraged to throw out a grandiose challenge to a match of a pound a peg (the game is scored by pegs placed in holes on the cribbage board beside the players). Finally he was encouraged to turn this into the biggest contest ever seen in The Grapes, a marathon game of 10,001 holes, the game to continue without pause until the last hole had been filled.

How easy it all must have been! The butcher at first boastful, at first complacent, at first unafraid, and thus gradually being forced into a position where the match would have to be played, for to back out would result in an intolerable loss of face. The onlookers applauding, the toasts drunk, the side bets offered and accepted – and the butcher finally going home to think over what he had done, and to wake up in the cold light of morning realising that he might well have saddled himself, through his conceit, with far more than he had ever intended. But he could not back down. The match would have to be played.

Yet his opponent was little more than a boy – and a fat, repulsive boy at that, the son of a fishmonger's widow from Temple Bar. And perhaps this clinched the matter. It was unthinkable that a small-time fishmonger from the East End could ever prove a match for a prosperous butcher whose clients included some of the highest in the land. This upstart youth must be taught a lesson. He must be taught how cribbage should be played.

The game lasted an entire night. It was watched by a large crowd of gamblers, supporters of one contestant or the other, and there was heavy side-betting on the result. And as in other incidents in Crockford's life, the issue was never really in doubt. A true professional, if albeit a young and relatively inexperienced one, was taking on an amateur – and as always the professional played better, thought more quickly and had more courage. As soon as the butcher began to find himself losing, his self-confidence began to desert him and he began to play badly; and the more he lost, the rasher he became, trying to extricate himself from his predicament by foolhardy play.

By the next morning it was all over. When the game ended, William Crockford had won £1,700, and the butcher was a broken man – his pride humbled and his business ruined by his losses.

Crockford now had capital and the next step was an obvious one: to open a gambling hell of his own, in the West End, to run it on business-like methods, honestly because that was the wisest thing to do, to make his premises as comfortable as possible and to provide his patrons with good food. And then to sit back and watch the bank make a profit, whilst at the same time investigating all the other methods of making money out of the rich, notably on the turf.

Two steps therefore became necessary. The first was to move into suitable premises as near St James's Street as possible. The second was to extend his activities to Newmarket, and perhaps to buy a second establishment there, so that he could obtain first-hand information about all that went on in the racing world. It would then be possible to insinuate himself into the profession of the 'legs', making a book and laying the odds against the horses owned by the nobility and gentry.

He probably did not sever all connection with the shop at Temple Bar. His mother was now becoming too old to run it and he therefore placed a manager in charge of the business, kept his eye on it and journeyed occasionally eastwards as far as Temple Bar to satisfy himself that it was being properly run; but his own attention was now turned to gambling. By retaining ownership of the shop, he furnished himself with a second string to his bow, for he knew that a run of unforeseen bad luck might yet cripple him. Even with bets so carefully assessed and major losses so carefully 'hedged', there was always the danger that some wealthy and ignorant young fool might make some absurd wager that succeeded. The professional gambler always fears luck in others, for it is a factor against which he cannot adequately guard. Fools can sometimes play ducks and drakes with the theory of probability and turn it upside down.

It is not surprising that he turned his attention to King Street, the scene of his first major triumph and a locality ideally situated for a gambling house. The proprietor of 5, King Street, a Jew named Livisne, sold him a quarter-share in his gaming room. The partnership was profitable enough, but the partners soon quarrelled over the division of the profits. There was also a rival gaming house situated next door, at No. 6, and the nightly disturbances which occurred at each, either as a result of the patrons fighting amongst themselves, of the proprietors fighting their patrons, or of the proprietors fighting each other, used to result in so much noise that the peace of the night was shattered and the neighbours began to complain. This, after all, was King Street, adjacent to fashionable St James's Street, the Palace and Pall Mall, and yet it could still become the settling ground for all numbers of disputes amongst all types of blackguards.

Letters written by outraged householders of the area to the newspapers give evidence of the indignation felt, but little seems to have been done. 'A door was suddenly opened, and a gentleman was thrust into the street by some ruffians, and dashed into the middle of it, upon his back, with great violence. On this, a lady screamed, who was accidentally passing in company with a gentleman . . . ' So runs one of these letters of protest. It builds up an engaging picture, and one is tempted to wonder what was the calling of the lady who happened to be passing down King Street in the early hours of the morning.

But despite all such goings-on, William Crockford was yet able to build up for himself a reputation as a reliable banker who always met his commitments. He had brought with him, as his aide, a skilful and cunning associate of his earlier days – a croupier named Gye, who watched over his interests. He could announce each night that the bank at hazard was of £500, and although this was nothing remarkable in that neighbourhood, it was big enough to satisfy the majority of his patrons. The time would come, as well he knew, when he would be able to advertise a bank very much larger than this.

The months passed, the profits multiplied, and the business flourished. He therefore began to look for other suitable premises so that his 'empire' might grow. More gambling houses were acquired, including one in Oxendon Street and others near St James's Street; and he also began to operate in Jerry Water's sporting tavern, The Tun, in Jermyn Street. His methods of attracting custom did not vary. They were based on the methods with which he had been so successful in the past – a display of big notes by the bank, implying that the money was waiting to be won by any backer brave enough to take a chance; and the seemingly liberal offer of long-odds against future events – the naming of the winner of the Derby many months before the race was run, and the coupling of it with that of the St Leger winner, a race staged nearly three months later still.

A clear picture of what Crockford looked like at this period, and of how he operated, is given in a contemporary poem that appeared in a pamphlet called, with ponderous wit, *Leggiana*. Here is how this particular 'leg' is described:

> Seated within the box, to window nearest,
> See *Crocky*, richest, cunningest, and queerest
> Of all the motley group that here assemble
> To sport their blunt chaff, blackguard and dissemble;

Who live (as slang has termed it) on the mace,
Tho' Crocky's heavy pull is, now, *deuce ace.*
His wine, or grog, as may be, placed before him.
And looking stupid as his mother bore him,
For *Crock*, tho' skilful in his betting duty,
Is not, 'twill be allowed, the greatest beauty;
Nor does his *mug* (we mean no disrespect)
Exhibit outward sign of intellect;
In other words, old *Crocky's* chubby face
Bespeaks not inward store of mental grace;
Besides, each night, he's drunk as any lord,
And clips his mother English every word.
His head, howe'er, tho' thick to chance beholders,
Is screw'd right well upon his brawny shoulders;
He's quick at thought, and ripe at calculation,
Malgré the drink's most potent visitation.
His pencil, list, and betting book on table,
His wits at work, as hard as he is able,
His odds matur'd, at scarce a moment's pains,
Out pops the offspring of his ready brains,
In some enormous, captivating wager,
'Gainst one horse winning *Derby*, *Oaks* and *Leger*.

The years passed. In 1805 Trafalgar was fought and won, allowing Englishmen to breathe freely once again and the wealthy to sleep easily in their beds once more. The gambling mania took on a further lease of life, and the era of luxurious living continued to flourish. Handsome donations were made to the Patriotic Fund that had been raised to help the dependants of those killed in the battle, and with the Englishman's conscience suitably eased by the liberal contributions he was happy to make to it (how pleasant it always is to be able to confirm one's patriotism by the donation of sums that one can well afford!), the world of Mayfair and St James's resumed its former carefree way of life.

It was not long afterwards that an important incident took place in the social life of the young bucks of Mayfair. A casual conversation over the port when the Prince Regent was entertaining a few of his friends to dinner at Carlton House gave rise to a discussion on the food that was served in the clubs such as

White's and Brooks's. The dinner which they had just finished had been an excellent one and had included a number of continental dishes, exquisitely flavoured and perfectly served. In reply to a query by the Prince, Sir Thomas Stepney declared that the dinners at both clubs were always the same – 'the eternal joints, or beefsteaks, the boiled fowl with oyster sauce, and an apple-tart – this is what we have, sir, at our clubs, and very monotonous fare it is'.

For answer the Prince rang the bell and sent for his chef, Watier, and asked him whether he would be prepared to organise a dining club where gentlemen of fashion could enjoy really good French cooking. Watier agreed to do so, and Watier's Club was opened in Bolton Row, off Piccadilly, with Madison, the Prince's page, as manager and Labourie, one of his cooks, in charge of the kitchen.

News of this new club soon spread throughout Mayfair, and the dandies and rakes hastened to join. The food was excellent and made the cooking at White's and Brooks's seem very dull and tasteless in comparison, and – as always – the moment the Club became famous and exclusive, everyone who was anyone wished to join it.

The next step was equally inevitable. As soon as Watier's had become the home of the rakes, it also became the home of gambling, for no young rake was content to join a club simply in order to eat, although this was important enough. The only way to end a perfect evening, after a gentleman had dined and wined in the best possible manner, was to sit down at a green baize table and call for cards or dice. At Watier's the game most in favour was Macao, and the play soon became very 'deep'. Macao is a card game not unlike *vingt-et-un*, in which only one card is dealt to each player and the winning number is 9 instead of 21. A player dealt a 9 has the equivalent of a 'natural' and is paid three times. (None of these games demanded much intelligence on the part of the players).

One of the chief members of Watier's, and also one of those who played deepest, was Beau Brummell. Brummell, although so fastidious in dress and so languid in manner, yet followed the gambling tradition of the 18th century by complaining bitterly when confronted with a run of bad luck. *Sang froid* was not for him when the cards were against him, and he could be as melo-dramatic as an actor on such occasions. Once, when his luck had been really atrocious, he called to the waiter and told him to bring a loaded pistol immediately. The inference was at once appreciated by all those present, who waited expectantly to see whether or not the Beau would blow his brains out. Brummell had good reason to believe that no pistol was available, but un-fortunately for him another member, a Mr Hythe, called his bluff by producing two loaded pistols from his pocket and push-ing them across the table to Brummell, who was forced to refuse them. On another occasion two players began to quarrel so bitterly that one threw a large bowl of counters in the face of the other.

Watier's soon developed a bad reputation. Its leading lights were Brummell, who soon became the dictator of the club, and his crony, Lord Byron. They were very conscious of the exclusive-ness of the place, and not only rejected all except the cream of Society but also country members as well, whom they felt might be insufficiently refined in their persons and might well bring mud into the premises on their boots.

News of what was going on at Watier's soon reached William Crockford, confirming all that he had already learnt – that exclusiveness coupled to the serving of the choicest foods and wines was the first requirement of a successful club, and that the second was the provision of gaming facilities, so that those who had eaten and drunk too much could be encouraged to bet too much as well. No obligation would ever need to be put upon them in order to make them gamble. This they would do of their own accord. The saying 'Give them enough rope and they will hang themselves' could be interpreted at a club such as this as 'Give them enough to eat and drink and they will ruin themselves'.

William Crockford followed the fortunes of Watier's with interest, and ideas began to form in his mind. His aim now was either to gain a foothold in Watier's itself, or else to start a similar club of his own, where the food was outstanding and the most exclusive set in London, such as that which Brummell and Byron were now leading, might be lured into its fold.

Trafalgar, in 1805, had ended the fears of invasion. Waterloo, in 1815, ended *all* fears. With Napoleon crushed and England supreme, there were those who confidently proclaimed that a century of peace might well lie before England. The country would become even more prosperous, the rich would become ever richer, and the way of life in Society would become ever more elegant, more comfortable and more impregnable.

In the January of 1820, 'the poor old, old King, George III' as Lady Sarah Lyttelton described him, died in his bed, still to all intents and purposes as mad as a hatter, as he had been for years, and the Prince Regent ascended the throne in his place. The advent of a monarch whose outlook to self-indulgence was already a byword, and whose immorality was famous throughout Europe, might have been taken as a sign that the golden age of dissipation which 19th-century England had inherited from the 18th might be prolonged indefinitely, but there were yet many who saw in this accession only the last brilliant explosion of the firework display. The urge towards respectability was now becoming unmistakable; and the character of the great Duke of Wellington brooded over London Society. Beau Brummell's disastrous escapades, and his flight to France in 1816 after he had been ruined by gambling and his extravagant way of life, had furnished a warning for many. The gambling age might last another 20 years or so, but it looked as if it might be ending.

But wars or no wars, the turf continued to flourish, and the lure of Newmarket and Epsom grew ever stronger. Here was a new field for the professional gambler to explore and exploit, either backing horses or by laying odds against them. In the old days gentlemen had bet only with gentlemen, and the system had worked none too well, for gentlemen were liable to cheat each other, and the younger set were also liable to bet far more than they could afford and then go bankrupt without being able to meet their commitments. Thus the need was felt at Newmarket and at other turf centres for a professional betting ring, with men of substance if not of breeding ready to assess the odds and to lay them. It was in this way that the 'legs' had come into being.

It had been Colonel O'Kelly who had largely led the way. He had capital enough to stand up and bet with the wealthy, and knowledge enough to manipulate the odds in his favour. The gentlemen layers who had preceded him had not for the most part had any knowledge of the mathematics of making a book, although a few of the canny ones such as 'Old Q' had been quick enough to ensure that when they made a bet themselves, the odds were in their favour. But bookmaking implied much more than this. A substantial bookmaker could become the changing-house for all bets, and by laying first one horse in a race and then another could give his backers a fair price and yet show a profit himself, no matter which of them won.

The face of Newmarket had changed. It had ceased to be the exclusive playground of the rich and had become instead the centre of a flourishing national industry – that of the breeding, training and racing of thoroughbreds, coupled with the laying of prices against their relative chances when these racehorses met in contests that were to decide not only how much money could be won over each, but which was in truth the best, so that this great national industry of thoroughbred breeding might be built up on the soundest of principles and English bloodstock might then be sold all over the world.

O'Kelly had entertained the fancy, raced against the fancy and gambled with them, always paying up when he lost; and in the end he was looked upon by the fancy as being almost a gentleman. The majority of the 'legs' who followed after him were unable to emulate him in this respect, although they tried to copy O'Kelly in the matter of grand living. For the most part they were rogues from the gutter, without principle and fully prepared to corrupt the turf in whatever manner seemed to suit their pockets best – either by bribing jockeys to pull their mounts in a race or dopers to nobble these mounts beforehand. A typical 'leg' whom the late 18th-century turf threw up was another Irish immigrant like Colonel O'Kelly, but a man who was quite without O'Kelly's charm. This was the notorious 'Captain' Dick England, an illiterate, cunning and ruthless bully – a big man who went through life threatening everyone in his path. He even assaulted O'Kelly once when the Colonel was an old man and crippled with gout, and very nearly killed him; and when O'Kelly sued for assault, he was only awarded a shilling's damages on the

grounds that both participants in the quarrel were men of doubtful antecedents engaged in a despicable profession.

Dick England set out to ruin those who gambled with him, and
succeeded in a number of cases. A wealthy young man, the
Honourable Damer, was bled to the tune of £40,000 and committed suicide rather than face his father when he was being
threatened by England with exposure and disgrace. Another
less well-born youth named Clutterbuck, a clerk in the Bank of
England, found himself in England's clutches and resorted to
forgery. He was tried, found guilty and hanged.

England was thus a typical bookmaker of the period – bad-
tempered, aggressive and dishonest. He finally killed one of his
clients in a duel after first assaulting him at Ascot and was forced
to flee to Paris, where despite his villainous aspect he was surprisingly mistaken for an aristocrat and only just escaped the
guillotine. After this experience he returned to England, a
chastened character if certainly not a reformed one.

Those who followed in his footsteps after the turn of the
century and who constituted the bookmaking world which
Crockford now entered were for the most part men of a similar
disposition. They were prepared to go to any lengths to stop one
horse from winning or to ensure that another should succeed;
and because many of them became wealthy, they were in a position to offer substantial bribes to the hirelings whom they employed to do their dirty work.

The first two decades of the 19th century witnessed the rise
to affluence of men such as 'Crutch' Robinson, Jem Bland,
Jerry Cloves, Myers Richards, Mat Milton, Tommy Swan of
Bedale, John Justice and John Gully. These were Crockford's
rivals when he took up bookmaking, and it is some measure of
his self-confidence that from the outset he was satisfied that he
could hold his own in such formidable company.

They were a villainous crew, differing only in their physical
aspect, but united in their determination to cheat their wealthy
and well-born clients and – whenever it seemed necessary – to
cheat each other. The important point was that the gentlemen
who raced at Newmarket and Epsom realised what crooks they
were dealing with, and how low these crooks were prepared to

stoop in order to make money, and yet these gentlemen were quite content to mingle in such company and to do business with such ruffians. Worse still, they were happy not only to associate with them and make friends with them but also to close their eyes to all the dishonesty that took place, and even to take part in it when the occasion arose.

In their youth, these members of the aristocracy and of the upper classes had usually spent much of their time in the company of the stable-lads and grooms employed on their country estates, and these servants had initiated them into the tricks of the racing world, and had taught their masters how to cheat.

What were they like, these fellow 'legs' of Newmarket with whom Crockford now began to associate? 'Crutch' Robinson was a little, wizened, monkey-faced north-countryman who had been kicked in his youth when working as a stableboy, so that he was forced to walk on a crutch. (Many of the bookmaking fraternity of the period had graduated from lowly positions in racing stables, which accounted for their shrewd knowledge of horses, jockeys and training methods.) 'Crutch' Robinson was the great opponent of favourites, especially those which are known in the racing vernacular as 'talking horses' – that is to say horses which have been 'talked' into favouritism because of rumours in circulation concerning the wonderful form which they have shown in their home gallops. What a horse does on a race-course, as he well knew, is often very different from what it can do at home, and 'Crutch's' opposition to such favourites was based on sound principles that are followed by bookmakers to this day.

Jem Bland was another of the 'legs' who had risen from the gutter and had learnt his trade whilst working as a post-boy and later as a livery-stable keeper in Wardour Street. He was noted for his foghorn voice, which could be heard booming out across the ring at Newmarket, bellowing the odds far louder than any of his competitors. He was quite illiterate and could not even sign his own name with anything other than an indecipherable scrawl. He could not read the bets which his clerk entered in the ledger, because figures were beyond him, but he carried every bet in his head and when the entries in the ledger were read out to him in the evening, he was able to check every one from memory.

His wife ultimately taught him a kind of primitive shorthand, composed of weird symbols known only to himself and to her. The rakes at White's and at Brooks's might lay their absurd wagers over the colour of the cravat worn by the next man rounding the corner from Piccadilly, or the likelihood of rain before nightfall, but Jem Bland could outdo them all when he opposed a horse which he considered to be outclassed. He once laid Mr Wyville £100 to a walking-stick against Theodore winning the St Leger, and paid up without demure when Theodore triumphed with some ease, the starting price being 200/1.

A rogue, of course, like all the rest – and one destined to end his days in luxury in a mansion in Piccadilly. Cunning seemed to run in the family, for his brother, Joe Robinson, made a fortune by 'cornering the market' in turnpike gates. A devious pair!

Jem Bland was conceived in the Crockford pattern, for both were pale and unhealthy, slovenly in dress and dirty in their habits. Both died rich men, but neither died half as rich as he should have done, for both were hoisted with their own petard in the end. 'Dog does not eat dog' was not a tenet of the underworld in their era.

These were the competitors whom William Crockford found in opposition to him when he first became 'a Newmarket man' and transferred some of his attention from operating gambling houses in the West End of London to laying the odds at Newmarket Heath.

Newmarket soon became his second home. It was a very different betting world from that of Newmarket today, for the speed of modern communications and the extent of racing intelligence that exists now has enabled the racing public to obtain a far more detailed knowledge of racing than existed during a large part of the 19th century. The betting public of today just did not exist in Crockford's time. The man-in-the-street might bet on the Derby, and know something about the runners, but in the 18th and early 19th centuries only the rich could afford to travel to Newmarket, and when a race was run there the man-in-the-street was kept in complete ignorance of the runners or the betting. The betting ring itself consisted merely of a few substantial bookmakers who were opposed by a few substantial backers. There were not many races run, not many horses in training, only a few trainers and not many spectators. Newmarket could only be reached by coach after a long and arduous journey of many hours. Runners from provincial stables were 'hacked' to a meeting, often taking several days on the journey. Surprisingly, no one had yet thought of improvising such a thing as a horse-box.

Because the racing press was still in its infancy, knowledge of what was happening in training, of racing form and the plans that were being made by owners and trainers for future events could only be obtained by secret intelligence, which was supplied by the touts who hid themselves on the training grounds and watched the trials, or as the result of the bribery of jockeys and stable lads. Open war existed between the betting ring and the trainers, and between the bookmakers and the backers. As in all wars, a most elaborate network of espionage, and counter-espionage, bluff and counter-bluff, was carried on continually.

Bribery of every sort was rampant. A jockey might be bribed, or a trainer, or even an owner. The starter was frequently 'got at' and various other methods were used in order to 'stop' a favourite from winning. Jockeys in the race could be paid to ride the favourite into the rails, to delay the start until the favourite had become unnerved, or to deny him a clear run. If necessary half-a-dozen useless animals might be entered for a race simply for the purpose of 'boxing' the favourite in.

This was certainly war, with huge sums involved. Today the betting market may be influenced by hundreds of thousands of small bets pouring on to the course in the hour or so before a big race is run, and these bets may represent the sum total of the opinion of the man-in-the-street, betting on what his morning newspapers have told him, or on something which he has seen as he watched the parade of the runners on his television set. No such factors existed in the early days of bookmaking. There were no telephones, and things seen on the course before the race were known only to those present to observe them.

It was thus a straight fight between the big backers and the big layers. The backers were for the most part the wealthy owners, of whom only a few were shrewd and knowledgeable. These included men such as the Duke of Cleveland, known as 'The Jesuit of the Turf', as clever as any man on the Heath, and the infamous 'Old Q'. There were also those who stood on both sides of the fence and who laid the odds and took them. These included the wealthy bookmakers who had become owners.

These were bad days, but they were also exciting days in which the drama of the Ring took place not only on the racecourse but was built up on whispered asides, hidden clues and the straws which showed which way the wind was blowing – the face of a jockey half-glimpsed in the back of a bookmaker's post-chaise as it rattled through a sleeping village at midnight; the sight of a stable-lad in a new pair of boots or of his mistress in a new hat.

Sometimes news of the breakdown of a hot favourite in a race such as the St Leger (in the long history of which more evidence of crooked riding, doping and skullduggery in general may be found than in any other race on the turf) would leak out almost at the last moment, and backers who stood to lose heavily on the horse would rush to the nearest livery stables and there pay big sums for the hire of a fast chaise which could carry them through the night to betting centres such as Sheffield or Notting-ham before the news could reach the bookmakers who were lodging there. And how the horses of these post-chaises would be flogged, and the drivers coaxed to urge them on with ever bigger bribes, lest the passengers should arrive too late and find the taverns already buzzing with the news!

Horses were frequently nobbled in the most shameless way, without any thought to the health and suffering of the animal itself. If they had to be stopped, they were stopped, even if it meant poisoning them to do so. The worst case of all was that which concerned a tout named Daniel Dawson who had lodgings opposite 'Old Q's' house in Newmarket High Street during the first decade of the 19th century and was a friendly enough fellow who was popular in the town.

It was in 1809 that a mysterious illness attacked horses using water troughs in the stables of J.Stevens. Two died, and others were badly affected. The Jockey Club offered a reward of 100 guineas for information that would lead to the conviction of the poisoner, but no one came forward. Two years later, the string belonging to Richard Prince were poisoned in the same way, and even troughs on Newmarket Heath were found to be contaminated. The water was tested and found to contain arsenic, whereat the Jockey Club, now seriously alarmed, raised the reward to 500 guineas – a sum large enough to tempt an informer. As a result, evidence was secretly supplied to the Jockey Club and Dawson was arrested at Brighton and brought to London. From there he was committed to the Cambridge Assizes of 1812, where a chemist's assistant named Cecil Bishop turned King's evidence and told of supplying Dawson with arsenic. Dawson was acquitted at his first trial on a technical point but was later re-tried, found guilty and sentenced to death, as the destruction of horses or cattle was a capital offence under the penal code of the day.

Bishop, in his evidence, described how he had used a fine syringe to squirt a thin stream of arsenic into the drinking trough of the Eagle Colt, owned by Sir Frederick Standish, after the horse had been seemingly locked up in safety in its box. He had then hurried back and told Dawson, who had passed the news on to the bookmakers who were paying him, and they were then able to put the information to good use by laying against the colt.

There was a strong move in Newmarket to have the death penalty commuted, for it was realised that Bishop had been as much to blame as Dawson but had saved his neck by turning King's evidence; and that anyway the real criminals were those for whom Dawson was working, and whom he had refused to name at his trial. One of these, it was strongly suspected, was Jem Bland. Lord Foley, who had lost his valuable mare, Pirouette, felt so strongly about the matter that he personally took up Dawson's case with the Home Secretary, who refused to alter the sentence.

The date of the hanging was fixed for noon on Saturday, 8 August 1812, so that the largest possible crowd might be able to attend. In fact, nearly 12,000 men, women and children surrounded the gallows, which had been erected on the top of Cambridge Castle. Dawson was now looked upon as something of a hero, for he had steadfastly refused to 'peach' on his employers, and when he was driven in an open cart up to the castle he was greeted with cheers. A contemporary source described how he died game, 'behaving with manly but religious fortitude', and his last words as he stood manacled on the scaffold were addressed to some of his cronies standing beneath him, to whom he shouted cheerily, 'Goodbye, my Newmarket lads. Sorry I can't shake hands with you!'

No doubt the 'legs' who employed him had paid him handsomely to keep his mouth shut, but his loyalty to them was commendable. It was doubtful if they were worthy of his sacrifice.

Crockford's great advantage was that he could calculate the betting odds more quickly and more accurately than most of his opponents, whilst he was equal in cunning to any of them. His disadvantage was that he had not been reared amongst horses, and had not that intimate knowledge of them which others possessed. However he had another advantage, that he did not share the ambitions of O'Kelly, and never sought to entertain the aristocracy in his home or to ape their grand ways. This helped overcome another disadvantage, that he himself, came under the magic spell of the turf, and like O'Kelly sought to write his name into turf history by owning famous horses and winning famous races.

No sooner had this magic of Newmarket and of ownership overtaken him than he became vulnerable. When he laid against other people's horses, he rarely made a mistake. But when he started to back his own, he was often caught in those very same traps that he, as a bookmaker, was for ever setting to ensnare others.

Once he had transferred his gambling interests to Newmarket, during the first decade of the century, it was not long before he made himself a person of importance in the little town. By 1809 he had bought Mr Panton's imposing house in the High Street, together with some 50 acres of land in the rear. He also bought a large farm on the east side of the town near the Lower Links' Wood, which he called Crockford's Farm. Finally he decided to go in for pig-breeding on an elaborate scale, and to this end bought a large estate some two miles outside the town. Here he built the most up-to-date sties and filled them with the finest

breed of pig that money could buy. The locals viewed this enterprise with astonishment and awe, but also with some doubt.
Pig-farming was a skilled occupation, and the fact that a man –
no matter how rich he might be – had once run a fishmonger's
business with success in London did not qualify him to set up as
a pig-breeder in the heart of Cambridgeshire. However 'the
great piggery' as it came to be known in the locality brought a
pleasant notoriety to its owner, who delighted in showing his
guests round it of a morning. At least it could be said of William
Crockford at this time that he might well have been mistaken
for a pig-farmer, whereas he could never have been mistaken for a
gentleman, the smell of pigs being not so very different from that
of fish, and the appearance of a pig-man being similar to that of a
man who sold fresh herring or cod.

The ultimate step, in order to establish himself as the complete
'Newmarket man', was to buy a string of valuable racehorses and
to go for ownership, and then to buy a stud farm and to go in
for breeding; for only in this way could he ever hope to meet the
aristocrats of the turf on equal terms. He first began to buy racehorses in 1811 and spent lavishly, but his successes with his string
were not encouraging.

During all this time when he was visiting Newmarket and owning racehorses, Crockford's interest in gaming houses was by no
means diminishing. A gambling club, as he well knew, could not
only provide facilities for the young sportsman to wager on dice
and cards, but also for him to back his fancies on the turf. Ante-
post lists, as we know them today, had not yet been thought of,
and the backer who fancied a runner in a race to be run weeks or
months in advance would approach his bookmaker and ask him
what price he was prepared to offer. (Not until the middle of
the 19th century, during the era of one of the most famous of
all Victorian bookmakers, 'Leviathan' Davis, were price-lists
introduced.) Crockford therefore determined to combine the
running of his gambling houses with the making of a book.
Manipulating a bank at roulette or hazard was far safer, for there
was really little risk attached, but making a book was a business
very much after his own heart, with the opportunities it offered
of duping the young men who crowded round him in the weeks

preceding the Derby or St Leger. He therefore opened a gambling club in Newmarket, at Rothsay House, which was opposite his private establishment in what is now New Station Road, and here he operated nightly both as banker and bookmaker whilst the Newmarket races were in progress.

By this time he was a man of substance, driving to and from Newmarket in a gorgeous carriage padded with down and silks, with powdered flunkeys in attendance and a magnificent pair of horses to draw it.

But during this period of increasing wealth and importance, when he lived and drove in splendour and could almost outdo the aristocracy in his mode of life, two things occurred which marred the image and undermined his self-esteem.

The first was the failure of two of his Newmarket ventures, for his racehorses failed to win races and his pigs failed to win prizes, so that in the end he was forced to reduce his commitments, to sell his stud, to limit his racing string and to abandon the piggery venture altogether.

The second threat to his self-esteem was something far worse, for the Newmarket scene was now beginning to be dominated by a rival whom he could not ignore; a man who had sprung from the gutter, as he had done, but who was now rapidly making a name for himself not only as one of the biggest bookmakers and backers on the turf, but also as one of the most popular and the most respected of sportsman. This was the ex-pugilist and ex-champion of England, 'Honest' John Gully.

To William Crockford, who had never resorted to fisticuffs in his life if he could possibly avoid it, whom no one had ever nick-named 'Honest' William, nor was ever likely to do so, and whose uncouth appearance and cringing servility when in the presence of the fancy made him despised by all, the proud demeanour yet manly modesty of John Gully was as a red rag to a bull.

Moreover William Crockford knew enough about life to recognise a fellow-crook when he saw him, and for all 'Honest' John's manly bearing, his upright carriage and noble mien, William Crockford formed the opinion that here was someone who might well prove himself to be as devious and as artful as any of his rivals. He might be 'Honest' John to the sporting fraternity, but to Crockford he remained just another 'leg'.

John Gully, like Colonel O'Kelly before him, had begun his career as an inmate of the Fleet Prison, from which he had been extricated by an unexpected benefactor, although not by a beautiful brothelkeeper like O'Kelly's friend. Thereafter no sportsman of his era enjoyed a more remarkable or more dramatic career.

Gully was born on 21 August 1783, at the Crown Inn, Wick, a west-country village between Bath and Bristol. His father was the landlord, who moved to Bath when John was still a small boy and set up in his business as a butcher. John took over the business when his father died, but could not make a success of it and soon ran into serious financial trouble. At the age of 21 he was committed to the Fleet Prison in London for debt. At this time he was a fine, upstanding young fellow, of exceptional strength and stamina, who had made something of a reputation for himself as a pugilist.

The Champion of England at this time was another west countryman, 'Hen' Pearce, known as 'The Game Chicken', a fighter of incomparable courage and – as it so happened – of a most generous nature. When news of Gully's plight reached Pearce, he determined that something should be done to save the lad from rotting away for years. When he visited Gully one day in the prison, he took with him a set of gloves and suggested that they should spar together so that he might assess the young man's ability. As soon as he had satisfied himself that Gully showed promise, Pearce put up a proposal to him: 'challenge me to a fight, and I will see to it that you then find backers who will get you out of prison and pay for your training. If you do well, your reputation will be made. Anyway you have nothing to lose.'

Gully readily accepted. He expected to be thrashed, but he realised that if he could make a game showing against the champion, all his money problems might be solved.

The fight took place at Hailsham, in Sussex, on 8 October 1805, before a large crowd of the fancy, which included the Duke of Clarence (later to become William IV), Beau Brummel and several members of the aristocracy. The patron who had come forward to launch the young fighter was Colonel Mellish, finest of the Corinthians, a close friend of the Duke and himself a fighter of peerless courage. Gully was beaten, as it was inevitable that he should be, but it was a splendid battle, and after 70 minutes of slogging during which Gully was punched repeatedly in the throat, Mellish threw in the sponge to save his man from further punishment, even though he had backed Gully heavily to win. At which 'The Game Chicken' walked forward, grasped Gully's hand and said, 'Thou'rt the best man I've ever fought.'

Within two months of this fight, Pearce was forced to retire, and Gully was then nominated as his successor. He was challenged for the championship by the Lancashire fighter, Bob Gregson, a man well over six feet in height and of huge strength, and the contest was staged on 14 October 1807, at Six-Mile Bottom, off the Newmarket Road. It was a sledge-hammer affair of fierce hitting, but after an hour – and in the 36th round – Gully dealt his opponent such a savage blow that he was unable to continue the fight. After this Captain Barclay bore Gully away in his carriage, and the next day drove him in triumph down the New-market racecourse. A return fight proved that Gully was un-questionably the better man, and with this point established he very wisely decided to retire. By now he was the proprietor of the Plough Inn in Carey Street, off Lincoln's Inn Fields, and his fame and popularity, to say nothing of the presence of his engag-ing young wife, ensured that the business quickly prospered.

A previous champion, Gentleman Jackson, had turned his reputation to good use after his retirement by teaching sparring to the fancy, thus earning himself a thousand a year. But John Gully had other ideas. He was at heart a Newmarket man, and his triumph in the ring at Six-Mile Bottom had made the ties between him and the town even stronger. He was also an excellent judge of a horse and a shrewd gambler, as well as being a sound man of business. But his greatest asset, as he well knew, was the confidence which his wealthy patrons now placed in his integrity, for in their racing activities they needed a go-between in their betting transactions – a man who could be trusted to place com-missions discreetly whilst mixing with the 'legs' on their own level. Such middle-men were hard to find.

John Gully therefore approached several wealthy owners

and suggested that he should be allowed to work their racing commissions. This meant that where a large bet was to be placed, he would spread the money in his own time and at his own discretion, getting the biggest price available and keeping the source from which the money came as secret as possible. The young bloods, in their unwise enthusiasm, loved to approach a bookmaker in the ring and bask in the notoriety of placing the biggest wager of the afternoon, but this was not the way in which the shrewd backers worked. Lord Foley, Lord Abingdon and, of course, Gully's loyal patron and supporter, Colonel Mellish, were at once happy to employ him as their agent.

A man who works a commission has access to information that can prove of great benefit to him. Here again, his discretion and integrity must be relied upon; but provided he serves his employers first, there is no reason why he should not benefit himself thereafter. Moreover the knowledge that one horse in a race is the probable winner makes it possible for the commission agent to exploit the situation by turning bookmaker and laying against the remainder of the field.

John Gully carried out his duties admirably. He made money for his patrons and he made money for himself. He abandoned the profession of publican and devoted himself fully to the turf. In this he was helped greatly by his knowledge of horses and his good judgement in assessing their respective merits. This at times could prove almost uncanny. He started backing Memnon for the St Leger nearly a year before the race, and six months before it he began laying bets that he could name both the winner *and* the second. The result of the race was exactly as he had predicted. And all this while he basked in the trust and even adulation of the gentlemen of the turf, who compared his open and honest manner with the sly and furtive habits of the other 'legs'.

Inevitably Gully came into contact with Crockford on many occasions and as inevitably the pair took an instant dislike to each other. Gully looked down his nose at the gross and ungainly ex-fishmonger; and Crockford sneered openly at Gully's fine ways and fancy friends. When they crossed swords, it was usually Gully who came out the better, for he was quite as cunning as Crockford, just as clever at calculating the odds, and far more knowledgeable when it came to judging horseflesh. He took up ownership, just as Crockford had done, and because of his greater knowledge he bought better horses and won races with them. He then took a page from Crockford's book by investing in house property, and outdid Crockford when he bought from Lord Rivers a splendid Newmarket mansion, Upper Hare Park. Indeed the Gully charm and manly bearing so impressed the seller that Lord Rivers insisted on making Gully a present of the farm-stock and all the farm implements. It was inconceivable that anyone might make a similar gesture when selling a property to William Crockford.

Meanwhile Crockford continued to own a few horses, and despite his failures he did not abandon all hope of winning one of the great races of the turf and thus establishing himself on an equal footing with the nobility as a result. Gully, of course, was dedicated to the same purpose, and their rivalry became more acute as each riding season came and went.

The prize above all other prizes was, of course, the Derby, and the rivalry between the two was brought to a head in 1819 when Crockford had good reason to believe that he had the probable Derby winner in his string. This was Sultan, a magnificent bay colt of the utmost courage, despite the fact that he carried 'the rogue's badge' of four white feet; and by the late spring of 1819 it seemed that Sultan had only one serious rival to face at Epsom, a colt named Tiresias, which was the property of the 4th Duke of Portland. The Duke at this time was one of the most popular and highly respected owners on the turf, who had been forced to reduce his racing interests considerably and who had only one other horse in training at the time.

Gully laid against Sultan and Crockford backed him. Each was motivated by prejudice, for Crockford believed that Tiresias could never prove a match for Sultan, whilst Gully – who had yet to experience the distinction of having a runner in the great Epson race – was anxious to convince himself that Tiresias was certain to win and Sultan to lose.

The betting before the Derby suggested that it was a two-horse race, for Tiresias was made favourite at around 2/1 while Sultan was offered at about half a point longer, and 7/1 was laid bar these two. The market, as is so often the case, provided an accurate forecast of the result, for Tiresias was sent straight into the lead and only Sultan ever looked like catching him. Tiresias was still well in front at the distance, but Sultan challenged so strongly in the last furlong that Tiresias was only just able to hold him off at the winning post, the distance given by the judge being 'half a neck'.

Gully smiled with undisguised satisfaction. Crockford cursed his luck, his trainer and above all his jockey, whom he maintained should have delivered his challenge sooner.

The aristocracy, on the other hand, were delighted by the Duke of Portland's success. He represented the very best type of owner (and in the years to come his son, Lord George Bentinck, was to earn for himself the same reputation), and although his string was small he was yet looked upon as the natural successor on the turf to the Derby's founders, Sir Charles Bunbury and the 12th Earl of Derby. The nobility were very conscious of the fact that the Derby was becoming the chosen arena in which the lower classes were seeking to rival their social superiors, and that the challenge from upstarts such as William Crockford, with plenty of money but no breeding or honesty, would become ever more threatening as the years went by. So far the Derby had largely remained the preserve of gentlemen at least, if not always of the aristocracy, and the notorious Colonel O'Kelly had been the only undeniable rogue to have won the race.

Now class had triumphed once again, and a duke's horse had beaten that of a fishmonger. Even so, it had been a narrow squeak, and the future of the Derby looked ominous. Sooner or later not only rogues and upstarts might be expected to win this English classic, but also foreigners as well. It was lucky that there were men such as the Dukes of Portland, Rutland and Grafton, and the Lords Jersey and Egremont, to repel the enemy.

Crockford was able to comfort himself, however, with the thought that there still remained the St Leger, the last of the season's classics and a race which was nearly as important as the Derby itself. Tiresias was not entered, and once again William Crockford backed Sultan heavily and once again Gully laid as heavily against it. Now for the first time Crockford was to be truly

hoisted with his own petard for Gully's secret information concerning Sultan's well-being was to prove more accurate than
that given to the owner himself. Crockford was assured by his
trainer that Sultan was fit and ready to run for his life, but Gully
was given reason to believe that – as has been the case with so
many other Derby runners – the strain of being prepared for yet
another punishing race was beginning to tell.

At the beginning of the St Leger week both Crockford and
Gully were still in London, and thus separated by more than 160
miles from the centre of operations. But they continued to bet
heavily on the outcome of the race. Almost on the eve of the race,
and shortly before his departure for Doncaster, Sultan broke down
in his final gallop and it was clear that he would have to be
scratched.

Messengers were at once sent post-haste to carry the news to
London, but Gully's information travelled faster, and for a few
hours he was able to continue to lay seemingly generous odds
against a horse which he knew could never run. Crockford
accepted these odds and then learnt soon afterwards that he had
been caught in a trap which was at that time a speciality of his
own. And his hatred of Gully was doubled.

What galled him, and continued to increase his hatred of his
rival, was the fact that Gully was still basking in the friendship
and esteem of the nobility and yet still making money out of
racing by trickery and double-dealing. One day he could be
seen fraternising with the highest in the land, his splendid presence
and hearty, honest laugh making him stand out amongst his companions, and the next – as Crockford well knew – he might be
glimpsed in the corner of a back-street tavern, in whispered conversation with some shifty-eyed blackguard. Indeed he was
already seen in close association with Robert Ridsdale, an ex-
boots from a Doncaster inn, who was fast building up for himself
the reputation of being the cleverest villain on Newmarket Heath
– a locality which specialised in producing villains of the deepest
infamy.

It would be incorrect to say of Crockford at this period that
he had learnt his lesson, and had realised that he would do better

to limit his sphere of operations to the field in which he was the acknowledged expert. In fact this lesson was never fully learnt, as his future history was to prove, but by the time that the third decade of the new century had been reached he had wisely come to the conclusion that he would be better occupied by concentrating on the running of gambling clubs in London, about which he knew everything, than of the running of racehorses at Newmarket, about which he knew little. He realised that he could never cut a dash on the turf, treating the aristocracy as his friends, as did John Gully. But he knew that he could achieve distinction in London by becoming the richest and most successful club owner in the history of gambling. By the 1820s, this had become his great ambition.

His first venture was a tentative one, and was none too successful, although it made him a great deal of money. Ever since its earliest days he had kept an eye on Watier's Club where the play had become so 'deep' that it put even the gambling at Brooks's into the shade. But Watier's had been going downhill rapidly under the influence of a wild and unprincipled set, and was now very different from what it had been when it was first started under the aegis of the Prince of Wales, to provide the gourmets of White's and Brooks's with a change from the dreary round of beefsteaks, boiled fowl and apple tarts which formed the staple diet of the club members in St James's Street.

Beau Brummell had long since left the scene and retired to Calais to avoid his debtors, and his erstwhile lieutenant, Lord Byron, was spending most of his time in Italy and devoting his attention to sex rather than to gambling. The set which had then taken up the Brummell mantle as leaders of fashion, and were known as the 'Exquisites', were now finding Watier's too crude, whilst the crooks who were manipulating the bank were too obvious in their methods and too greedy in their outlook. However it seemed to Crockford that with the proper management it might yet be possible to revive the former glories of Watier's without lessening its potential as a money-making enterprise.

Foremost amongst the crooks who were manipulating the bank of Watier's was a certain Josiah Taylor, an astute operator whose chief failing as a club proprietor was that he had not the

Crockford the Shark – a sketch made by Rowlandson when William Crockford was first making his name in the gambling hells of fashionable London. Rowlandson himself was a confirmed gambler.

Crockford's birthplace – the old bulk shop in the shadow of Temple Bar.
Traitors' heads were impaled on spikes above the Bar.

The playground of Crockford's childhood. Temple Bar from Butcher's Row –
a slum that was 'a nesting place for the plague and fevers'.

Newgate Gaol, where public hangings provided free entertainment.

Crockford's Club in St James's Street in 1828, the year of its opening.

The premises today, now the home of the Devonshire Club.

The gaming room at Crockford's, renowned for its decorum and the gentlemanly behaviour of the players.

A gambling hell of the period, a place of altercation and violence.

The two rivals –
William Crockford,
ex-fishmonger and
despised 'leg';
John Gully – ex-pugilist
and honoured sportsman.

Layers at Ascot in the Victorian era, after William Crockford had made bookmaking respectable.

Discipline à la Kenyon.
The Lord Chief Justice flogs Lady Buckinghamshire for flouting the gaming laws. Lady Elizabeth Luttrell and Mrs Sturt stand in the pillory.

Doncaster Racecourse – the rogues' paradise.

intelligence to appreciate that if the club's reputation became too bad it might well destroy itself. Crockford, who was by now a person of importance in the gambling circles of London and Newmarket, suggested that Taylor and he should go into partnership, and this they did, operating a hazard bank with great success and making a great deal of money.

Taylor, however, soon proved himself to be both an unreliable and an untrustworthy associate. Unknown to his partner, he succeeded in buying the lease of the club's premises in Bolton Row, and having done so he then demanded a bigger share in the bank. Crockford was not a person to allow himself to be cheated in this way. He decided that the sooner the partnership was broken up the better, and he therefore severed his connection with Watier's and with Taylor.

He considered that the time had come for him to realise his life's ambition by opening the finest gambling club in London, yet for a while he held back, hesitating before he finally committed himself to so bold an enterprise. He was determined that his new club should be in St James's Street, and as a start he bought No. 50 and opened a gambling club there. Becoming bolder, he bought the house next door, and gradually the Master Plan began to take shape.

His desertion of Watier's and his move back to his old love, St James's Street, did not escape the attention of the wits of the day, one of whom wrote the following lines:

> Crockford, voting Bolton Row
> On a sudden, *vastly low*,
> And that gentlemen should meet
> Only in St James's Street,
> Broke his quarters up, and here
> Entered on a fresh career.
> Promising the scene, and new –
> First he purchased houses two;
> Then, no sooner said than done,
> Two were blended into one.

He still retained his interest in several other gambling houses in the district, and continued to make a great deal of money out of them, but financial difficulties were arising. Gone admittedly were the days when he could only put up a bank of £500. Now his nightly banks at each of his bigger houses stood at least at five or ten thousand, on which he was content to draw an estimated profit of about 1½ per cent. The play at each of these houses was 'deep', however, and he was being faced with the problems of bad debts and of the occasional lucky winner who could threaten the bank's solvency.

Gaming was in theory forbidden by law, although it was practised so openly, and there was therefore the further danger that a disgruntled loser, especially one who felt that he had been cheated, might try to evade his commitment or alternatively get his revenge on the bank by initiating a private prosecution. A number of foreigners were frequenting the London gaming hells at this time – exiles from France, minor officials from the various embassies, tourists visiting the capital and sundry others – and they were often in danger of being cheated because of their inability to understand all that was going on.

A crisis was finally reached in Crockford's affairs when a certain German baron lost heavily at one of Crockford's gambling hells and decided to revenge himself on its proprietor by taking him to court. An indictment was preferred and a true bill found; and William Crockford was summoned to appear at the Clerkenwell Sessions.

Crockford countered by playing his usual sly tactics for dealing with such an enemy. His spies, covertly investigating the baron's finances, found that he was nearly destitute and reported back to their master that threats of exposure and its resultant disgrace, with hints at possible strong-arm methods as well, would be certain to soften up the baron, who would soon be happy to settle out of court for a relatively small sum. This might well have been true, but unfortunately for Crockford the baron met with a shrewd adviser, who warned him against being browbeaten and told him to stand out for a large sum. Thus Crockford's bluff was called, and the day of the trial arrived without any settlement having been reached.

Crockford's chief lieutenant at this time was still the man named Gye, an ex-groom porter from a cheap gaming house in

Jermyn Street where Crockford had met him in the earlier days, and a very cunning operator indeed, who knew everyone in the underworld and who also knew just how far it was possible to go in attempts to silence an enemy of the bank. Gye now reported to his master that the time had come to accept defeat and to try and settle out of court.

On the day of the hearing, Gye arrived at the Sessions to appear on Crockford's behalf, and found that the case was low on the list. He therefore got into conversation with the baron, casually suggested a visit to a neighbouring tavern, and there plied him with drink until a mellow atmosphere had been created, when he made a generous offer to settle out of court. The baron demurred. He could not, he said, come to any such decision without the guidance of his adviser, whereat Gye played the trump card which so seldom fails. He produced from his pocket a large wad of notes, tossed them down on the table and then added a ticket for a passage from England back to the Continent, with all expenses paid.

The baron hesitated and was lost. The wad of notes was pressed upon him, he was hurried into a coach that was standing waiting outside, and carried off to the docks where he was established in a comfortable cabin on board a vessel due to leave for France within the hour. Thus there was no prosecutor in court when Crockford's case was called.

The interesting point about all this was the effect which it had on William Crockford. He was now in his middle forties happily married with a large family kept discreetly in the background, and living a life of luxury, and the thought of serving a prison sentence had frightened him a great deal. Indeed it was said that he took to his bed on the morning of the trial and did not leave it again until several weeks after the news of Gye's success had reached him. By nature William Crockford was both cautious and calculating; and in his childhood at Temple Bar he had seen enough of the prison world to view it with horror. One of the reasons why he had withdrawn from the partnership with Taylor at Watier's was because he felt that the activities of the bank there were bordering on the criminal, and now this further crisis had caused him the gravest alarm. His aim was to found a respectable club, to which only prominent and respectable citizens belonged, so that he would not be threatened again with fears of prosecution.

More and more he was becoming convinced that cheating did not pay, and he was determined to restrict his dealings with the underworld to bribery and corruption connected with the turf, where it was very difficult for anything to be proved (for if a poisoner like Daniel Dawson could be persuaded to keep his mouth shut, even on the scaffold, then money could buy the silence of others as well). His two chief ambitions on the turf were firstly to win the Derby by any means possible, and secondly to get his revenge on John Gully, also by any means possible. But otherwise he was anxious only to present himself as an honest man operating an honest club for honest gentlemen of Society.

There were other disturbing incidents that caused him alarm at much the same period. The game which had ruined the German baron had been roulette, a craze for which had recently swept London; and continental visitors, and in particular the wealthy French *nouveaux riches* thrown up by the Revolution, gambled heavily and lost substantially at the game.

The theory of probability is mathematically sound, but it does not operate except over a long period. In roulette, for example, the number of times red or black comes up in ten thousand spins will be very nearly the same, but that does not mean that the same equality will be shown on fifty spins of the wheel or a hundred. A run of a dozen of one colour is not unusual, and a run of 20 or more is by no means unknown. And it is when such a run develops, and backers have the good sense to *follow* the run rather than to back against it (they very seldom do) that they can double their money at every spin. Thus one pound becomes more than a thousand after a run of eleven consecutive even-money chances.

Such runs usually destroy the backer, but they can also destroy the bank. Limits may be fixed for the amount that can be won on any one spin, or even in an evening, but if the run continues into the next gambling session, the bank may well be in danger of being broken.

It was soon after the successful conclusion of the Clerkenwell Sessions affair that Crockford suffered just such a run of bad luck.

It was not that any one night proved particularly disastrous, but rather that several heavy gamblers struck a long winning sequence simultaneously. According to the writer of his biography in *Bentley's Miscellany*, there came an evening when the £5,000 with which the bank opened represented nearly all the ready cash that William Crockford was able to find; and that not long after play began – the game being hazard – £3,000 of that was quickly lost. Crockford then left the gaming room and walked into the Green Park, opposite Piccadilly, and there waited for the news to reach him that he had been wiped out. But in fact the news, when it did reach him, pacing miserably up and down under the plane trees, was of the bank's triumphant comeback. Any run of luck must finally come to an end, and the theory of probability must come to the rescue of the bank if only it can hold out. At the close of play that night the bank was showing a profit of over £20,000 and before the winter season was over this had been increased to more than £200,000.

Once again the interesting aspect to the whole affair is the effect which all this had upon Crockford himself. Here, again, as in the case of the threatened lawsuit, he did not reveal himself as the inscrutable gambler, remaining unruffled in the face of impending disaster, but rather showed himself to be unnerved at the prospect of failure. No doubt the courage of his youth had by now deserted him. Yet as a professional gambler he knew that he must continue to bet boldly and to maintain his reputation as a bookmaker who could accept the largest of wagers and who was ready to pay up without hesitation if he lost. To reduce his commitments at this stage, when he was on the brink of becoming London's leading layer, could only lead to disaster, for once he showed anxiety about the size of the bets which he was accepting, his patrons would assume that his financial situation had become insecure, and then the centre of 'deep' play would be transferred elsewhere.

But Crockford was getting on, and the time might come when he felt too old to take on the wealthiest members of Society single-handed. If he was to achieve his ambition, then his Master Plan must soon be put into operation. There could be no further delay; no further holding back. The time had come for him to screw his courage to the sticking-point, and to convince himself that he could not fail.

He therefore began to buy up still more property at the top of St James's Street. Thus Crockford, 'voting Bolton Row, on a sudden vastly low', bought the lease first of one house, then two, and finally of three. These he fitted up lavishly, and he began to operate in direct competition with Watier's and with his former partner, Josiah Taylor. Soon it became apparent to fashionable London that Taylor's fortunes were on the wane and that Crockford's were waxing mightily. And soon Watier's was forced to close down and Crockford was left with the field to himself.

In 1826, he completed the strategy of his Master Plan by buying the *fourth* house in St James's Street, so that he now owned a lengthy frontage on the street in exactly the right position. And it was in 1826 that the Master Plan was finally put into operation, when he called in an architect and informed him that all four houses were to be razed to the ground and in their place was to be built the most sumptuous and the most magnificent gambling house in Europe, with no expense spared, so that the cream of Society, of the Court and of the Government might make it their rendezvous.

It was to be a club for gentlemen to meet together under the most pleasant of circumstances; and special attention was to be paid to the kitchens, because the cooking provided at this club was to be unequalled even in Paris itself.

Gambling facilities were also to be provided, for the passing amusement of the members when the inclination took them. At the time it may have seemed to the architect almost as if the provision of these gambling facilities had been but an afterthought to the grand design. The same view may well have been taken by many of the members after the club was completed. Indeed it must almost have appeared to them as though a benevolent philanthropist – an ex-fishmonger with a heart of gold whose ambition it was to bring happiness, sociability and comfort into the lives of his superiors – had decided to glorify St James's Street solely for their benefit and without a thought for himself.

William Crockford was at pains to encourage them in this

belief. Never before had this Uriah Heep of a man shown more servility to his patrons, or fawned more obsequiously on his superiors. He almost contrived to present the demeanour of simple honesty that was the speciality of his rival, John Gully, when dealing with the aristocracy.

4

THE MASTER PLAN
Pandemonium in St James's Street

The year of 1827 marked the turning point in the career of William Crockford. During it he was able to complete his Master Plan for becoming the creator of the most magnificent gentleman's club in Europe. In it, also, he was able to bring to a most satisfactory conclusion some unfinished business in connection with John Gully. Gully had outwitted him over the St Leger of 1819. In the St Leger of 1827 Crockford was able to gain an ample revenge, and at only a moderate cost to himself in bribery and corruption. By an act of cold-blooded and calculated dishonesty, he succeeded in depriving Gully of around £45,000, of which £20,000 went into Crockford's own pocket. He was also able at the same time to cause Gully to suffer a far greater humiliation and disappointment than he himself had suffered when Sultan had been withdrawn from the race a few days before it was run in 1819.

It is true that at the beginning of the year he had no expectation that the enemy might be delivered into his hands by the time the Doncaster meeting came round in the autumn. Throughout the summer he had only one concern, and that was the demolition of the four adjoining houses which he had bought in St James's Street, and the employment of an architect who would cause to be erected in their place a mansion which – if not quite comparable in size to the Palace of Versailles – should certainly bear some similarity to it and which should definitely outshine, in the splendour of its decorations and the sumptuousness of its trappings, the residence of the English monarchy which stood at the southern extremity of the street.

In the years to come the home of the great Duke of Wellington at Apsley House, Piccadilly, was to become known as 'No. 1, London'. As far as Crockford was concerned, Crockford's Club, rather than St James's Palace, was to become 'No. 1, St James's Street'. In this he was unquestionably successful; and it was not surprising, under the circumstances, that George IV should have turned his attention to the transformation of Buckingham House into a royal palace before the end of his reign, for his Palace in St James's Street was made to look like the house of a poor relation in comparison.

From the outset William Crockford was determined that his club in St James's Street should dwarf all other buildings in the vicinity. Indeed he may well have had in mind the creation of a building which might look – and in fact become – as significant in London life as that which had gradually risen during the 18th and early part of the 19th centuries in Threadneedle Street, not far distant from his birthplace at Temple Bar, and which he had so often passed in his youth when on his way to the Billingsgate Fish Market. This was the Bank of England.

In searching for an architect who would do full justice to his grandiose scheme, William Crockford considered only those candidates with the highest qualifications, both socially and professionally. Nash, of course, was the obvious choice, but Nash, besides being very expensive, was also at this time rather in the pocket of the sovereign. He had been George IV's favourite architect during the Regency days, when he had made a great deal of money. Indeed he had made so much money that some of his rivals had wondered just where it had all come from, and there were those who hinted at the fact that Nash's delightful and accommodating wife had in fact proved so accommodating to the Prince that her husband had been rewarded liberally for the broadmindedness of his outlook as well as for the breadth of vision which he had shown architecturally when designing Regent Street.

But Nash, as Crockford well knew, had his faults. His sense of grandeur was somewhat limited, and so were his powers of imagination. He was an old man by this time (although not too old for chasing women) and was nearing the age of retirement. And anyway he was busy on half a dozen projects in and around

London, redesigning Buckingham House and turning it into Buckingham Palace, and rebuilding Carlton House Terrace, as well as replanting and laying-out St James's Park and producing designs for the United Service Club in Pall Mall.

The ideal man would have been another favourite of the Prince Regent's, James Wyatt, the most talented of a long family line of architects and more reliable than Nash in many ways; but James Wyatt had been killed in an accident on the Bath Road, when the coach-and-four in which he was sitting had been involved in a triple crash with a man on horseback and a post-chaise travelling at excessive speed in the opposite direction. Wyatt had been thrown against the door-handle and his skull had been crushed. That had been the end of a distinguished career, as well as a salutary commentary on the dangers of the growing traffic congestion on the roads.

However, James Wyatt had left behind him a large family which had included two sons – Benjamin Dean and Philip – both of whom had inherited much of their father's talent, if not his character and rectitude. In fact they were a pair of black sheep, forever running up debts and getting themselves into trouble over drink and women, but Ben, in particular, had some sound ideas. They worked in amicable partnership, with Ben the senior, and this caused some surprise for they should by rights have been rivals. Philip had always wanted to become an architect, but Ben had gone gallivanting off to India as a young man, and had later become private secretary to Sir Arthur Wellesley in Ireland. But he had given up this post in 1809 and returned to London just at the time when a competition was being held for a design for the new Drury Lane Theatre (the old one having been destroyed by fire), and he promptly sent in an entry. Philip, encouraged and advised by his father, had also gone in for this competition, but when the winning design was announced it proved to be that of Ben. James Wyatt was furious, for it seemed to him that his eldest son had no real interest in architecture whereas it did seem that it might provide Philip with a worthwhile career which would keep him out of debt. But these two sons had always proved a sore trial to him and he was soon content to wash his hands of the pair of them.

Working together with surprising industry, and revealing 'great competence but small invention', they soon began to make a name for themselves in fashionable London. Ben, on the death of his father, had succeeded him in the post of Surveyor to Westminster Abbey, and had soon afterwards carried out some restoration there. The pair had then been given the task of completing the reconstruction of York House (later to become Lancaster House) for the Duke of York; and as a result of the influence wielded by Ben's former employer, Sir Arthur Wellesley, now the illustrious Duke of Wellington, they had also discussed with him the possibility of redesigning Apsley House, his home in Piccadilly. Finally, in 1825, they had been given the lengthy task of reconstructing Londonderry House, in Park Lane, for the 3rd Marquess of Londonderry. Thus, by 1827, when William Crockford had finally completed his purchase of Nos. 50–53, St James's Street, they were being generally recognised as two of the most successful architects operating in Mayfair.

Two other factors may have influenced William Crockford when he decided to offer the work of designing his new club to Ben Wyatt. Ben's father, James, had been responsible for bringing into being the new frontage to White's Club nearly 50 years earlier, when he had furnished the place so lavishly and decorated it so elaborately that the great ball which had been held to celebrate the occasion in 1789 was still the talk of the town. White's, with its now famous bow window, was on the opposite side of the road to Crockford's new premises; it would be gratifying to dim the memory of that great opening of 1789 by an even greater display when the new Crockford's Club opened its doors in 1828.

The second factor was that Ben Wyatt had been chosen some years previously as architect for redesigning and furnishing a house in Brook Street, Piccadilly, by one of William Crockford's unintentional benefactors, the Old Etonian rake, Ball Hughes, who with Colonel Mellish had for years held the reputation of being the wildest and 'deepest' gambler in London. Indeed St James's Street gossip had always whispered that Crockford's fortune had originally been built on the £100,000 which he was said to have won in a single sitting of hazard off Ball Hughes and Lords Thanet and Granville.

Whether or not this was true, Crockford had certainly gambled a great deal in the past with Ball Hughes, and had been impressed by the young man's panache, his flamboyance and his attitude of reckless abandon in the face of mounting financial misfortune. He had certainly earned for himself the nickname of 'The Golden Ball'. When instructing Ben Wyatt to decorate and furnish the house in Brook Street, Hughes had given him *carte blanche* to do as he liked, regardless of cost, and this grand gesture had greatly impressed London Society; as indeed had the buhl furniture, the elaborate draperies, the ancient statues, bronze figures and countless *objets d'art* which Ben Wyatt had then seen fit to assemble there. William Crockford knew little enough about marble, buhl or *objets d'art;* but his chief concern was to appoint as his architect a man who would think in the grand manner and thus be able to bring the Master Plan to glorious fruition.

The choice was therefore made. Ben Wyatt, aided by his brother Philip, was instructed to draw up plans for the ex-fishmonger's consideration. Ben gratefully accepted the commission, which would ensure a period of prosperity for both of them and banish for a time the ever-recurrent threat of bankruptcy. At the same time he resigned his post as Surveyor to Westminster Abbey, feeling perhaps that this task was hardly in keeping with his new employment as creator of a sumptuous gambling hell in St James's Street.

Meanwhile fashionable London was thrilled at the news which filtered through to them of what was being planned. Some facetiously referred to the magnificent new building which was being planned as 'Fishmonger's Hall'. Others described it as 'The Pandemonium'. But William Crockford kept his counsel and said little. They could laugh at him if they wished, but the time would come when he would amaze them. In the meanwhile he opened temporary accommodation for his patrons in Pall Mall, and continued to provide them with every facility for gambling, and himself with a rapidly increasing balance at the bank. The run of bad luck which had so alarmed him in the years before did not recur. In 1827 he moved forward inexorably towards the completion of the Master Plan.

But although it remained his policy throughout 1827 to

say little of his project, and to allow his patrons to make whatever they liked out of the many rumours which were circulating in St James's Street and Piccadilly, the magnitude of the operation could not be concealed. Once his workmen had moved in, to pull down the old buildings and to start erecting the new, the orderly calm of St James's Street was destroyed. The workmen were not armed with pneumatic drills, but from the views expressed at the time one might have supposed that they were, for Londoners raised their hands in horror. They cursed William Crockford mightily, and taking up their pens, they began to write indignant letters to the press.

There is no doubt that the workmen's activities completely disrupted the traffic in St James's Street throughout the summer and autumn of 1827, and the culmination of it all occurred when – as a result of the endless digging and laying of drains – the building of the Guards' Club, immediately adjoining the site on its northern extremity, fell in with a great crash on 9 November, filling the street with dust, hurling débris across the pavement and, worst indignity of all, exposing the intimate interior of the club to the public gaze, so that the bedrooms and indeed the very beds of numerous illustrious guardees were seen naked and ashamed.

This, it was widely felt, was really too much. The club had only been opened in 1813, and had been established for the benefit of the three regiments of Foot Guards, who ran it in a very orderly and military manner and used it as a guardhouse for the convenience of officers carrying out duties in the locality. It was a dignified and highly respectable establishment and its members limited themselves to such decorous recreations as whist and billiards. The realisation that some blackguardly ex-fishmonger had seen fit to undermine their premises as well as their ordered way of life and that, by digging his damned drains, had brought their club-house crashing about their ears, caused many a soldierly heart to beat with fury beneath its red tunic. This was a nation's reward for the gallantry of Waterloo!

However members of the neighbouring clubs, and especially those which were in no danger from the excavations, took great delight in gazing upon the ruins, commenting upon the beds which lay poised to fall from shattered floors, and uttering ribald

observations upon the whole affair. It was an irreverent age and
many were the witticisms made at the expense of the unfortunate
inhabitants of the club, none of whom appears to have been in-
jured in the cataclysm. The Irish poet, Thomas Moore, who at
this time was very much a member of London Society, recorded
the incident in verse which delighted everyone except the Guards
themselves, who considered it in poor taste.

> 'Mala vicini pecoris contagia laedunt'.
> What can these workmen be about?
> Do, Crockford, let the secret out,
>   Why thus your houses fall.
> Quoth he: 'Since folks are not in town,
> I find it better to pull down,
>   Than have no pull at all.'

> 'See, passenger, at Crockford's high behest,
> Red-coats by black-legs ousted from their nest;
> The arts of peace o'er matching reckless war,
> And gallant Rouge undone by wily Noir!

>   'Impar congressus' ...
> Fate gave the word – the king of dice and cards
> In an unguarded moment took the Guards;
> Contriv'd his neighbours in a trice to drub,
> And did the trick by – turning up a club.

>   'Nullum simile est idem.'
> 'Tis strange how some will differ – some advance
> That the Guards' club-house was pulled down
>   by chance;
> While some, with juster notions in their mazard
> Stoutly maintain the deed was done by hazard.

The Committee of the Guards' Club demanded financial
satisfaction from Crockford, who reluctantly decided that it
would be advisable for him to make a handsome contribution
towards the rebuilding of the establishment, a number of whose
members, he foresaw, might one day be visiting him next door
and losing their money to him at hazard. For William Crockford
was nothing if not far-sighted.

In the meantime he declined to make any statements about his own club, other than to indicate that the outcome of all this building would be a mansion more splendid than any other in London (and certainly much more magnificent than the Guards Club had ever been). He allowed rumour to spread on its own. Many prominent members of Society looked down their noses on the whole enterprise, and announced that they would have nothing to do with anything so vulgar and ostentatious. But Crockford smiled to himself, knowing that it had ever been thus and that those who criticised most strongly would probably be amongst the first to accept his invitation to the grand opening.

Meanwhile his army of workmen continued to labour night and day. Indeed the night life of the locality, which had always been active and varied but which had usually been carried on discreetly under the cloak of darkness, now found itself flooded with illumination, and the whole street was so full of flares and blazing torches that the regular business of the brothels, taverns and gambling houses was impeded by the large crowds of sight-seers who came merely to gaze and to wonder, and with no intention of spending their money on the dubious amenities on offer to them.

Those who had already nicknamed the establishment 'The Pandemonium' had every reason to justify the title for pandemonium reigned in St James's Street throughout the year of 1827, and the excitement reached its crescendo as the opening day of 2 January 1828, drew ever closer. Meanwhile Crockford's rivals in the gambling-house business either scoffed at the whole enterprise and argued that he would never recover the money that he had laid out, or else watched the progress of the new building with growing apprehension. If it *were* a success, then it would soon be putting a large number of them out of business.

William Crockford watched his building grow with quiet satisfaction, but there were other events which occurred during the summer and autumn of 1827 which increased this mood of well-being and which suggested to him that this was indeed destined to be his lucky year. If there was one thing which gave him greater pleasure than the contemplation of the rise of his club it was the contemplation of the fall of John Gully.

The setting was Doncaster, the event the running of the St Leger and the cause of his catastrophe was William Crockford.

The Derby of 1827 had seen the largest field ever to go to the post for the great race, when 23 runners had lined up to face the fall of the flag which would send them on their way. The betting on the race had naturally taken a wide range, but the market had been complicated by the fact that Lord Jersey had owned two of the most fancied runners in Glenartney and Mameluke. If, as was strongly suspected by several well-informed backers at the time, he had the winning of the race with either of them, which was the one that would carry his money?

It was just the sort of situation which so often occurred during the running of the big betting races of the 19th century; and it was just the sort of situation which gave rise to what Harry Edwards, one of the jockeys concerned, was wont to refer to as 'putting the double-dodge on the swells'. But the swells were not above a bit of double-dodging themselves, and few of the swells of that period were more skilled in the art than George Child Villiers, 5th Earl of Jersey. In 1825 he had won the Derby with Middleton, who had never been seen on a racecourse before and whom the Ring had fielded against with confidence before the 'off' because they knew that a lad in the stable had been 'got at' and had just allowed Middleton to drink a bucket of water (when in fact he had swallowed a large sponge in the water as well). This, however, had failed to stop the colt, thus proving him to be an animal of robust constitution, to say the least, although he was never seen on a racecourse again.

Glenartney was a full brother to Middleton, but he was not being ridden by Jem Robinson, the jockey who had ridden such a dashing race to bring Middleton and the sponge home by a comfortable two lengths. Robinson, in fact, was riding Mameluke, and Harry Edwards, the exponent of the double-dodge, was on Glenartney. Expert opinion favoured Glenartney as being the better of the two, but racecourse rumour had it that his jockey had backed Mameluke to win. Lord Jersey solemnly announced that the pair were untried against each other at home (a phrase that has been in common usage amongst owners and trainers for more than 200 years) but that he considered Glenartney held a slightly better chance. But racecourse rumour had it that he, too, had backed Mameluke to win. If this was so, then Harry Edwards was for once on the side of the swells, and he and Lord Jersey were doing a bit of double-dodging on the Ring. The betting public were in two minds, but on the day Glenartney was heavily backed at 5/1, while Mameluke was easy at nearly double this price.

Horses cannot talk, and jockeys and owners can be as silent as the grave, so none may say with any certainty whether the Derby of 1827 was cleanly run. The simple facts are that two furlongs from home Glenartney was out in front with the race seemingly at his mercy but that Mameluke came through to beat him 'cleverly' at the finish.

'To win cleverly' is another of the traditional phrases of the turf. It can be so pregnant with meaning, and in this case it no doubt was.

The race gave rise to much argument, but there was one expert at Epsom that day who was convinced that Mameluke was a very good horse, whether or not he had won as the result of a double-dodge. This was John Gully. When he met Lord Jersey at Ascot a short time later, he bought Mameluke from him for 4,000 guineas, although Lord Jersey later refused an offer from another source of 5,000 guineas for Glenartney.

John Gully was now convinced that he had bought the winner of the St Leger in the autumn, and he made one condition when the terms of the sale were being made: the news that Mameluke had passed into his ownership must remain secret for a further 24 hours. During this time he approached William Crockford and asked him casually to lay a price against Mameluke for the last classic. The reply was '10/1', and Gully just as casually took £10,000 to £1,000. He then made further complicated wagers with his rival, in one of which he undertook to name 10 horses whom Mameluke would beat in the race; and in another 9 horses. In the end Gully stood to win around £45,000 if Mameluke won the St Leger, even if some of the side bets were unsuccessful. And as soon as the wagering was concluded, Gully revealed that Mameluke was now his.

Crockford was indignant, and as the day of the St Leger approached he sent out his spies to discover just how good Mameluke might be and what were his prospects in the race. Their report was alarming. Mameluke was a great horse and a virtual certainty for the St Leger. His only weakness was his temperament, for he was an excitable and bad-tempered animal who could become almost uncontrollable if jostled at the start or subjected to unnecessary delays.

Crockford pondered the problem, and John Gully, who guessed exactly what was going on in his rival's mind, determined to take every precaution to safeguard his colt. But Crockford himself was fully aware of the fact that there are other ways in which a race might be 'fixed' besides those used by stable lads with buckets of water or poisoners with syringes of arsenic such as the late Dan Dawson. He first of all made it his business to become acquainted with the starter; and he then let it be known amongst some of the owners and jockeys concerned with the race that those whose entries proved unmanageable at the start, so that the start was unduly delayed, might expect a liberal reward.

Of all the great races that take place in England, the St Leger has the worst record for double-dodging. Just why this should be so is not apparent, but the student of turf history who cares to examine the records of the race since its inception in 1776 will find repeated evidence of roguery of every sort. The crooks of racing seem to have set this one event aside as their especial province; and many curious things seem to happen to St Leger favourites even before they reach the start.

Mameluke at least reached the start, but he was given a very rough passage as soon as he was there. He was ridden by Sam Chifney Junior, who must have realised very early in the proceedings that everything possible was to be done to prevent his horse from getting a clean break. Whenever he found himself in a good position to start, half the remainder of the field would be facing in the wrong direction, and it soon became apparent that the starter himself had no intention of allowing Mameluke to do himself justice. He insisted on holding back the start whilst the rest of the field made ineffectual efforts to get in a line, for they included – as Thormanby was later to remark when describing this infamous race – 'half a dozen half-trained and half-broken brutes who were sent to the post with instructions to their jockeys to keep back whenever Mameluke started'. John Gully, watching poker-faced in the Stand, must have realised at once what was being done, and who was behind the doing of it. His enemy, William Crockford, had bribed not only other jockeys in the race but also the starter himself, and since Mameluke was such a bad-tempered horse these delaying tactics were certain to reduce him to impotent fury.

There were seven false starts and it surprised no one to see that when the starter did finally send them on their way, Mameluke was left many yards behind the rest and was facing the wrong way. Yet despite this he ran a magnificent race, and although left with so much ground to make up he threaded his way through the field and despite jostling and interference on every side he only just failed to catch the leader, the Hon. Edward Petre's bay filly Matilda, who just held on to win by a length.

The preliminaries to the start had been so scandalous that the starter was dismissed, but he had no doubt expected this, and had been well rewarded for his work. Not quite every man had his price on the turf in those days, but certainly jockeys and racing officials were not difficult to buy.

Gully made no official protest, and he paid his losses to Crockford without comment. He knew that he had been cheated, and he knew also that there was nothing which he could do about it. 'Is it convenient for you to settle?' asked one of his creditors at Tattersalls on settling day. 'It is always convenient,' replied Gully haughtily, 'but it is not always pleasant.' His only act in defence of his colt's reputation was to challenge the owner of Matilda to a match, offering him a 7-lb pull in the weights. Mr Petre, like so many other over-optimistic owners, was quite ready to accept the challenge, but his trainer told him succinctly that he had won the race by a fluke, and that he should pocket his winnings, which amounted to some £15,000, and thank his good fortune for what had happened (or alternatively thank William Crockford, although he probably did not say this in so many words).

John Gully has always been looked upon in racing as a sportsman and a gentleman, and his demeanour after being so badly cheated over the St Leger of 1827 has always been cited as evidence of this sportsmanship.

Well, perhaps ... Or can it have been that he realised he had been outwitted, and in accordance with the code of the underworld he took no official action against his enemy but decided instead to bide his time, and to get his revenge in his own way?

Perhaps William Crockford eyed his rival with some apprehension. He had deprived Gully of £45,000, nearly half of which had been diverted into his own pocket; and Gully, as he well knew, would not be willing to accept such treatment with docility. Gully might not openly protest, but secretly he would be certain to plot revenge. Thus Crockford knew that it would be necessary for him to watch his step, especially in matters concerning the turf. Gully had always shown himself to be a dangerous and implacable enemy. Still, the money which Crockford had won made a useful contribution to the rising costs of the building and furnishing of his new club. Its growing magnificence was a stimulant to his self-esteem, and he could not resist the temptation to gloat over Mameluke's defeat and Gully's discomfiture.

The date of the grand opening of Crockford's Club in St James's Street was fixed for the second day in the new year of 1828, and once matters at Doncaster had been settled to his satisfaction in the autumn of 1827, Crockford was able to settle down to making his final plans.

Two main considerations kept him fully occupied. The first was the setting up of an administrative body that would run the new club; the second was the need to ensure that the official opening was carried through without a hitch. He was determined that the fiasco which had resulted when Almack had opened his new club in St James's Street more than sixty years before, when the building was still incomplete and the walls were still dripping with damp, should not be repeated. Moreover there were other, more recent, occasions which would have to be equalled, if not eclipsed. In 1789 White's, on the opposite side of the street, had organised a ball to celebrate the king's recovery from madness which had been a magnificent success, and in 1814 they had staged another in order to celebrate the country's triumphs in the war against Napoleon. On this occasion they had borrowed the Duke of Devonshire's mansion, Burlington House, and the Prince Regent, the Emperor of Russia and the King of Prussia had all attended (at a cost, to the club, of some £10,000).

William Crockford was mindful of these precedents; and he was also mindful of the fact that, unlike these elegant goings-on at White's, he would be forced to expect antagonism in high places and a good deal of ill-natured criticism of his efforts. It was becoming increasingly clear to him, as the year of 1827 moved on towards it end, that both the organisation of his new club and its official opening would have to be stage-managed with some dexterity if his enemies were to be deprived of the satisfaction of seeing him humiliated.

The newspaper comments in this winter of 1827 were for the most part hostile in tone. *The Times*, in its issue of 29 November, noted with disapproval that amongst the names of the aristo-cratic members of the new club were also to be found those of 'doctors, surgeons, parsons, wine merchants and brewers' and it coldly observed that 'the counting house and the hazard table do not well accord'.

In a later issue it noted with approval that 'The establishment of the Pandemonium in St James's Street under the entire super-intendence of the fishmonger and his unblushing patronizers, lately called forth the opinion of the highest personage in the kingdom, who expressed himself in a manner which reflected the utmost credit on his head and heart' – a denunciation which appears to have caused at least one nobleman in the royal presence to deny hastily the rumour that he had become a member.

The Literary Chronicle and Weekly Review, in its issue of 15 December, sourly observed that Crockford was already known to be worth in the region of £300,000 and it forecast that this sum would be substantially increased if his new venture proved a success.

Meanwhile contemporary writers drew attention to the fact that although times were bad and the country was faced with numerous difficulties, and although its financial state was in a parlous condition and the mood of its people was sullen and discouraged, there was yet evidence throughout Mayfair, and above all in St James's Street, of wanton extravagance and idle dissipation. 'Everybody admitted that the nation was ruined,' wrote the author of a novel called *Whitehall*, 'and yet, if you visited their palace-like theatres, they were full . . . in fact every place where money was to be spent displayed crowds of people, who could all testify to the melancholy fact that there was no money in the country.'

Worse still, for many upper-class Englishmen, was the evidence that money could now buy a position in Society. Wealth was being amassed in trade or on the Stock Market, in the Ring at Newmarket or – lowest of all – in the cockpits of London; and the aristocracy were failing dismally in their social obligations by accepting these upstarts without resentment.

William Crockford was in complete agreement with all such reactionary views. He had no use for democracy, and having used his own wealth to buy himself a position in Society he had no desire to see anyone else achieve a similar elevation, and least of all such upstarts as John Gully. He was prepared to allow representatives of trade and the professions to join his new club, but his real interest lay only with the upper classes. In the matter of enrolment of new members he acted on a simple precept, which may best be translated as that of 'setting a peer to catch a peer'. It was a policy that was to prove highly successful. His aim was to obtain the maximum publicity for the new club whilst seemingly seeking to avoid it, and to ensure its success by the patronage which he could build up.

In accordance with the traditions on which Almack and others had operated throughout the 18th century when initiating such ambitious social enterprises, his main concern during 1827 had been to form a 'Management Committee of Noblemen and Gentlemen' who would give the club a social status and establish confidence in its respectability. Perhaps he realised that in the years to come, when the enterprise was fully on its feet, he might find such a committee a hindrance to his plans, but its formation at the outset was essential. He was able to persuade such leaders of the sporting world in Society as the Earls of Chesterfield, Sefton and Lichfield to join this committee, in order to help formulate the rules of the club and 'to preside over the ballot box'. The Duke of Wellington was known to be in favour of the new club (although he was opposed in principle to gambling) and prominent continental visitors such as Talleyrand were anxious to join, although he was perhaps hardly the type to arouse confidence, being one of the biggest rogues in Europe.

The entrance fee was set at 30 guineas, which was the highest in London, and soon the Committee's selectivity in their choice of the new members made election to Crockford's more difficult – and therefore more desirable – than election to White's, Boodle's or Brooks's. By February 1828, *Bell's Life in London* was able to announce with truth that 'The most distinguished noblemen in the country are members of the club.'

Thus William Crockford acted upon the oldest and soundest rule of salesmanship: do not place yourself in the position where you must go cap-in-hand to your patrons, but rather in the position whereby they must come to you. And throughout all these lengthy preparations, the emphasis was always on the respectability, the good taste and the comfort of the new club, where gentlemen might meet gentlemen under the most congenial circumstances, and then comport themselves as gentlemen should. Throughout he was at pains to emphasise publicly and often that this was *not* primarily a gambling club but rather a social club, whilst acting on the private knowledge that in the era in which he lived it could scarcely be the one without the other. He might equally well have stated – although he did not – that this was not primarily a dining club either, but rather a social club, yet one of the main reasons for becoming a member of the new Crockford's was the fact that it provided the best food in London, cooked by the best chef in Europe.

At White's and Brooks's they might still serve their long-suffering *habitués* with the eternal joints, beefsteaks and boiled fowl but at the new Crockford's such delicacies as *pâtés*, *omelettes à la confiture*, *filet de sole* and *éperlans frits* were available in abundance, washed down by the finest French and Rhenish wines. It was not surprising that the members of both these rival clubs hastened to become members of the new Crockford's.

It was while he had been in partnership with Taylor at Watier's that Crockford had first experienced the cooking of the club's French chef, Louis Eustache Ude. Indeed it had been said at the time that one of the reasons why he had originally taken a share in Watier's was so that he could experience the delights of Ude's cooking whenever he wished. He had kept his eye on Ude ever since then, and when the Master Plan had first started to form in his mind he had at once added Ude to his list of the essential adjuncts of the new building.

When salary was discussed, Ude haughtily demanded a higher payment than any other chef in London, together with the freedom to order whatever he liked and to cook in whatever manner he chose. Crockford readily agreed to these terms. His architects had been given *carte blanche* to produce the most magnificent of rooms; and he was prepared to give his chef *carte blanche* to produce the most magnificent of meals. Reports varied as to how much he agreed to pay Ude, but the sum was probably in the region of £1,200 to £2,000 per year, out of which Ude had admittedly to pay his own kitchen staff, which included three male cooks, two kitchen-maids and at least two scullions.

Even so, this was an astonishing salary for the period, when the wages paid to ordinary domestic servants in the big houses seldom exceeded twenty pounds a year; and the news of this remuneration soon spread around Mayfair and caused a flutter of excitement, which was precisely what Crockford intended that it should do. Meanwhile the fortunate chef gave evidence of his new status by purchasing a house in Albemarle Street, 'contiguous to the scene of his official duties', and there installed his family.

Eustache Ude was a typical French chef – hot-tempered and highly temperamental, an artist who was fully conscious of his skill. Various stories were in circulation concerning his antecedents (it was said that he had started his professional career as a jeweller), and it was generally believed that he had been a *chef de cuisine* to Louis XVI before the Revolution. He was far too good a cook to have suffered any persecution during the upheaval however, and after the Revolution he was thought to have taken a post with a member of the Bonaparte family. Finally he was persuaded to come to London as cook to Lord Sefton, who was a

famous horseman, a prominent clubman and a noted gourmet.
(He and Ude were said to have together concocted what was
later to be considered one of Ude's most celebrated dishes, an
entrée of soft roes of mackerel baked in butter and served with a
rich cream sauce.) Another of his famous dishes was one that he
created for the young Lord George Bentinck, to whom he used
to serve a most delicious sweet made with fresh stoned cherries,
and which he christened *Boudin de cerises à la Bentinck*.

Ude could prove very quarrelsome at times, and was not
above remonstrating excitedly with diners who did not appreciate his *specialités*, or – worse still – who summoned the waiter
and complained of being overcharged for one of his culinary
masterpieces. William Crockford was fully alive to all these
failings and quite happy to tolerate them; Ude, as he well knew,
was a showman and the future of the new club was dependent
on an initial display of showmanship.

The poets who were so busily writing their odes to the new
establishment were quick to include references to its celebrated
chef. The difficulty which Crockford had at first experienced
in persuading Ude to join his staff is evidenced in the lines –

> First, he turned his conjuring book
> For a spell to raise a cook.
> Thrice invoked, an artist came
> Not unworthy of the name;
> One who with a hand of fire
> Struck the culinary lyre,
> And through all its compass ran:
> Taste and judgement marked the man;
> Ever various, ever new,
> Was this heav'n-born *Cordon bleu*.

This, then, was the situation when the new Crockford's Club
first opened its doors on the night of Wednesday 2 January 1828,
and the fashionable world of Mayfair crowded into the vestibule,
bearing the ornate invitation cards that had been sent out by its
proprietor, and rubbing shoulders with the existing members of
the old Crockford's Club who were only too happy to display
the splendid appointments in their new premises, and to point

out the superb decorations which were said to have cost some
£94,000.

What exactly was it like, this Crockford palace? What had
the brothers Wyatt achieved during their year's labour, and what
had the London navvies contrived to build, after they had spent
months in knocking half St James's Street down and months
putting it up again?

The exterior, facing on to the western side of St James's Street,
and only a few yards down from Piccadilly (which brought it
within the parish of St George's, Hanover Square) was simple
but impressive. It consisted of two wings and a centre, with four
Corinthian pillars and surmounted by a balustrade along its whole
length. The ground floor had Venetian windows, and the upper
floor large French windows. It was a three-storey building, with
a short flight of four stone steps leading up to the main entrance.
There was a bay window on the right-hand side.

Not a *bow* window, mark you, for this was by tradition the
sole perquisite in St James's Street of White's; but in the years to
come the members of Crockford's were to sit at this bay window
and survey the London scene before them with the same judicial
interest as those who sat in White's bow window on the opposite
side of the street, although never with quite the same haughty
disdain. The bay window at Crockford's was quite a convivial
meeting place for members, but at White's it had ever been a
shrine – 'that sacred semi-circle', as Disraeli was to describe it,
where no man under 40 dared to enter and which the junior
members looked upon, as Bourke once said, with the same awe
as they looked upon the throne in the House of Lords.

The visitor mounted the steps and entered the new Crockford's
Club with suitable hesitation. Beneath him (and quite unknown
to all except a few) were capacious cellars suitable for later development as a cockpit, and providing also a secret exit from the
Club in case of a police raid, but it was the main entrance hall,
with Roman-Ionic *scagliola* columns with gilt capitals which
first caught his eye as he entered the main vestibule. To his right
and left were the dining-room and reading room respectively.
Facing him was the grand staircase, in spiral form, and suspended
by four Doric columns which led to a 'quadrangle' above with

entrances to the main apartments. Towering above this grand staircase was a ceiling perforated with luminous panels of stained glass which supported, at their centre, a large dome from the middle of which was suspended a glittering chandelier, the whole illuminated by the latest form of gas lighting.

The dining-room, on the right of the entrance, was a majestic room flanked by marble pillars, but the room which commanded the chief attention was 'The State Drawing Room', a magnificent room on the first floor which, to quote *Bentley's Miscellany*, baffled perfect description on account of its beauty that was so splendidly enhanced by decorations in the most florid style of the school of Louis XIV.

The room presents a series of panels containing subjects, in the style of Watteau, from the pencil of Mr Martin, a relative of the celebrated historical painter of that name: these panels are alternated with splendid mirrors. A chandelier of exquisite workmanship hangs from the centre of the ceiling, and three large tables, beautifully carved and gilded, and covered with rich blue and crimson velvet, are placed in different parts of the room. The upholstery and decorative adjuncts are imitative of the gorgeous taste of George the Fourth. Royalty can scarcely be conceived to vie with the style and consummate splendour of this magnificent chamber.

The implication of the last sentence, which admittedly was written some years later, probably was not lost on the king and his architect, John Nash, then busy together designing Buckingham Palace. It had been Crockford's intention to put the royal mansion in the shade, and this he had succeeded in doing.

But despite his seeming purpose of creating the most ornate, the most fashionable and the most select club in London – and no doubt in the world – the real purpose behind the enterprise was, of course, to make Crockford's the centre for all 'deep play' among English gamblers, and to siphon off the money that was being taken by the bankers at White's, at Brooks's and at all the other gambling clubs in Mayfair. Thus was 'the Ascot of gambling' created – and not even the Royal Enclosure was ever destined to be more select than Crockford's Club in St James's Street.

The real centre of this mansion therefore – the engine room as it were, or the Operations Room if one looks upon it as the place from which the major assault was to be initiated – was the gaming room itself, which was situated on the second floor, overlooking St James's Street, and was of modest proportions. Here was the spider's lair, where Crockford himself used always to sit during the hours of play, watching the flies that were being enticed into his web.

This gaming room was his lair, but the mansion itself was Crockford's monument to his self-esteem. It represented all that he had set out to achieve – a building which was the very reverse of the gambling hells of his boyhood, and of the back alleys of St James's and the Strand. And indeed the very reverse of the ill-tempered ill-mannered gambling of the 18th century, when gentlemen forgot they were gentlemen and cheated each other, quarrelled with each other, demanded satisfaction on the duelling ground from each other and cursed fate and their ill-luck when they lost.

In all this William Crockford can almost be seen as one of the first of the Victorians. It is ridiculous to think of him as either a gentleman or a sportsman, yet Crockford's Club, in its dignity and elegance, helped to usher in the era of Victorian self-control and gentlemanly good manners. And Tom Duncombe, 'King' Allen, Ball Hughes and all the rest who came to gamble at Crockford's were themselves the leaders of a new outlook to gambling and to gentility as well. Perhaps it was the influence of the Duke of Wellington, the leader of Crockford's and one of the first exponent of English *sang froid*, that brought about this revolution in gambling, for revolution it certainly was. Not for another 50 years would Victorian imperturbability and reserve reach their zenith in the behaviour of the aristocratic heroes glorified in the novels of Whyte-Melville, the chronicler of the stiff-upper lip, but Victorian equanimity in sport was yet cradled in solemnity of the gaming room at Crockford's Club. Here it was established that the essential qualities of a gentleman were not only to hold his liquor but also to lose – or to win – with dignity.

It was not an imposing room, this gambling room at Crockford's. Indeed the writer in *Bentley's Miscellany* could describe it as comparatively small, but handsomely furnished:

In the centre of the apartment stands the *all-attractive Hazard Table*, innocent and unpretending enough in its form and appearance, but fatally mischievous and destructive in its conjunctive influence with box and dice. On this table it may with truth be asserted that the greater portion, if not the whole, of Crockford's immense wealth was achieved; and for this piece of plain, unassuming mahogany he had doubtless a more profound veneration than for the most costly piece of furniture that ever graced a palace. This bench of business is large, and of oval shape, well stuffed, and covered with fine green cloth, marked with yellow lines, denoting the different departments of specu-lation. Round these compartments are double lines, similarly marked, for the odds or proportions between what is technically known as the *main* and *chance*. In the centre on each side are indented positions for the croupiers, or persons engaged at the table in calling the main and chance, regulating the stakes, and paying and receiving money as the events decisive of gain and loss occur. Over the table is suspended a three-light lamp, conveniently shaded, so as to throw its full luminous power on the cloth, and at the same time to protect the eyes of the croupiers from the light's too strong effect. At another part of the room is fixed a writing-table or desk, where the Pluto of the place was wont to preside, to mete out loans on draft or other security, and to answer all demands by successful players. Chairs of easy make, dice-boxes, bowls for holding counters representing sums from 1 to 200, with small hand-rakes used by players to draw their counters from any inconvenient distance on the table, may be said to complete the furni-ture, machinery, and implements of this *great workshop*.

By the terms of Crockford's agreement with his committee he was bound to put down a bank or capital of £5,000 nightly *during the sitting of Parliament* – a curious commentary on the man-ner in which the Committee considered the Club should be run. (When Parliament was in recess a smaller, downstairs room was used for hazard.) Should the bank suffer a long losing run, Crockford was not permitted to terminate play until the whole of his £5,000 had been lost. If it was all lost, he could continue or close the gaming room according to his wish. In practice he was usually prepared to increase the bank to £15,000 or £20,000 in a night, but when he found himself opposed by really heavy gamblers enjoying a run of luck he would often exert his right to close down for the evening.

Finally, despite the respectability of this Management Committee, the overlordship of the Duke of Wellington and the overriding air of gentility which pervaded everything, there is reason to suppose that some of these committee members enjoyed 'a cut' of the bank's profits – which admittedly had been the custom with the organising committees of the fashionable gambling clubs of the past, and notably of that run by Crockford's predecessor, Almack.

As already noted, the annual subscription for the Club was 30 guineas, and the membership was between 1,000 and 2,000, but in addition there were people such as visiting diplomats, ambassadors of foreign countries, members of the European aristocracy and the like who were granted temporary membership whilst in London. Any member of White's, Brooks's or Boodle's was automatically eligible for Crockford's.

The staff of the Club, apart from those employed in the gambling room, but including Eustache Ude, consisted of some 30 or 40 employees, with a different staff of waiters for day and night service. All were dressed in livery and had impeccable manners – except only for Eustache Ude, with his tendency to quarrel with diners who had the temerity to question the quality or flavouring of the food.

The gambling room staff were quite separate, and were highly trained, secretive and expert in their work. This they had to be, for they worked always under the close but seemingly unobtrusive supervision of Crockford himself. 'The whole and sole direction and control of the department and operations of play were under the experienced professorship of the proprietor,' wrote the anonymous correspondent in *Bentley's Miscellany*, and to all those who knew Crockford it would have been inconceivable that it should ever be otherwise, for Crockford wished to know everything that was going on, who was winning and who losing, and how his staff were administering the bank. He therefore sat 'snug and sly' at his desk in one corner of the room, where he commanded a full view of all that was happening, 'watchful as the dragon that guarded the golden apples of the Hesperides'.

His main function, besides ensuring that no one was cheating him, was to furnish loans to those who needed further cash with which to play, but such loans were only forthcoming to those whose credit was known to be beyond question, because of their social standing; because Crockford's secret intelligence service had reported to him that their bank balance was sufficient; or – in the case of a young gambler – because a wealthy parent was in the background, who could be relied on to pay up rather than to face a scandal.

It was said of Crockford at this time that he was a walking Domesday Book, in which was recorded the whole financial history of the great families of England. He knew the day and almost the hour when heirs were born to wealthy fathers, and so could calculate how long it would be before the infant with all its great expectations might grow up to become a prospective client of the bank and a member of Crockford's Club. Some of this information he kept to himself, locked away in the neatly tabulated ledger which he called his mind, but some he was prepared to divulge for the information and guidance of his Management Committee so that when they had considered the social desirability of some new candidate, Crockford could then fill in for them the more mundane details – the rent-rolls of father and grandfather, the mortgages, the debts and the financial scandals, the codicils that had been added to wills, and the contents of these wills themselves. Just as his rival and enemy, John Gully, knew the pedigree of every horse in training, its breeding, stamina index and racing characteristics, so William Crockford knew the pedigrees of all the young gamblers in London. Often, indeed, he knew a great deal more about an heir's prospects than did the young man himself.

But inevitably, as the years went by, he found that despite all his precautions he was yet faced with the problem of numerous bad debts, and in the end – some seven years after the club's formation – he was forced to bring in a rule that gamblers must play with ready money, although he continued to oblige some of his more distinguished and reliable clients in private. But needless to say he was always willing to accept a settlement in kind, providing always that he felt he was getting a bargain, and he was thus happy to accept jewellery, pictures and property in lieu of payment. It was as a result of this that he later acquired a large building adjoining the Travellers' Club in Pall Mall; and Lord Seagrave was said to have made over to him a fine house in Bruton Street after suffering heavy losses in the gambling room.

To all of this, a notorious rogue of the period, the self-styled 'Lord Chief Baron' Nicholson, in his memoirs, was able to add an interesting footnote when he observed that a thriving business was carried on by the pawnbroker's shop in Green Street, off Leicester Square, wherein might be encountered some of the highest in the land when faced with the necessity of raising ready cash at short notice.

The 'Baron' wrote more warmly of Crockford than did most of his contemporaries, and he even referred to Crockford's benevolent disposition. The two crooks no doubt had sympathy with each other's activities, and it seems that Crockford's generosity was chiefly extended to others of their tribe. He never helped a rich young wastrel who suffered a run of bad luck, but he might on occasion extend a helping hand to members of his staff when they fell on hard times.

One point about the Crockford régime which delighted the 'Baron' was the punctiliousness shown in the gaming room on a Saturday evening. The moment the clock struck midnight, all play was suspended for 24 hours, and Crockford himself would have been horrified at the suggestion that gaming should be continued on the Sabbath.

Even at the height of his wealth and importance, Crockford remained wholly without grace or elegance, his manner servile, his gaze shifty and suspicious, his speech slurred and his bow both clumsy and absurd. And like Uriah Heep he remained always outwardly humble. It was said of him at the time that he never lost the hackney coachman's manner of speaking, and a fragment of dialogue from a contemporary description of him – from John Mills' *D'Orsay or the Follies of the Day* – reveals his willingness to lend and the manner in which he did it:

'Excuse me, my Lud, did I hear you say as how you had no more ready money? My Lud, this 'ere is the bank (pointing to the bank) if your Ludship wishes it £1,000 or £2,000 is at your Ludship's service.'

'Really, Mr Crockford, you are very obliging; but I don't think I shall play any more tonight.'

'Ashgrove,' said the Earl of Kintray, 'Ashgrove, do accept Mr Crockford's liberal offer of the £2,000; perhaps you may win back all you have lost.'

'Nothing, I azure your Ludship, vill give me greatur pleasur than to give you the moneys,' said Crockford.

'Well, let me have £2,000.'

Crockford dipped his fingers into the bank, took out the £2,000 and handed it to his Lordship. 'Per'aps your Ludship vould obleege me with an IOU and pay the amount at your convenians.'

'I shall be able to pay it you in a couple of months,' said his Lordship, handing the ex-fishmonger the IOU.

'Your Ludship's werry kind – werry.'

The description of Crockford himself which the book also includes presents a slightly more flattering portrait than that traditional one which will later be quoted, in which he is seen in his heyday at Newmarket, 'his cheeks whitened and flabby, his hands without knuckles, soft as raw veal and as white as paper.'

Here, 'in a gorgeously furnished and well-lighted room' he is shown as remaining apart from the players and seemingly almost aloof to all that is going on but watchful and cunning yet almost benevolent withal:

A little in arrear of the players a tall and rather spare man stood, with a pale and strongly marked face, light grey eyes, and frosted hair. His dress was common in the extreme and his appearance generally might be denominated of that order. The only peculiarity, if peculiarity it can be called, was a white cravat folded so thickly round his neck that there seemed to be quite a superfluity of cambric in that quarter.

A smile – it might be of triumph, it might be of good-nature, of satisfaction, of benevolence, of goodwill – no, it could not be either of these, save the former, and yet a smile was there. He was the proprietor of this leviathan of earthly hells, and it would be passing strange, indeed, for one who had drawn his mammoth fortune from extravagance and reckless folly to wear a look other than as a jay bends to the egg he is about to suck. But there he stood, turning a pleasant – it almost amounted to a benevolent – look upon the progress of the hazard, and at each countenance of the players.

Thus Crockford watched over his new empire, saw it flourish and allowed his nimble, mathematical brain to calculate the night's winnings, the week's winnings, the year's winnings – the winnings of a lifetime.

His chief lieutenant, 'his steward, agent and factotum', was still his old associate, Gye, a man as cunning and devious as he was himself, who had worked in partnership with Crockford for so many years, had followed him through the ups and downs of gambling and who had saved him from prison when he had been summoned to appear on indictment at the Clerkenwell Sessions.

Gye had feathered his nest as the years went by, and now he was a 'warm' man, with a fortune that was whispered at nigh on £30,000 as a result of his salary, his own private speculations, and the secret information which his position enabled him to acquire about the clients, their habits and their racehorses. But despite the manner in which Gye had saved his master from prosecution at Clerkenwell, there was no love lost between the two. Crockford watched Gye with a deepening suspicion. He knew of the fortune that Gye had amassed, and he resented these secret operations. Sooner or later, as Crockford well knew, Gye would overstep himself. When that occurred, Gye could expect no sympathy and no mercy from his employer – and well he knew it.

Seated in a high chair beyond the hazard table, and in the opposite corner of the room to Crockford at his desk, was his 'inspector', groom-porter or general supervisor', a Mr Page, who performed the duties of a *chef* at a modern roulette session, and who acted also as a sort of auditor and debt-collector. He had a rake with which he gathered in and paid out the stakes made by the gamblers, and he saw to it that the pace of the play never slackened and that the rattle of the dice in the box – that sound which had such a stimulating and even erotic influence on compulsive gamblers – was never silent. Since he was responsible for supervising the play and receiving and paying out the money, it was essential that his accuracy and impartiality should be acknowledged by all the players; and this respect he certainly commanded. Even Crockford himself would never have overruled a decision of Page's, whose salary, it was said, amounted to some 50 guineas a week.

No servant of the Club was ever allowed to enter the hazard room once play had started; and no interruption that might affect the concentration of the players was ever permitted. The general atmosphere in the room was one of quiet decorum, although the players were allowed to call out the number they sought. (There was, of course, no smoking permitted, and the building did not even contain a smoking-room. White's Club did not open one until 1845, Brooks's not until 1881.)

The cost of running the hazard room was substantial, for besides the wages paid to Page and Gye, there was the not inconsiderable cost of the dice themselves. These were made from finest ivory and were bought by Crockford at a guinea a pair. Three new pairs were provided for the opening of play every night, and the old ones were never used again. The total cost of dice alone *per annum* was therefore in the region of £2,000.

By a further tradition of the Club, which Crockford had instituted from its opening, the players in the hazard room ate 'on the house'. To this end, there was a coffee or supper room leading from the grand vestibule where the gamblers could congregate either before or after their play and where Ude's finest dishes were assembled for their benefit. Indeed it was in this supper room that he really excelled himself, and the cold buffet was laid out in fine display. Wine, also, was free. This seeming generosity cost Crockford about £50 a night.

Those members who never gambled were naturally reluctant to partake of these free luxuries, and they ate in the large dining-room. But even here the cost of a meal was not excessive. Dinner – which was served in the early evening between four-thirty and six – would cost in the region of half-a-guinea. Supper, which was available for the ordinary members between about eleven and one-thirty in the morning, would be a little cheaper. One of the biggest altercations in which the temperamental Eustache Ude was ever involved arose out of the fact that a member dining early, and by himself, had ordered a red mullet, for which Ude had charged him two shillings, plus a further sixpence for the superb sauce which Ude had concocted for it with his own hands. This extra sixpence the member refused to pay. 'The imbecile must think that red mullets come out of the sea with my sauce in their pockets,' shouted Ude in gallic frenzy.

That Crockford's new club should prove a success from its inception was a foregone conclusion. He had not taken the risks that Almack had taken in the previous century when Almack, in the terminology of the turf, 'had hit the front too soon'. But Almack had yet succeeded in the end, despite the coldness of the weather and the dampness on his walls on the opening night, and the efforts made subsequently in some quarters to boycott his enterprise.

Crockford had his enemies too, of course, but they had little influence. The only thing which might have retarded his progress in this opening year of 1828 and in the years that followed was another long run of bad luck such as he had encountered once before. This he feared, as all bankers must fear it, but it never materialised. From the start, the play in his famous hazard room was extremely 'deep' and players such as Lord Sefton, Ball Hughes and Scrope Davies gambled immense sums from the outset without ever hitting a really lucky streak. In 1829 Creevey noted that Lord Sefton had broken the bank at Crockford's on two successive nights and carried off more than £7,000, but Lord Sefton was a typical Crockford loser, in that he remembered when he won, but quickly forgot when he lost.

Thus William Crockford, seated in snug seclusion in his corner of the gaming room, increasingly observant but seldom being observed, must have preened himself over his success in founding a great and fashionable club that bore his name, and over the cunning which enabled him to enrich himself nightly at the expense of these wealthy men of Society. With his famous white cravat folded thickly around his neck, and a smile of benevolent approbation on his face, he must have appeared to the players as but part of the furnishings of the room. They knew that 'Old Crocky's' gaze was fixed upon them, and they joked about it amongst themselves as they flung down the ivory dice on the rich green cloth.

Thus the hunted browsed happily in their reserve whilst the hunter laid his snares and traps all around them.

5

THE CROCKFORD SET
The Daredevils and the Dandies

No one can describe the splendour and excitement of the early days of Crockey. . . . The members of the Club included all the celebrities of England, from the Duke of Wellington to the youngest Ensign of the Guards; and at the gay and festive board, which was constantly replenished from midnight to early dawn, the most brilliant sallies of wit, the most agreeable conversation, the most interesting anecdotes, interspersed with grave political discussions and acute logical reasoning on every conceivable subject, proceeded from the soldiers, scholars, statesmen, poets, and men of pleasure, who, when the 'house was up' and balls and parties at an end, delighted to finish their evening with a little supper and a good deal of hazard at old Crockey's. The tone of the club was excellent. A most gentleman-like feeling prevailed, and none of the rudeness, familiarity, and ill-breeding which disgrace some of the minor clubs of the present day, would have been tolerated for a moment.

It was thus that Captain Gronow described the scene at Crockford's Club in its golden era, which covered the fourth decade of the century. The quotation underlines the point which has already been made – that in a curious way Crockford himself may be seen as one of the first Victorians, because he introduced a note of decorum and gentility into the world of gambling, in St James's Street at least, if not at Newmarket or on Epsom Downs.

The influence of the Duke of Wellington must, of course, have been considerable in establishing this atmosphere of restraint and quiet good manners. The Duke, then in his early sixties, was the most respected personality in London Society. He was never disdainful or aloof, and he mixed freely and easily amongst young and old, but no one was ever in doubt that he stood head and shoulders above his contemporaries. Sir Walter Scott once wrote that he had never felt awed or abashed except in the presence of one man, 'The Duke of Wellington, who possesses every mighty quality of the mind in a higher degree than any other does, or ever has done'. At this period the Duke was still an imposing figure, still straight and slim, and still perfectly dressed, as befitted one who had been known in Spain during his fighting days as 'The Dandy' and later in London as 'The Beau'.

His principles were rigid and high-minded, and he never gambled. It is a little surprising, therefore, to find him associated with Crockford's Club from the outset. Perhaps he felt, as Admiral Rous was later to feel, that betting was but a means of levelling out disproportionate fortunes; or he may have considered that since gambling clubs were inevitable in Society, it was better to have one run on the lines of the new Crockford's than in the manner of the gambling hells of the back streets. Moreover he would have been one of the first to appreciate the need for a really select and comfortable club which could provide a meeting place for all the prominent members of Society and where men of intelligence from the services and the political and diplomatic worlds might meet for friendly and informal discussion.

The Duke was, of course, the senior member of the club, but as he took no part in the gambling life which went on there he cannot be considered as a typical 'Crockford man'. The majority of the gambling set at the club were young, or in early middle age, with a sprinkling of senior members who were ready to bet as heavily as the juniors.

Who were they, then, and what were they like – this gambling élite of Crockford's Club in its hey-day, during the fourth decade of the century, a century that was in the end to see the eclipse of a way of life which was peculiarly their own?

Two of the most influential members of the new club, and both of them founder-members of the management committee, were the Earls of Sefton and Chesterfield. Of these, William Philip Molyneux, 2nd Earl of Sefton, was in every respect 'a Crockford man'. Of roughly the same age as the proprietor, he was one of the most famous sportsmen in England, being a great horseman, a fine whip who drove a splendid team of bay horses, and a man of taste and breeding. Gronow referred to him as 'the vigorous Sefton' and Greville observed that he 'filled a considerable space in Society' and that 'his natural parts were excessively lively, but his education had been wholly neglected'. Like 'Old Q' before him, he had the greatest scorn for all intellectuals and for those who gained their knowledge from books, but his great wealth and dominant personality made him a leader of the aristocracy. He was not a wit, but he was a great droll; a man with an infinite capacity for laughter and for making others laugh. At the time that Crockford's opened he was still committed to a long feud with George IV, because there had been an occasion when Arthur Paget, a close friend of the monarch's, had fallen in love with Lady Sefton and – to quote the words of Greville – 'the King had pimped for Arthur' and had contrived to get Sefton out of the way on some pretext or other so that the lovers might 'amuse themselves'.

Lord Sefton probably lost more money at Crockford's than anyone else, which is to say that he lost a great deal. The total must have approached nearly a quarter of a million, and Gronow declared that after Sefton's death in 1838, by which time he was senile and half-mad, Crockford obsequiously approached his eldest son, and informed him that there were still debts to the tune of £40,000 outstanding. The new Lord Sefton – a man of honour and as great a sportsman as his father – accepted the liability, although he may well have had his doubts about it, and he paid Crockford the money.

Sefton's fellow-committee member, George Stanhope, 6th Earl of Chesterfield, was a much younger man who had succeeded to the family estate in the year of Waterloo, when he was still a minor. He was a less attractive character than Sefton, wilder and more dissolute. Greville, who was a close friend of most of the Crockford set in these early days, spoke of his 'idleness, folly, waste and constant progress to ruin ... He lies in bed half the day, and rises to run after pleasure in whatever shape he can pursue it.' This was a young man very much after Crockford's heart – a typical 'pigeon', waiting to be plucked.

Yet no one can have entered the fashionable world at this time under more favourable auspices than George Stanhope. George

III and Queen Charlotte had been god-parents at his christening, which was performed by the Archbishop of Canterbury; and not only Chesterfield House but the whole of South Audley Street had been brilliantly illuminated in celebration of the event, which took place at night when the street itself was lined by members of the Life Guards.

Unfortunately his career thereafter set an example that was to be closely followed 40 years later by the luckless Harry Hastings, 4th Marquis of Hastings, who was ruined by Hermit's Derby. Both were orphaned at an early age and both were sent to Eton, from where they emerged with no intellectual knowledge, no knowledge of life and no aptitude for anything except the squandering of money. That Chesterfield should have joined Crockford's at the age of 22 was tantamount to financial suicide – which is no doubt what William Crockford had in mind when he invited the young Earl to become a member of the Management Committee. Under the guidance of Charles Greville, he entered upon a turf career with all the enthusiasm and impetuosity of Harry Hastings, and was soon picturing himself as the owner of a Derby winner, but it was not long before Greville found him intolerable and ended the friendship.

When he opened his Pandemonium in 1828, William Crockford must have calculated in his mind which of the young rakes who hurried to join the Club and to gamble at his tables were most likely to ruin themselves and to enrich the Club's proprietor. No doubt it was quite a long list, with a question-mark placed against several of the names. But at the head of it may well have been the name of George Stanhope, 6th Earl of Chesterfield. *His* ruin was inevitable.

Another big gambler at Crockford's in the late 1820s was Lord Alvanley, a close friend of Sefton's and one of the leading dandies of the Crockford set. At the time it was generally thought that he had already lost the bulk of his fortune at Watier's before ever Crockford enticed him into his web, but there was still plenty of money left for Crockford to take from him. A wit, a noted eccentric (he always read in bed by candlelight and then threw the lighted candle into the middle of the room when he wished to go to sleep), a noted gourmet who loved Ude's cooking (he had a curious obsession with apricot tart, which he insisted on eating almost daily), he was perhaps best remembered in Society for the way in which he and Sefton had continued to befriend Brummell after the Beau had ruined himself so sensationally and had retired to live in poverty and squalor in Calais.

Then, of course, there was that notorious Old Etonian, Edward Hughes Ball, another crony of Greville's, who had inherited a fortune which brought him in an income of £40,000 a year on the death of his celebrated uncle, Admiral Sir Edward Hughes, in 1819. Sometimes he called himself Hughes Ball and sometimes Ball Hughes, but to the Crockford set he was always known by his nickname of 'The Golden Ball'.

Here was another ideal type of member of the club for William Crockford, to whom anyone with an income of £40,000 a year *and* a propensity for gambling was as a gift from heaven. He was another of the Crockford dandies, and as this was the great era for amateur coaching, 'The Golden Ball' invested in an elaborate chocolate-coloured coach with four cream horses and two, immaculately turned-out grooms.

Ball Hughes was the man who had employed the Wyatt brothers to decorate his house in Brook Street, and whose taste for things ornamental but impractical led him to fall madly in love with a 15-year-old Spanish dancer named Mercandotti, who was thought to be either the mistress or the illegitimate daughter of Lord Fife (some felt that she might even be both). She was the leading attraction of the 1822 season at the King's Theatre, but failed to appear there one night when Ball Hughes abducted her, which she had anyway been expecting him to do. He then married her, which was no doubt a good deal more than she had expected of him under the circumstances.

> Instead of partner for the night,
> She partner soon became for life,

wrote one wag about the incident, whilst another produced the epigram:

> The fair damsel is gone; and no wonder at all
> That, bred to the dance, she is gone to the Ball.

As a dandy, Ball was no more than a pale imitation of Beau Brummell, whom he had always greatly admired, and Ball's eccentricities tended to be rather childish. He remained something of a joke in Society, and although he tried to turn his hand to everything, he showed aptitude for nothing, for he had not even the deportment or presence for dandyism, despite all his flamboyant displays. His contemporaries viewed his antics with toleration, and his only claim to distinction in his daily perambulations up and down St James's Street seems to have been summed up by one observer of the scene who remarked that 'The Golden Ball' was the only man he knew who could carry off a white waistcoat before luncheon.

Turf historians have maintained that the best of the younger set at Crockford's in these early days of the club was the noted sportsman and popular man-about-town, George Payne, another Old Etonian and one who had inherited a vast fortune when still a minor. Born in 1803, he was already the Sheriff of Northampton by the time Crockford's opened its doors in 1828. He was caught inevitably in the Crockford web and lost a great deal of money at the club, playing as 'deep' as almost any man there.

A club member once approached Crockford and asked him which of the two champagnes served, Mousseux or Sillery, did he himself prefer. To which the old man replied, after some thought, 'Vy, I don't much care – but I like George Payne better than either.'

Opinions vary on George Payne, and one sees him in different lights. He was lovable – there seems no doubt about that – and a charming and delightful companion. In his own country of Northamptonshire he was looked upon as the ideal squire and a model M.F.H. (he was twice Master of the Pytchley).

'Other districts have had and still have their names to swear by. The West Riding of Yorkshire has its George Lane Fox, and Gloucestershire its Duke of Beaufort, but there never has been and never will be but one George Payne.' Thus spoke one of his country neighbours. He was strongly built, handsome, friendly and a good mixer, which was one of the reasons why the tenants on his country estate, Sulby Hall, were so devoted to him. He was orphaned at the age of six, and in all inherited three fortunes, as well as a legacy of £25,000 from his friend, the irascible Lord Glasgow; and he lost the greater portion of this money in gambling, for his passions in life were the turf and playing cards, on both of which it was his custom to wager very heavily. Sir John Astley, writing of him in *Fifty Years of my Life*, declared that 'George Payne was endowed with every attribute of a sportsman and a polished man of the world. He never married, but he was by no means indifferent to female charms', an observation which seems to have been borne out by persistent rumours that he kept a private harem of young girls. His close friend, throughout a long life, was Admiral Rous, and the Admiral was a man of aggressive rectitude and highly critical of social irregularities.

Yet there seems always to have been some doubt about George Payne, as there has been about another Society idol of the period the colourful Viscount D'Orsay. George Payne had first entered Crockford's orbit when, at the age of 21, he lost £33,000 on the St Leger of 1824. He had been secretly advised at the time by John Gully that he could lay with confidence against one of the fancied runners, a black colt named Jerry, because John Gully himself was also doing so. Jerry, Gully assured his young confidant, would be 'taken care of', and the young man could therefore oppose the colt with absolute confidence.

In all fairness to Gully, this piece of turf intelligence which he passed on was based on a reliable source. The informant, indeed, was none other than his crony, Robert Ridsdale, well known as the slipperiest customer on Newmarket Heath. Ridsdale had whispered to Gully that he had Jerry's jockey, Harry Edwards, 'in his pocket' and that the colt would be 'pulled'.

But the betting talks in racing, and sometimes it even shouts its information abroad. The owner and trainer of Jerry were fully satisfied with their horse's home gallops and they began to back him accordingly, only to discover that the more they invested, and the better the colt went in his trials, the longer became the price which they were able to secure against him.

The inference was clear. Someone was about to betray them. But who? The answer was given by one of those curious chances which occur in life. A friend of theirs who was standing in a darkened street one night chanced to look up just as a post-chaise rattled by, but in the gloom he was just able to glimpse the faces of the two occupants, deep in conversation in the back of the carriage. One was Jerry's jockey, Harry Edwards – the other was Robert Ridsdale. Thus the answer was given. Edwards was dismissed and an honest jockey substituted; and Jerry won the race.

The whole incident was typical of the manner in which the highest in the land were allowing themselves to be drawn into the malpractices of the turf by their association with the scum of Newmarket Heath.

George Payne was both a wild gambler and a bad gambler, always chasing his losses when he was heavily down, and always giving others a chance to chase theirs when he was heavily up at their expense. In the size of his wagers and the extent of his gambling, he ran second only to Sefton. Like so many other compulsive gamblers, he could never make up his mind for certain when assessing the form in a big handicap, and would end by covering more than 20 runners out of a field of 30. And since he was both unlucky *and* a poor judge of form, he usually failed to find the winner even then! He dabbled in the stock market – about which he knew nothing – with equally disastrous results, and it was only when he played cards that he seemed to demonstrate a natural flair and a certain judgement.

But here again, the doubt arises. Was he after all the perfect sportsman, the gentleman who would never cheat, and who could never tell a lie? The Victorian era opened – as it was destined to close – with a major card scandal involving some of the highest in the land, with open allegations of cheating, and George Payne was destined to become involved in the first of these two *causes célèbres*, as were several other prominent members of Crockford's.

The case was that of Lord de Ros versus John Cumming, when Cumming, Payne, Brooke Greville and Lord Henry Bentinck together charged Lord de Ros with cheating. The case was heard at Westminster Hall before the Lord Chief Justice; and Sir John Campbell, defending de Ros, gave Payne a rough passage in the box, describing him as 'a professional gamester', and concluding with the bitter allegation that 'having started as a dupe he soon crystallized into something worse'.

George Payne was infuriated by this, as indeed he had good reason to be, and he attempted to horsewhip his accuser, but here again the doubt arises as to whether anyone who was so deeply involved in the heavy gambling of the period could possibly have kept his hands clean. Certainly any man who gambled heavily at cards had perforce to know all the stratagems of play, and had to rely upon at least astuteness.

A gentleman gambler also had to be ruthless at times. This is illustrated by a story told by George Payne at this period. It was said that he and the young Lord Albert Denison, afterwards the first Lord Londesbrough, sat up all night at Limmer's Hotel on the eve of Lord Albert's wedding, and that Payne deprived the groom of £30,000 before accompanying him round the corner to St George's, Hanover Square, for the marriage ceremony.

George Payne was also an eccentric, and was very extravagant in his mode of life. He had a passion for travelling by post-chaise, which was said to cost him a £1,000 a year.

Payne, Lord Sefton and Charles Greville, the diarist, were lifelong friends and spent many evenings together at Crockford's. Between them they had, perhaps, too many of Nature's gifts. They had too much money – and too little common sense. Greville, whom they nicknamed 'Punch', had been born in 1794, and like 'The Golden Ball' was an Old Etonian. He was not one of the original Crockford members, and probably did not visit the club until two years after it was opened.

The Old Etonian element at Crockford's was as strong as it had been at White's in the previous century, when George Selwyn and Horace Walpole had ruled the roost there, but Crockford's at its opening was not without a representative from 'The Hill'. Chief amongst these Old Harrovians was Tommy Duncombe, whom Gronow remembered with such affection in a paragraph of his memoirs which has become a part of the Crockford saga:

In the play-room might be heard the clear ringing voice of that agreeable reprobate, Tom Duncombe, as he cheerfully called, 'Seven', and the powerful hand of the vigorous Sefton in throwing for a ten. There might be noted the scientific dribbling of a four by 'King' Allen, the tremendous backing of nines and fives by Ball Hughes and Auriol, the enormous stakes played for by Lords Lichfield and Chesterfield, George Payne, Sir St Vincent Cotton, D'Orsay, and George Anson, and, above all, the gentlemanly bearing and calm and unmoved demeanour, under losses or gains, of all the men of that generation.

Tommy Duncombe was a typical Crockford member, a man of many parts and many interests – a dandy, a fop, a politician, an ex-Coldstream Guardsman and a dedicated gambler. Born in 1796, he spent three years at Harrow between 1808 and 1811 where he boldly opposed the establishment and was several times flogged as a result. Gazetted as an ensign to the Coldstream Guards, he was dispatched to Holland in the winter of 1813, but was sent home again without ever becoming involved in the activities of Waterloo. He took up a political career in 1820, although singularly lacking in any political qualifications except for his inherent love of opposing those in authority. A month after Crockford's opened, he made his maiden speech in the House during ministerial explanations and astonished everyone by the fluency with which he delivered it (although this was afterwards explained when it was learnt that de Ros had not only written the speech for him, but had even coached him in every pause and gesture). Not surprisingly, he made many enemies, not the least of whom was the Marquis of Salisbury, partly because of his radical views, and partly because of his unashamed methods of getting himself elected. He was later returned as the member for Hertford, having used his fortune for purposes of bribery and corruption (his five contests for the borough were said to have cost him £40,000).

He lived for pleasure, and indeed voted for it in the House, one of his proposals being that an annual fair should be held in Hyde Park, but he could also declaim with passionate vehemence, and in spite of his dandyism he was well able to hold his own in the rough-and-tumble of a noisy debate. 'Tom Duncombe,' wrote Greville on one occasion, 'made one of his blustering Radical harangues, full of every sort of impertinence, which was received with immense applause.' Later on he was used as a go-between when the master-builders became involved in a quarrel with their workers; and Cubitt, head of the building firm, asked him to work towards a reconciliation. Thus Tommy can be looked upon as a father of our modern industrial conciliation machinery, a title which would certainly have astonished him at the time.

In some respects he may be seen as an inferior edition of Charles James Fox, who was also a dedicated gambler and an ardent speaker, and who also passed through a stage of extreme dandyism; and no doubt both of them were inspired by that same rebellious attitude towards conformity as is seen in the young of today.

Tommy Duncombe was not one of the heaviest gamblers at Crockford's, but he was certainly one of the most regular attendants in the gaming room. As with so many of the others, gambling exercised its spell over him, and he could not tear himself away from the tables.

> There's Tommy Duncombe, who, at play,
> Thousands has often thrown away;
> And yet, unwilling to refrain,
> More thousands has won back again.

One of Tommy's closest friends in the Crockford circle was another of what one might describe as 'the butterfly brigade'. This was Count D'Orsay. He was a Frenchman, the second son of one of Napoleon's generals. This General D'Orsay had been nicknamed 'Le Beau D'Orsay', and was said to have been the most dashing and the most handsome soldier of his era. Unfortunately all that he seemed able to hand on to his second son was this family tradition of good looks, for his son was no soldier. Indeed the distant sound of cannon was quite enough to send him hurrying in the opposite direction, and his idea of a gallant assault was to ravish a beautiful young girl in her boudoir – without, of course, exposing himself to any danger. He had charm, astonishing good looks of a rather effeminate kind, delightful manners and a way with women. He also had vitality, wit and gaiety, and quite an outstanding talent as an artist, but he remained nevertheless, a cad. A delightful cad, admittedly, but a cad none the less. The Crockford set were fascinated by him, but the

French contingent in London would have nothing to do with him.

Were it not for the fact that – as is the case with so many handsome cads – he was permanently in financial straits and therefore unable to gamble as heavily and as frequently as he might have wished, Count Alfred Guillaume Gabriel D'Orsay could be remembered as a typical member of the younger set at Crockford's. Crockford could smell out a shaky bank balance with all the certainty of a terrier at a rat-hole, and so he never therefore looked upon the Count as one of his plumper 'pigeons'; but he welcomed him none the less because the Count was so popular in Society; even if he had not much money himself, at least it could be said of him that the majority of his friends had a great deal.

He had been born in 1801, and was therefore only 27 when Crockford's opened its doors to him – which was more than could be said of the doors at White's, which had been slammed very firmly in his face not long before when he had sought membership there. Certainly his behaviour had not been un-blemished up to this moment, because he had left the French army in haste in 1822 when on the point of being posted to Spain, and having resigned his commission, he had joined the Earl and Countess of Blessington on a tour of Italy. Lady Blessington was fascinated by the young French aristocrat, and after engineering his marriage to her step-daughter, she promptly set about seducing him herself, whilst at the same time encouraging the young married couple to investigate the more remarkable paths of love-making, assisted on some occasions both by herself and some of her friends.

His reputation, when he joined Crockford's, could hardly have been worse. 'On these peculiar circumstances, I shall not dwell,' observed Gronow somewhat sententiously. 'They are known to all, and cannot be palliated.' They were, however, quite happily palliated by the younger Crockford set, who looked upon the Count as the leader of the effeminate school and nicknamed him 'the last of the dandies'. And even Gronow spoke with enthusiasm of the beauty of his feet and ankles.

To those who find today the appearance of the modern young man to be often offensive on account of its effeminacy, Gronow's description of Count D'Orsay may come as a salutary reminder that nothing is new, for Gronow wrote of 'his dark chestnut hair which hung naturally in long waving curls'. Like that other French eccentric, the Chevalier D'Eon, who had appeared in London Society during the 18th century alternatively as a man and a woman, D'Orsay was yet tall, strong and magnificently built, a fine athlete, a good horseman and an excellent swordsman (as indeed was the Chevalier D'Eon). Indeed he was a pleasant young man in almost every way – except for the fact that he was a cad. Duncombe, to him, was always 'Mon cher Tomie' and there is no doubt that Duncombe helped him often when the Count was unable to meet his debts.

Another of the Count's cronies and one of his great admirers was Byron, who once described him as having 'all the air of a Cupidon déchaîné, and being one of the few specimens I have seen of our ideal of a Frenchman before the revolution'. Indeed his contemporaries in Society generally found D'Orsay a fascinating personality. R.B.Haydon, in his diary, described him as 'a complete Adonis, not made up at all. He bounded into his cab and drove off like a young Apollo with a fiery Pegasus.' Lord Lytton said of him that he was 'the most accomplished gentleman of our time'.

Gronow always maintained that D'Orsay would have been a very different person had he not lived so long under the corrupting influence of the Blessingtons; and there is little doubt that his astonishing good looks kindled the desires of the homosexuals, who were as numerous in the fashionable world of that period as they are today; and the real truth about the Blessington affair may well have been that it was Lord Blessington, and not his wife, who was chiefly attracted to the young Count. He certainly merited his title of 'last of the dandies'; and he alone can justifiably be compared with Beau Brummell.

This, then, was Crockford's Club at its zenith, during the reign of William IV; and the personalities which have been described in the last few pages may be said to represent the type of gambler whom the new club attracted. This, too, was St James's Street, now brought to its fullest splendour by the erection of so imposing an edifice.

These, then, were the members who nightly thronged the palatial rooms and feasted on Ude's cooking and on the camaraderie of the brilliant and cosmopolitan company which they encountered. The senior members, led by Lord Sefton; the junior members led by the dissolute Old Etonian, Lord Chesterfield, the dare-devil George Payne and the madcap 'Golden Ball'; the dandies led by the exotic Count D'Orsay; the rebellious would-be politicians, with Tommy Duncombe at their head; the literary clique, led by Charles Greville, Creevey and the wit and poet, Henry Luttrell; the eccentrics, the gourmets, the doctors, surgeons, parsons, even the wine merchants and the brewers; the honorary members from the ranks of the politicians and the diplomatic corps; the evil old roués such as Talleyrand; and the ambassadors of France, Spain, Russia, Portugal and Austria; the military men, such as General Alava; the foreign aristocrats, such as the Duc de Palmella and Count Pozzo di Borgo; and finally, and above all – and *really* above all, since he was the greatest man of his age – the great Duke of Wellington himself.

Here was the cream not only of London Society, but also of European Society. Here, too, were some of the richest men in Europe – nay, some of the richest men in the world. And here were the heaviest of all gamblers.

This was Crockford's Club, and this was the centre of the spider's web.

6

THE FINAL PHASE

Resignation and Retirement

What can the poor fly demand from the spider in whose web he is enveloped? – Admiral Rous.

What indeed! And yet, as England entered the fourth decade of the 19th century, a decade that was to see the crowning of a young Queen and the dawn of the great Victorian era, the writing was already upon the wall for William Crockford. He had come far in his journey from Temple Bar. He had amassed great wealth and was destined to amass still more; but the goddess of retribution waits for us all.

Dog does not eat dog, so they say, but the same code of ethics does not apply to spiders, who are often happy to devour each other. Crockford, moreover, had many enemies – enemies amongst men who were as avaricious and unscrupulous as himself, and whose memories were as long as his own. Sooner or later it was inevitable that they would catch up with him – probably when he was growing old, and when his judgement had become less astute – and then they would do their utmost to bring him down in just the same way as he had brought them down in the past – by trickery, bribery and the double-dodge. His old opponent, John Gully, had still a few scores to pay off. He had not forgotten what had happened to Mameluke in the St Leger. As for the Newmarket boys, they too, were awaiting their chance for the enemy to be delivered into their hands.

But all this was still in the future. In the 1830s, when Crockford's Club was growing daily more fashionable and more select, Crockford himself could watch the nightly profits from the bank increase whilst yet relying on the turf to enlarge his fortune, for he was still pursuing his artful methods of laying what seemed to the uninitiated to be extravagant odds against the materialisation of some far-distant double. He was still travelling to and from Newmarket in the utmost luxury for the main meetings. He still ran his bookmaking business in the town, and the best-known and most often-quoted description of him is of this Newmarket life of his, written by one who knew him well:

Rolling in a melodiously hung chariot, and assisted up a flight of steps, which led to a mansion as large as Apsley House, by one or more of his powdered lackeys, the old *cidevant* fishmonger, and the aristocratic hall-keeper, entered his gorgeous *Web* as we passed, from our gallop on the Downs.

We well remember the old gentleman, as we will endeavour to show by a draft upon memory. His cheeks appeared whitened and flabby through constant night-work. His hands were entirely *without knuckles*, soft as raw veal, and as white as paper, whilst his large flexible mouth was stuffed with 'dead men's bones' – his teeth being all false, and visibly socketed with his darling metal, as was foully developed when indulging himself with a hideous laugh with his friend Gully, or other 'congenial' over the delicious flavour or odour of some little 'plant' or lucky *coup*.

On a settling-day, old Crocky sat him down at the seat of custom, and generally had some thousands of Bank of England notes pinned to the table before him by the dainty, flexible fingers we have noticed; having the heavy figures secured by the thumb; the fifties, twenties, and tens under his three longer 'prongs', and a sheaf of 'fivers' under the guardianship of his little finger.

It is not an attractive portrait, and least of all in its reference to 'dead men's bones', for the history of false teeth is one of the more unpleasant aspects of 18th- and early 19th-century dentistry. In Crockford's day extraction was still generally considered to be the only cure for toothache, but John Hunter, the 18th-century London surgeon, had introduced the practice of transplanting human teeth from one jaw to another; either the teeth of the poor into the mouths of the rich, which was a most expensive operation, costing up to £500, or else the teeth of a corpse into that of a living body. The shortage of good-quality human teeth, however, had been largely overcome during the Napoleonic wars, for the far-sighted and well-to-do dentists had kept their agents operating in the battle-fields to extract the teeth of healthy young men who had been killed in the fighting.

More interesting is the reference to 'his friend Gully'. Gully was not his friend at this time, and never had been, but they met frequently and were companionable enough when they found themselves on the same side of the fence, as when some piece of turf roguery was being planned, or some plot being hatched for double-dodging the swells. Not that Gully did not consider himself to be anything but a swell himself at this time, having allied himself with the aristocracy, if not with the angels.

By 1830 Gully had fully entered into partnership with the infamous Robert Ridsdale, and they were sunk deep in many devious and dishonest practices. Now Gully's whole ambition was to win the greatest classic race of them all – the Derby – and in its winning add not only a greater lustre to his social position but also a great deal of money to his steadily mounting fortune. Each season now, he and Robert Ridsdale carefully planned out their campaign on the turf, with the Derby as their principal objective. They entered their colt, Little Red Rover, for the race of 1830 and backed him to win a fortune, but although he came into the straight in front and looked the probable winner, he was run out of it by Will Chifney's Priam. Priam was undoubtedly a very good horse, so Gully's judgement in believing that Little Red Rover, despite his rather weedy appearance, was also a good one was certainly justified; there was not a lot in it at the finish.

Two years later Gully's objective was achieved – through the instrument of St Giles, a colt which ran in Ridsdale's name and one about whom little was known, as his form in public had not suggested any particular ability. Gully and Ridsdale, however, whilst protesting that he was an unknown quantity, yet saw fit to back him to win themselves a total of £100,000, which was sufficient to bring him with a run in the market and caused him to start favourite on the day.

He won easily and his delighted owners pronounced him to be 'a rattling fine 3-year-old'. The Ring, when it paid out, qualified this statement in only one respect, declaring St Giles to be a rattling fine 4-year-old, and therefore not even eligible to run in the race; and they added that it looked very much to them as if several jockeys in the race had been 'squared'. But these things could not be proved, so nothing could be done. Crockford paid out substantially over the race, but the backing of St Giles by the Gully-Ridsdale confederacy had been too significant for its implications to be ignored. Gully's colt, Margrave, who then seemed to be of little account, came a long way behind St Giles in this Derby of 1832, but with St Giles a non-runner in the St Leger, Margrave won this last of the season's classic races without any difficulty, and another fortune – somewhere in the region of £40,000 – was won by the Gully-Ridsdale partnership.

But thieves usually fall out in the end, and since the pair were certainly concerned in what was little more than an elaborate plan for stealing money on the turf, Gully and Ridsdale finally separated. Margrave had run in the St Leger in Gully's name and colours, so Gully took the larger share of the winnings. Ridsdale protested vehemently, and spread scurrilous stories around Newmarket about Gully's double-dealings. When they met later in the hunting-field, Gully gave Ridsdale a horse-whipping, whereat Ridsdale took him to court for assault. Gully failed to justify his actions, and was fined £500. Gully then called Ridsdale a rogue – which was certainly true – and announced that in future he would associate only with gentlemen, a high-minded statement which was soon belied by his joining forces with one, Harry Hill, of whom it was said that if he ever laid against a horse with confidence, it could be assumed that the animal was probably already doped, and soon likely to be dead. A dirty customer, in speech and body, and nearly as big a rogue as Ridsdale!

This partnership between Gully and Hill was later destined to develop into 'The Danebury Confederacy', which was probably the most successful turf-gambling syndicate of the 19th century, for Hill acted as a layer of the odds while Gully appeared in his old role of backer. When they had a horse in their stable which they knew to be 'dead meat' – a term used to define a horse that was sick, lame, nobbled or for other reasons unlikely to do itself justice in a race – Hill would get up and lay the odds against it. But if a *coup* was in the offing, and they had something really to back on, then Gully placed the commission and Hill avoided any commitments on that particular animal. Thus in a race such as the Derby of 1832, Margrave was 'a dead 'un' since the stable commission was being worked on St Giles. It was a murky business, and one not unknown today, where 'the dead meat market' still attracts a few gamblers addicted to this particular aspect of turf necrophilia.

William Day, in his *Reminiscences of the Turf* published some 50 years later, quotes a contemporary description of the scene between the 'legs' on the eve of Margrave's St Leger, 'all yelling and blaspheming in concert, or rather discord', when to see:

Gully's threatening, overcharged brow, with Crockey's satanic smile and working jaw, surrounding the table, as the party explained, was to view a picture worthy of the pencil of a Rembrandt. Old Ord, of *Beeswing* notoriety, also mounted the table, howling drunk, and unshaved for a fortnight, and denounced the gang as a crew of robbers and miscreants, for whom the gallows would be too good; at which the room only applauded ironically or groaned approval. Then Jemmy Bland, an atrocious 'leg' of the ancient top-booted, semi-highwayman school, and old Crockey got set by the ears like two worn-out mastiffs, and had a few words through their false teeth. The *quasi* fishmonger, paddling his arms in his peculiar way, brought some of his early Billingsgate to bear, and floored old Jemmy, after a few rounds, with some withering slang and not-to-be-parried innuendo, though the opponents made a fight of it to the last.

It is not an attractive picture, this thieves' kitchen at Doncaster, and yet at about this same time John Gully was able to command the respect and indeed the friendship of the nobility, and became so highly thought of that he decided to enter politics. To this end he sold his stately mansion, Upper Hare Park, at Newmarket, and bought the even larger and more imposing estate of Ackworth Park, near Pontefract. As a result he became the member for this pocket borough in December of 1832, and the career of John Gully, gentleman, politician and statesman began.

This was rather too much for Crockford – and several others too – to swallow. Greville, in his *Memoirs*, noted that 'The

Borough elections are nearly over and have satisfied the Government. They do not seem to be bad on the whole, but some very bad characters have been returned; among the worst, Gully, Pontefract.' However Greville, too, was gradually coming under the influence of 'Gully, the gentleman' and later observed that 'he has gradually separated himself from the rabble of bettors and blackguards of whom he was once the most conspicuous.'

Perhaps one is being unfair to the memory of John Gully, whom turf historians are wont to eulogise. At his death, 30 years later, the Mayor and Corporation of Pontefract and 'an immense concourse of gentry' followed his coffin to the churchyard and all sporting England mourned his passing. He has been referred to as 'Glorious John', and held up as an example of all that was finest in the 'noble art'. It may have been so. But William Day, the son of John Gully's trainer, old John Day, was later to write of Gully with scorn and indignation. 'He was of tyrannical and overbearing disposition, extremely avaricious, and, like men of his class, not over-scrupulously nice in the acquirement of wealth. He knew how to worship the rising sun.' So one is left to ponder the problem of John Gully's rectitude, and to consider his friendship with men such as Ridsdale, Harry Hill and the money-lender, Henry Padwick. Can the leopard change his spots or the blackleg his skin?

There is no doubt that the turf was in a bad state at the time, with men such as Crockford, Gully, Ridsdale and others involved in so much bribery and corruption. Both Greville and Gronow, who provided so many illuminating comments on the state of England at this period, were shocked by the many examples which they encountered of the lust for wealth producing dishonesty on the part of the avaricious, and ruin on the part of the inexperienced.

I grow more and more disgusted with the atmosphere of villainy I am forced to breathe . . . it is not easy to keep oneself undefiled. It is monstrous to see high-bred and high-born gentlemen of honoured names and families, themselves marching through the world with their heads in the air, all honourable men, living in the best, the greatest and most refined society, mixed up in schemes which are neither more nor less than a system of plunder . . . The sport of horse-racing has a peculiar and irresistible charm for persons of unblemished probity. What a pity it is that it makes just as strong appeal to the riff-raff of every town and city.

The comment is by Greville, and it foreshadowed the ultimate scandal which sooner or later had to occur, when a great race such as the Derby would be turned into a fiasco by the villainy of nearly all the parties concerned with it, and the new Victorianism would arouse a public outcry, and the demand that gentlemen on the turf should behave as gentlemen and not as rogues.

But William Crockford cared for none of these new virtues. Nevertheless, he could appreciate that change was in the air, and thus although his image at Newmarket, Doncaster and Epsom remained that of an unscrupulous 'leg' who was ready to become involved in any nefarious scheme which held promise of a profit, his image in St James's Street was that of the dignified and law-abiding proprietor of London's most fashionable club, who expected that his patrons should behave at all times with integrity and decorum.

At Doncaster he cursed and caroused; but in St James's Street he continued to sit, snug and sly, in the corner of the gaming room of his club, watching members of this greatest and most refined society ruining themselves with imperturbable elegance against the background of his marble pillars and glittering chandeliers.

But even he may have seen the writing on the wall. A new era must dawn, in which the rich would be less rich, and inherited wealth would have to be watched over with greater care. No matter. By the middle 1830s he had reached 60, and his fortune was already made. By the time that the rich had come to their senses, or the politicians had stepped in to restrict their gambling, he would have made all the money he needed and could happily retire.

Not that he was now as wealthy as he might have been. The club was a gold-mine, but greed and that fatal temptation which causes so many successful business-men to launch out into other fields had together resulted in a set-back to his fortunes. He had burnt his fingers years before at Newmarket, when he had not only gone in for breeding racehorses but also pigs, neither of which he had known anything about at all, and he had only succeeded in making himself look ridiculous as a result. He had seen the red light soon enough then, but there still persisted in him the urge to try something new. Thus he left the sphere in which he was the complete professional and entered one in which he was but an inexperienced amateur, and set out to increase his empire in St James's Street by the building of a fashionable bazaar – an edifice which held a peculiar fascination for 19th-century England, being as it was the forerunner of the modern department store.

In this project he revealed, admittedly, the ability to show initiative and enterprise, for bazaars were only just beginning to become popular. The first really successful English bazaar had been opened in Manchester by John Watts, a farmer of Didsbury, at the turn of the century, and when *The Manchester Guardian* had produced its first edition in 1821 it had carried an advertisement for the new Bazaar.

At much the same time The Royal London Bazaar had been opened in Liverpool Street with great success, so that by 1830 *The World of Fashion* magazine could write of it 'You may purchase any of the thousand and one varieties of fancy and useful articles, or you may lounge and spend an agreeable hour either in the promenades or in the exhibitions that are wholly without parallel to the known world.'

Perhaps William Crockford read that comment. If he did, the last few words would certainly have attracted his attention, for he was by now a specialist in the field of buildings that he considered to be wholly without parallel to the known world. The basis of such an enterprise was to erect a large building on a suitable site and then to act as its proprietor, hiring out counters and stalls to various local shop-keepers. *The World of Fashion* had declared that The Royal London Bazaar provided an essential amenity for 'the many thousands of highly respectable inhabitants of the Liverpool Street area, where they could immediately obtain all the variation of Fancy, Elegant, and Useful articles'. In 1832 William Crockford decided to provide the highly respectable inhabitants of Mayfair with a similar amenity in St James's Street.

In the spring of 1830 he applied to the Commissioners of Woods and Forests for a lease of what he deemed to be an admirable site at the south-eastern extremity of St James's Street, on the corner of his old and happy hunting-ground, King Street, now becoming daily more respectable. On the opposite side of the road was the new St James's Hotel, Boodle's Club was a little further up on the same side of the proposed site, and Brooks's Club only a few yards away. Just round the corner from the Bazaar would be Pall Mall. An ideal situation in every way.

Money, as always, was of no object to him when it came to building, and the Commissioners of Woods and Forests were happy to grant the lease of the ground for the erection of 'a large and handsome building', especially when they learnt that this building was to be designed by James Pennethorne under the supervision of John Nash.

So far, so good; but then William Crockford's luck began to run out. George IV died on 5 June 1830, and this really marked the end of Nash's career, for he had always sheltered under the rather excessive patronage of 'Prinny', and now he had no one to protect him from his enemies. James Pennethorne was then an up-and-coming young architect, but he ran into trouble over the new building, partly due to the fact that he found it impossible to evict an obtuse property-holder living in Crown Court. However Crockford pressed on with his plans, and the building was finally completed in 1832. Soon after the foundation stone had been laid, he realised that it was going to cost him a great deal more than he had intended, and thereafter he supervised every aspect of its construction. 'Every brick, plank, and other material,' it was recorded 'was bought at the best market, and every hour's work paid for under the advantageous terms of contract' but the cost still continued to rise. By the time the building was finished, it had taken more than £20,000 out of his pocket.

It looked impressive enough when completed and was certainly well in keeping with the architecture of St James's Street. It was opened with much publicity in April of 1832, 'under very favourable auspices, in the full fashionable season. For a time its novelty attracted, and crowds of visitors gave it patronage and support; but, the novelty over, and curiosity subsiding, traffic fell again into its ordinary channels, and the business of the St James's Bazaar became inadequate to the high rents demanded for the counters or standings in it. From this cause it became a total failure in its original design.'

Thus *Bentley's Miscellany* described the complete failure of Crockford's business enterprise, and the writer may well have summed up the situation correctly when he suggested that Crockford had made the mistake of believing that because the area of King Street had always been lucky to him in the past, it would continue to be so in the future. He failed to appreciate that an area in which a gambling house flourished might not be an area suitable for a shopping centre.

For a time the Bazaar was used for exhibitions and a celebrated conjuror and sleight-of-hand expert known as 'The Wizard of the North' gave popular demonstrations of how card-sharpers preyed upon a gullible public. One might have supposed that Crockford would have been none too enthusiastic to see such demonstrations given in the very heart of an area dedicated to card-playing, but he may have felt that he could afford to ignore such a performance, which certainly called forth some ribald comments from the younger players in the clubs up and down the Street (some of whom were able to benefit themselves by learning how to cheat more dexterously).

The Bazaar remained open for a year and then had to be closed because it was losing so much money. It became a St James's Street white elephant, and remained empty for six years. Crockford blamed its failure on changes in fashion and the shopping public's fickleness, but in reality the Bazaar probably failed because he had chosen the wrong site, and anyway had no knowledge of this sort of commercial enterprise. He had burnt his fingers again, yet strangely enough he had not the sense to profit by the experience. For the remainder of his life he continued to dabble in money-making ventures which he did not understand, including the stock-market, and thus drained away a large part of his fortune.

The only profitable aspect of the Bazaar was that he used its cellars for a time as a store-room for the club's large selection of wines, which was said to be the finest and most extensive in London, and he also carried on there the business of wine merchant, so that some of his favoured clients could buy from him – at a price – the vintages which they particularly liked and which they could not otherwise obtain. His stock was considerable, and it was rumoured at one time to be worth nearly a quarter of a million. This wine-merchant's business flourished, and it was still in existence after his death.

It is interesting to note that it was run under the management of three of Crockford's sons. In this he made an exception to his rule that his family should be kept separate from his business; for like Colonel O'Kelly before him he discouraged his heirs from having anything to do with gambling.

By this time he was a married man with a large family, and living in the utmost respectability in a house which had been decorated for him by the Wyatt brothers at 26, Sussex Place, in Regent's Park. The secrecy which he always preserved over his private life, and the fact that neither his wife nor family were ever seen in the neighbourhood of St James's Street, has left his biographers with a blank as far as all his family affairs are concerned. He lived in two worlds, keeping the world of his domesticity quite separate from his gambling world in St James's Street. Even his sharpest critics, and the many novelists, poets and satirists of the day who were for ever tilting at him and describing his activities on the turf or at Crockford's Club, with constant references to his low origins, never made any reference to his family life. Probably this was because they knew nothing about it.

His wife, Sarah Frances, was no doubt a quiet and retiring woman who knew her place – which, as far as her husband was concerned, was in the bosom of her family. According to the writer of the Crockford obituary in *Bentley's Miscellany*, she had at one time been a governess in the employment of a lady of wealth and fashion. The young Crockford had met her when she was thus employed, and having seduced her mistress he probably then seduced her as well and married her, having decided that she was a quiet and reliable girl whom he could trust to keep in the background and to run his home whilst at the same time furnishing him with every satisfaction in the nuptial bed. As a young and middle-aged man he was virile and sexual, and despite his uncouth manners, or perhaps because of them, he had encountered a number of women who were ready to oblige him. No doubt he was a domineering lover; and probably an unfastidious one as well, being of the opinion that all women look alike in the dark. He had fourteen children by Sarah, which suggests that his sexual activities were pursued with gusto after marriage; and he may well have kept one or two mistresses on the side. But if he did, no mention has ever been made of them in the many contemporary comments which were written about him. No doubt he satisfied himself with the tavern trollops whom he encountered when carousing with his evil companions at Doncaster and Newmarket. So he may well have refrained from any indiscretions on his own doorstep in St James's Street or at Regent's Park. All this throws an interesting sidelight on his character, for it is never easy for a notorious personality who is constantly in the public eye to keep his private life a secret.

William Crockford succeeded in doing this because he was, after all, a devious and secretive personality, sly and self-effacing. He left it to men like John Gully to advertise their growing wealth and influence by making a great show of domesticity, attending the balls given by the county, and appearing at them with such a modest and self-effacing demeanour that they were able to bask in the limelight whilst seemingly attempting to avoid it. This was not Crockford's way. He may perhaps have wished to be like them, but he had never been looked upon as 'a sport' by the aristocracy, and his crude manners, coarse appearance and vulgar speech made it impossible for *him* to enter the limelight at a fashionable ball.

News had reached him at this time of the coming-of-age celebrations of the young Lord Milton, heir to the Earldom of Fitzwilliam, which had been held at Wentworth House, near Rotherham, in Yorkshire. Every celebrity in the county had been present, and the mansion and park had been brilliantly illuminated for the reception of the distinguished guests who had arrived in more than 500 carriages.

The young Earl had stood at the head of the grand staircase

to welcome them; and the most distinguished figure of all to mount this staircase had been a tall, broad-shouldered man of aristocratic mien who had supported on either arm two young girls, dressed simply but exquisitely, and of such beauty that all eyes had been turned upon them. The young Earl had received them with obvious pleasure, and when the trio had later entered the ballroom a whisper had gone round amongst the county gentry, who did not recognise this trio, and assumed that they must be one of the young Earl's aristocratic friends from Mayfair. Could it be the Earl of —? Or perhaps the Duke of —?

In fact it was Mr John Gully the ex-pugilist, and two of his daughters. William Crockford was not impressed when he heard the story. John Gully was putting on airs, now that he was an M.P., and as to the two daughters, the fellow was as fertile as a rabbit, had married twice and had produced 24 children in all, so that his supply of young daughters for occasions such as this was almost inexhaustible. Crockford himself, who had only married once and produced little more than half as many children, and who had always kept them in the background, could view such refined ostentation with secret scorn and derision; for it did not do to criticise Gully too openly in public now that he was the darling of Society.

The years passed by, and Crockford's Club in St James's Street grew ever more fashionable, and its proprietor ever more wealthy. Even the staff were enjoying exceptional prosperity, and the waiters alone were said to receive up to £1,000 in gratuities to divide amongst themselves at the end of each season whilst the head waiter could expect £500 just for himself.

Yet the Crockford Empire was beginning to crumble, rent by internal quarrels and personal jealousies. Gye, the old retainer and partner in many a dishonest enterprise in the past, having amassed his fortune of nearly £30,000, became too big for his boots, and launched out as a betting man of the turf, talking knowledgeably of handicap weights and secret trials, and even offering attractive odds to the members of the club who had horses engaged in the big races.

This was too much for William Crockford, who considered

the making of a book on future events the exclusive prerogative of himself, and so Gye was peremptorily dismissed. He left without regret, announcing boldly that he was quite capable of succeeding on his own; but he had never been more than a second-in-command, and he had none of Crockford's flair. He became a speculative builder in Essex, failed dismally, and returned to open a rival club in St James's Street, and failed dismally in this also. Crockford hounded him without mercy, and before long both his health and fortune ebbed away. In the end he became paralysed and destitute, and was carried off to the workhouse, where he died and was buried in a pauper's grave without receiving a penny piece from his former employer.

His place was taken by a small-time crook and gambler named Dasking, who had been an associate of Crockford's in the old days, when he had worked as a groom-porter in a gambling hell in Oxendon Street, run by an Irishman named O'Hara. He proved an efficient substitute for Gye, whom he attempted to imitate in some respects, by quietly amassing a small fortune on his own; so that within a few years he had made around £10,000. This profited him little as he died soon afterwards, but at least he was able to enjoy the benefits of a funeral commensurate with his newly-acquired wealth.

That temperamental and irascible Frenchman, Eustache Ude, followed in the wake of Gye soon afterwards; and for much the same reason, having grown too big for his boots, a common enough complaint amongst master chefs, who must of necessity divide their time between bending over hot stoves, tasting highly-flavoured dishes and receiving the nearly idolatrous praise of delighted patrons in the dining-room. The heat and highly-flavoured food made him short-tempered, and the idolatry made him explosively resentful of any suggestion that his cooking had failed to reach the highest possible standards. Previously he had informed the Management Committee that he was worth £4,000 a year to the club, and had been given it – a truly astounding wage which must have given him a higher income than many of the club's members.

He became so difficult in the end that Crockford finally dismissed him as summarily as he had dismissed Gye; and Eustache

Ude shook the dust of St James's from his feet, declaring that he would never again walk on the same side of the street as Crockford's Club, an oath which he observed until his death.

He was miserable in retirement. Benjamin Disraeli, in a letter to his sister, referred to Ude's exile but wrote that he might yet be allowed to return from his Elba. This was not to be, even though his successor, Francatelli, was a failure.

Disraeli went on to repeat a conversation he had heard between Ude and Sir George Wombwell, whom he had told of his misery. 'Hah!' he said, 'I have not been into my kitchen once; I hate the sight of my kitchen. I dine on roast mutton dressed by a cookmaid. Do not be offended, Mr W., if I do not take my hat off to you when we meet; but I have made a vow that I will never take my hat off to a member of the committee.'

'I shall always take my hat off to you, Mr Ude,' was Sir George's reply.

The empire was beginning to crumble from within. Outwardly, the club was flourishing, and indeed as the fourth decade wore on it seemed to be able to attract an ever-widening circle of famous people – aristocrats, diplomats, very important personages, politicians and the literary lions of the day. The spirit of the club seemed as lively as it had ever been, but its proprietor was growing old. He was in his sixties, and he had led a hard life. He still retained his zest for making money, but he was fast losing his enthusiasm for many of his other interests.

In his dismissal of both Gye and Ude he had been supported by his Management Committee of Noblemen and Gentlemen, but by now he was finding that this committee was proving steadily more irksome to him. Its members had been chosen principally as figure-heads, but they were becoming increasingly determined to influence the general running of the club. At times they were quite dictatorial in their attitude to him, but he was fully aware that he still had the whip hand over them. They could, in theory, dismiss him – or at least ask him to resign – although they would then have to buy him out. But where would they find another proprietor as rich as himself, or one who would be willing to put up a nightly bank of such a size?

He knew that if he announced his retirement they would soon find themselves in a pretty fix, faced by the break-up of the club of which they were all so proud, and in which they could enjoy themselves to such good purpose. At first he had only to hint at this ultimate step in order to silence them; and at first they knew that he had no real intention of putting such a threat into action. But as he entered his sixties his health began to fail, and his resentment against them grew stronger.

His interest in the turf was also waning. However his ambitions were re-kindled by the events of 1836. In 1819, when he was in his prime, his colt Sultan had come very near to winning the Derby for him at Epsom. It had been a great disappointment when Sultan's tremendous challenge in the last furlong had been resisted – but only just – by Tiresias, but they had told Crockford then that Sultan would make a splendid sire, and that his offspring might well accomplish what he himself had just failed to achieve. Now, in 1836, it seemed that this promise might well be fulfilled, for the Earl of Jersey owned a son of Sultan, named Bay Middleton out of an Oaks winner, Cobweb, whom he esteemed so highly that he had backed the colt for the Derby as a two-year-old and before he had ever been seen on a racecourse.

Such an act showed an unwise impetuosity, but rumours of what this colt might achieve were soon confirmed when he started his racing career as a three-year-old. After Bay Middleton had won the first of the season's classic races, the Two Thousand Guineas at Newmarket, he became a hot favourite for the Derby. Here, it was generally conceded, was a great horse in the making.

As the day of the Derby approached, rumours concerning his well-being were spread about, and Crockford may well have wondered whether John Gully was up to his old tricks, but Bay Middleton's owner remained adamant in his view that this was the best three-year-old colt in England and that he would prove this at Epsom.

One of the biggest crowds that had ever been seen at a race-meeting assembled on the Downs that afternoon, among them the Prince of Orange and his sons, as well as the Duke of Cumberland. It was a royal occasion.

Some Derby winners struggle bravely to beat their opponents. but some treat their opponents with scorn, sweeping past them with effortless ease when the winning post is in sight. Bay Middleton was such a winner. Never at any time was the result in any doubt, and on that afternoon he proved his owner's assertion that here might well be one of the great Derby winners of all time.

In William Crockford's cold and unemotional heart, there stirred a feeling of exultation. This great horse had sprung from the loins of *his* great horse, Sultan. For once his pale face was flushed, and there was fire in the dull, grey eyes. He promised himself that one day, before he died, he himself would own a great horse, and would see him triumph at Epsom as Bay Middleton had done, overwhelming the opposition with his speed and resolution.

A year later, when the Derby of 1837 was run at Epsom (and won by an indifferent outsider of Lord Berner's named Phosphorous who was not in the same class as Bay Middleton), the new Victorian era had already begun. Not that it seemed of any special significance at the time. The old king, William IV, suffering dreadfully from asthma, had whispered his last dying wish that he might live to see the sun set on the day of Waterloo, 18 June, and this wish had been granted. But he was dead within 36 hours, and on 21 June 1837, the young Victoria was proclaimed Queen from an open window in St James's Palace. A slip of a girl, fragile-looking and delicate, and not yet out of her 'teens, the occasion cannot have seemed of any great importance to William Crockford, in spite of all the junketings up and down St James's Street, with the loyal toasts drunk again and again in Crockford's, Brooks's and White's – and especially at White's, where Lord Melbourne was one of the leading lights.

Yet the presence of a woman on the throne must have its significance. There would be no more of the Regency laxity now – and a new decorum might well spread throughout London Society. Change and reform were in the air, and people were talking of the need for a more careful and cautious way of life. The heavy gambling that had ruined so many of the famous families of England during the last century was at last being seen as a social evil – a disease that, like the plague, would sooner or later have to be stamped out.

More alarming still, as far as William Crockford was concerned, was the undeniable fact that the aristocracy were showing signs of running out of money. The gambling in St James's Street, even at Crockford's, was growing less 'deep'. It could hardly be expected to revive with a rather prim and sober-minded young woman on the throne – and self-willed as well, if her demeanour at her inauguration were anything to go by.

And yet, in this year of 1837, a year so pregnant with change and the implications of things to come, Crockford's Club seemed to stand unshakable, as celebrated, as select and as dignified as it had ever been. That there might ever be a St James's Street *without* this club was unthinkable. It would be like Westminster without the Houses of Parliament. The great foreign diplomats continued to belong to Crockford's 'as a matter of course', as Gronow observed, the Peninsular and Waterloo heroes still thronged the rooms, led by the Duke himself, whilst the brilliant young writers of the day, Bulwer Lytton and the flamboyant Jew, Benjamin Disraeli, 'displayed at that brilliant supper table the one his sable, the other his auburn curls'.

Disraeli at this time was second only to Count D'Orsay in the brilliance of his dress and the elaborateness of his toilet. And indeed, in the years to come there were those who could maintain that he, rather than D'Orsay, should have been remembered as 'the last of the dandies'. A showman, of course, as Beau Brummell had been. The two had some points in common, both being upstarts who had forced their way into Society, and both having the gifts of eloquence, charm and self-assurance which enabled them to carry off this invasion with panache.

Disraeli and D'Orsay had been close friends from the day, in 1832, when they had first met at a dinner at Bulwer Lytton's house in Hertford Street. Bulwer had just made his reputation with his novel about the dandies, *Pelham;* Disraeli had just made his with *Vivian Grey*. Disraeli had arrived on this occasion in green velvet trousers, a canary waistcoat, buckled shoes and lace cuffs, and D'Orsay had looked him up and down, at first in astonishment but later with growing approval. The fellow was clearly a bit of a bounder, but then so he was himself.

Thus deep called to deep, and the two became close friends. It was not long before D'Orsay suggested that Disraeli should seek election to Crockford's, but the flamboyant young man shook his head in doubt. A Jew a member of that select coterie? And with *that* Management Committee controlling the entry of all new members? In 1834 he wrote to his wife that he would have liked to have joined but he was certain that he would be blackballed if his name were ever put forward.

Still, he was a frequent visitor to the club – often in the most distinguished company. By 1834 he was able to note in his diary:

I have become this year very popular with the dandies. D'Orsay took a fancy to me and they take their tone from him. Lady Blessington is their muse and she declared violently in my favour. I am as popular with first-rate men as I am hated by the second-rate.

The patronage of two such leaders of fashion as D'Orsay and Lady Blessington ensured him a full complement both of friends and enemies. Both men were still the centre of scandal in their conflicting world of sexual virility and impotence, passion and frigidity, dignity and licentiousness.

Inevitably, the young novelist found plenty of material for his books in this fashionable world, and especially in the sphere of Crockford's with its diplomatic and political influences as well as its affinity with all that represented the culture and good breeding of English Society. When, in the years to come (*after* he had been elected to membership of this select circle), Disraeli came to write his novel *Sybil, or The Two Nations* (the allusion being to the Rich and the Poor) it was not surprising that he should use Crockford's Club as the background for his picture of how the rich lived and gambled. Indeed *Sybil* opens with a description of Crockford's which still stands as the best ever written of that illustrious gathering.

It was the eve of the Derby of 1837. In a vast and golden saloon, that in its decorations would have become, and in its splendour would not have disgraced, Versailles in the days of the grand monarch, were assembled many whose hearts beat at the thought of the morrow, and whose brains still laboured to control its fortunes to their advantage . . . The gleaming lustres poured a flood of soft yet brilliant light over a plateau glittering with gold plate, and fragrant with exotics embedded in vases of rare porcelain . . . It seemed a scene and a supper where the marble guest of Juan might have been expected; and, had he arrived, he would have found probably hearts as bold and spirits as reckless as he encountered in Andalusia.

The style is somewhat florid, as was its author, but the picture conjured up is vivid and accurate. This was Crockford's in its golden era.

This year of 1837 was one of great portent for the future. Not only because of the accession of the young Queen; not only because the gambling fever seemed to be dying out, and with it the era of the dandies; not only because the Derby had been won by an outsider, in a race which had been started for the first time by flag, and run for the last time on a Thursday; not only because the vast crowd that had assembled on the Downs had been told that by the following year they would be transported there by the new railway trains; not even because change was in the air and the Industrial Revolution was gaining impetus with every month that passed; but rather because bad times and hard times were ahead. The Whigs as a party were finished, their long reign ended, and the financial situation was such that Peel was able to describe their Chancellor of the Exchequer as 'seated on an empty chest by the side of bottomless deficiencies, fishing for a budget'. The phrase has a modern ring to it, when modern Chancellors so often find themselves in a similar position.

Responsible men throughout England were becoming increasingly aware of 'the Two Nations' which Disraeli was to describe in Sybil. The middle classes were rapidly increasing their wealth, while the lower classes were growing poorer. In the north of England these poor were being herded into the new factories, there to work until their degrading labours destroyed their health and finally killed them. In the south, even despite the New Poor Law in 1834, the rural community was near to starving.

It was not a time for profligacy in Mayfair, dandyism in St

James's Street or wild and irresponsible gambling in the fashionable clubs. These things would continue, of course, but not in the style of the past.

William Crockford assessed the situation dispassionately; and the desire to retire grew stronger within him. The hunter who had entered the game reserve so boldly had now killed all the game. The time had therefore come to withdraw, although he had no antlered heads to hang upon his wall, he yet had his bank balance to remind him of victories won and victims slain.

By now he had lost much of his former interest in the running of the club. The Management Committee exasperated him, and were becoming even more unpractical in their administration of the club's affairs. The depth of play was decreasing and bad debts were steadily mounting; and his rivals were robbing him of business, because it was no longer an advantage to run the biggest hazard bank in London.

Finally, and perhaps worst of all, the reformers were gaining ground with their agitation for having the gaming laws revised. The time must come when the police would be forced to take stronger action (and therefore be forced to refuse the routine bribes that had formerly kept them quiet), and although their powers of entry and investigation were still limited, this state of affairs could not be expected to continue. Betting on horses – which was still legal – remained substantial, but the fascination which dice and cards had once held for the wilder members of Society was undeniably lessening. In short, the era of 'hell and hazard' was coming to an end.

His final and irrevocable decision came in 1840. Chief amongst the many reasons which prompted it was that in this year his terms of agreement with the Management Committee had run out and were due for renewal. The original terms, to which he had submitted readily enough at the outset, had been that he should operate the bank and organise the gambling, and that the Committee should administer all other aspects of the club, deciding not only how it should be run but also who should be elected to membership. In short, his function was to put up a nightly bank of £5,000 and to be grateful to it for an aggregate profit of around 1½ per cent.

Now, in a brief but servile address, he informed the Management Committee that he had had enough, and was getting out. It would have to find someone else to take his place.

No one learnt the news with greater regret than Benjamin Disraeli, for he had at last been elected to membership; and he wrote in agitation to inform his sister of the doleful news:

One great resignation has occurred. Last night Crockford sent in a letter announcing his retirement. 'Tis a thunderbolt, and nothing else is talked of; 'tis the greatest shock to domestic credit since Howard and Gibbs. Some members are twelve years in arrear of subscriptions. One man owes £700 to the coffee-room; all must now be booked up. The consternation is general. Moors that were hired are given up, and yachts destined to the Mediterranean must now lie in harbour.

All fashionable London began asking how the club could continue and who could take Crockford's place. The Management Committee searched vainly for the answer. No one else had either the capital or the experience to accept such a position, and Crockford's would quickly lose its stature once it became known that its bank was no longer the biggest in London, for the heavy backers would drift away.

It may well be that William Crockford, in his first ultimatum to the committee, was doing no more than hold a pistol to their heads. He was saying that he found their terms restrictive and was no longer prepared to accept them; and possibly the committee at first decided to call his bluff, by announcing that they would find a successor. Wealthy business tycoons of the City were approached, and tall stories were told of the huge profits that were to be made by becoming the banker at Crockford's, but no one was prepared to run a bank as big as that which Crockford himself had put up. For a time two of Crockford's lieutenants in the gaming room, Page and Dasking, continued to operate the bank on a much smaller scale, and it is possible that Crockford still maintained an interest in it, having thus achieved his aim by retiring from the position of being the wealthiest banker in London, and therefore the one whom everyone was trying to bring down. But he was not the man to remain ostensibly in charge of the bank when it had ceased to enjoy its old status. He therefore left his snug corner in the gaming room, and his white cravat and podgy figure were seen there no more. The great hunter had withdrawn from the game reserve, and had left others to the ignoble task of chasing what little game there was left to chase.

Had he retired completely from all his activities and settled down to a life of ease, concentrating solely on his life's ambition to win the Derby, he would have finally died a much richer man than he did. But unfortunately for his wife and his 14 children he now used his newly-acquired leisure to speculate even more widely than before; and he even extended his interest into a sphere which John Gully was finding lucrative and became interested in – of all things – an alleged gold-mine in Flintshire.

This surely was evidence that he was getting old, and that his judgement had become impaired. He took on as his partner a man who was glib of tongue but palpably a rogue, and listened to all his high-sounding talk of alluvial and mineral deposits, scientific reports, engineering plans for sinking shafts and boring tunnels, and all the hocus-pocus which is part and parcel of the sales talk of engineering crooks; and having invested heavily in the project, he was given more professional talk, informed that deeper shafts should be sunk and even more money invested, only to find in the end that the whole scheme was bogus and the land on which he had expended so much money was almost devoid of any mineral resources.

Finally he fell out with his partner and they agreed to partition the land; whereupon the portion which he was allotted was found to be even more barren than had been expected, whilst that which his partner was given proved, after all, to have some value.

It is remarkable that such facts should have to be recorded in writing a life of William Crockford – a man who throughout his gambling career had proved himself to be one who cheated others whilst seldom being cheated himself. These continued reverses, coming as they did when he no longer had his club to bolster up his losses, so that he could see his once great fortune now diminishing before his eyes, undoubtedly produced a violent and injurious reaction. Bitterness and frustration have ever been the enemies of good health, especially in old age, when they are brooded over and more deeply felt, and William Crockford became daily more querulous and restless. His blood pressure grew higher and his breathing became more stertorous.

However he had two interests which continued to bring him stimulus. The first was his determination to win the Derby before he died; the second was to find himself a new house – preferably in the very heart of aristocratic London, where his neighbours would all be titled and where he could live in a splendour that not even John Gully could match. The most desirable location, in every respect, was the new Carlton House Terrace, which had taken the place of the old Carlton House.

Throughout the 18th century the Mall, fashionable London's most fashionable promenade, had been dominated at its western end by Buckingham House and at its eastern end by Carlton House, hard by the Horse Guards Parade and Whitehall. Each had looked at the other – from a respectable distance. Each had been flanked on the one side by the delightful trees and waterways of St James's Park, and on the other by the splendid buildings and gardens of St James's Palace and Marlborough House.

Each mansion had been the home of royalty in the 18th century, for George III had bought Buckingham House from Sir John Sheffield (after an attempt had been made to use it for the British Museum) in order that it might be a home for Dowager Queens; and Carlton House, which had been built at the beginning of the 18th century by the 1st Lord Carlton, had later become the home of the Prince Regent, who was given it on his 21st birthday by his father.

This was his home, and this his peccadillo. He spent huge sums on altering it and restoring it, and he continued to change and redesign it for the next 30 years. Indeed it was to him what Crockford's Club was later to become to St James's Street – the most fashionable meeting place in London, and it became, as Gronow was later to remark, a centre for all the great politicians and wits of the Regency, where Beau Brummell displayed his starched cravats and the great Duke of Wellington talked with quiet objectivity of the ebb and flow of events at Waterloo.

Not that it was ever very much to look at; and Gronow went

as far as to describe it as one of the most ugly edifices that ever disfigured London, which was rightly condemned by everybody who possessed taste. He spoke of it being blackened with dust and soot, and tartly observed that it was constantly under repair but yet was never improved. The Prince Regent enjoyed initiating these alterations but strongly objected to the workmen who made them, for he had no love for the lower classes, and least of all for the British workman.

Nevertheless, despite its ugliness and lack of taste, Carlton House remained the Prince's proud possession. After Nash, acting on the Prince's instructions, had rebuilt Buckingham House (although the money voted by Parliament had only been for its repair), he was instructed to turn his attention to Carlton House, which was also rebuilt under his supervision. It was finally demolished in 1826, when the columns of its portico were transferred to the front of the National Gallery, and its place was taken by two blocks of terraced houses, also designed by Nash and with their erection superintended by his young assistant, James Pennethorne, who was also responsible for the construction of Crockford's ill-fated Bazaar in St James's Street.

Throughout all this time Nash's great interest was the laying-out of St James's Park, so that by the time he retired, soon after the death of his patron, George IV, the design for the whole area from Carlton House Terrace across the Park to Buckingham House was largely his brain-child.

As soon as Queen Victoria turned Buckingham House into Buckingham Palace and took up residence there, Carlton House Terrace became the smartest address in London. It was for this reason that William Crockford turned his attention to this most desirable of properties when he decided to retire. Sussex Place, in Regent's Park, had been a genteel enough address, but Carlton House Terrace was infinitely grander.

It is curious that a man who had always avoided the limelight and had tended to avoid a close personal relationship with his aristocratic patrons, should have launched out in this way during the last few years of his life. But Crockford may have felt that his retirement from Crockford's Club had resulted in some loss of prestige, and that this could only be restored by living in the grandest possible manner; or he may even, at this late stage in his career, have decided to outdo John Gully. It seems unlikely that his wife, Sarah, kept for so long in the background, can have influenced him in any way towards a move into the very smartest of residential areas; or that his fourteen children, also kept so discreetly in the background, should have urged him to take so grandiose a step.

There is one fact which may have accounted for his move. In buying No. 11, Carlton House Terrace in 1842 from Baron Monson he may have been prompted by no other motive than his love of getting a bargain.

No. 11 had been occupied from the day of its completion by Frederick John, 5th Baron Monson, who had lived there as a young man from 1831 to 1834. Thereafter, for some unexplained reason, it had been allowed to lie empty, year after year. In 1842, when William Crockford bought it, it had been unoccupied for six years, and was available at a reasonable price. The social standing of the Terrace was evidenced by those whose houses adjoined this desirable property. No. 10 was the home of Sir Mathew White Ridley, the 3rd Baronet, and No. 12 that of the Marquess of Cholmondeley, while the Dowager Marchioness lived in No. 13 and the Earl of Lincoln in No. 14.

It was certainly a fashionable area, which had been much improved in its amenities as a result of the changes that had taken place to the north of Pall Mall since Nash and his associates had started to give a new face to that part of London. When William Crockford had first taken to visiting the West End, and while he was making his fortune in and around St James's Street, St James's Square and Waterloo Place had been filled with gambling hells and brothels, and even as late as 1816 the residents in St James's Square had complained to the authorities because prostitutes would ply their trade around the Square of a summer evening, thus attracting licentious young drunks who shouted rude oaths and made rude gestures.

But the enlargement of Carlton House (whose main entrance had then been on Pall Mall and not the Mall) had eliminated Waterloo Place, and now the street-walkers were drifting northwards to the Haymarket and the Burlington Arcade, which were destined to remain their favourite haunts throughout the Victorian era. The Park, too, was now far more respectable than it had been in Boswell's time, when the services of the sixpenny tarts were readily available to all comers after dark, and thus offered strong competition to their sisters parading in Waterloo Place.

That the young Queen should live adjacent to such areas of immorality was unthinkable. The Mall became respectable and Carlton House Terrace became the home of the rich and the élite.

It also became the home, in 1842, of William Crockford.

7

THE ULTIMATE SCANDAL
Death by a Derby Favourite

Thus it came about that William Crockford, in late middle age, abdicated his throne as emperor of the gambling world of London, and became instead a gentleman in retirement, living in affluence at No. 11, Carlton House Terrace, within sight of the Queen's own home at Buckingham Palace and with windows overlooking the Mall along which she was wont to drive in her royal carriage on state occasions.

It is doubtful if William Crockford ever gazed down upon her with any emotion; certainly not with one of patriotism, although perhaps with one of resentment, seeing that she stood for so much which was opposed to his own way of life. But the young Victoria herself must sometimes have glanced up at that splendid terrace of houses and wondered why such an enemy of Society should be permitted to live there, in the midst of the fashionable world which he had done his best to ruin. She had already shown her spirit by her refusal to change the Ladies of the Bedchamber after Melbourne's government had been overthrown in 1839; and in February of 1840 she had been married to Prince Albert, who looked upon the Crockford world of dissolute extravagance with abhorrence.

In the summer of this year of her marriage she had visited Epsom with him, and elaborate preparations had been made in the Grand Stand to receive her. But although the weather had been perfect, the visit had not been an unqualified success. The ill-feeling which had been aroused by the young Queen's seemingly heartless treatment of Lady Flora Hastings' false pregnancy had not been forgotten, and the mob on the hill were in an unpatriotic mood. They did not look upon their sovereign with any affection, and thus each party viewed the other with resentment.

But the stewards and members of the Jockey Club welcomed the Queen with enthusiasm. The Grand Stand had been specially repainted and decorated to receive her, and their aim was that both she and her husband should be persuaded to bestow the royal patronage on the turf.

The rift between royalty and the turf had been a long one. The Escape affair of 1791 had caused bitterness and suspicion; and as a result of it the Prince of Wales, later George IV, and the Jockey Club had fallen out, so that the Prince had said that he would never go racing again. It had been a case of in-and-out running, with suspicion falling – not altogether unjustly – on the Prince's trusted jockey, old Sam Chifney, who had lost a race on Escape that he should have won, and then won on Escape when by all known form he should have lost. Many years later, a deputation from the Jockey Club had waited on the Prince at Brighton, and had invited him to bury the hatchet, but he had remained adamant. He did not boycott racing for the rest of his life, but showed no further enthusiasm for it.

Now, at the Derby of 1840, with a new monarch on the throne, there seemed hope that racing would once again become the sport of royalty. But the sulky behaviour of the crowd, the evil reputation that still clung to the betting ring and which must have been well known to the Queen and her Consort, and the fact that rogues such as Crockford and Gully had made a fortune out of the turf, often by cheating, and yet were accepted by the aristocracy as a necessary part of the racing scene, must together have made the young Victoria look upon the noisy, angry Epsom mob with distaste and even with disgust.

The optimists amongst the Jockey Club members declared afterwards that the day had been a great success, but the pessimists shook their heads and expressed the view that Epsom would be lucky if it ever saw the Queen on Derby Day again. It never did.

In this same year, William Crockford celebrated his 65th birthday. By now he looked and felt an old man. He had come a long way since his birth at Temple Bar. He seldom visited the East End of London now, but occasionally he would order his carriage and drive up the Strand as far as Temple Bar. The whole area was changing rapidly, but the old fish shop and Temple Bar itself remained the same as he had remembered them in his childhood. He still owned the fish shop and the house, and he refused to allow any changes to be made to them.

Thus in one curious and even sentimental way he clung to his past. At least he had never been ashamed of his antecedents; he had never pretended to be a gentleman, or aped gentlemanly ways as his rival, John Gully, had done.

By the beginning of 1844 the Victorian era was fully launched and the Crockford era was dying. By the end of the year it was dead. At the beginning of that year there were those who could talk and write enthusiastically of the great brotherhood of the turf, and of the spirit of sportsmanship and integrity which inspired it; by the end of the year such noble phrases were meaningless. At the beginning of the year a man could still gamble freely at roulette and hazard in the gaming houses of the West End; by the end of it this freedom had been curtailed, and was soon to be terminated for more than 115 years. At the beginning of the year William Crockford, now a weak and ailing old man, seemed to have the great prize of the Derby Stakes within his grasp; by the end of the year he too was dead, killed by a Derby favourite, the prize snatched from his grasp. In January the Derby itself was looked upon throughout the racing world of Europe and the United States as the supreme test of a thoroughbred; by December it was looked upon as a wretched fiasco, a horse-race dominated by the influence of rogues.

This year of 1844, which to our historians has in the past seemed of no particular importance, opened significantly for the Crockford world and the world of gamblers in general with the appointment of a Select Committee of the House of Commons, under the chairmanship of Lord Palmerston, for the purpose of making a full inquiry into the whole question of gaming; it was felt that the existing gaming laws were contradictory, unrealistic and unobserved, and that the continued existence of the gambling hells of London constituted a public scandal. Victorianism was beginning to develop, and with it an added respect for the law and an increasing resentment against the ways in which it was being openly flouted.

This committee sat during the early spring, and a number of expert witnesses were called to testify before it, including not only judges of the High Court, magistrates, lawyers and the Commissioner of Police himself, but also representatives of the aristocracy and of the sporting world, including Admiral Rous and William Crockford himself. The Select Committee terminated its enquiry in the middle of May, but shortly before it ended its investigations – and no doubt because of the publicity which the evidence given before it was receiving – the police, acting on the orders of the Commissioner, staged a series of raids on the gaming houses of the West End of London, and no fewer than seventeen were invaded by the constables, and some 79 defendants were brought before the magistrates and fined sums from a pound to three pounds. Notably, the only gaming house in the area that was *not* raided was Crockford's.

The Commissioner of Police, who had already given his evidence, was recalled and asked to explain this. He replied that Crockford's was a general club, and not specifically a gaming club, and that many of its members never gambled at all. He also implied that since Crockford's Club was the meeting place of gentlemen and of the aristocracy, it was not the sort of place to be subjected to the indignity of being raided. All this was well known to the members of the Select Committee, who appear to have accepted his explanations as reasonable. Yet at the time Crockford was the defendant, at the suit of common informers, facing penalties in respect of alleged offences against the existing gaming laws.

The members of the Select Committee were men of the world, who had a shrewd knowledge of all that was going on in the gambling houses of London, and no doubt the evidence given by the judges, lawyers and magistrates did not tell them very much which they did not know already. They were probably more interested to discover what was the attitude of those who were a part of this sporting world of gamesters and racehorse owners, and to try and learn from them just how much went on behind the scenes; and possibly to extract from them an admission of just how serious the gambling mania still was in London, especially amongst the rich and in a fashionable club such as Crockford's. Two of the most important witnesses whom they called, therefore, were Admiral Rous and William Crockford; the one known to be a gentleman of the highest integrity, the other known to be the proprietor of London's foremost club and suspected of being one of the most unscrupulous rogues on the turf.

Admiral Rous commanded universal respect. He and his ally, Lord George Bentinck, were rapidly becoming the acknowledged arbiters of turf affairs and the guardians of the good name of racing. They were accepted as spokesmen of the Jockey Club.

Admiral Rous had been born in 1795, and his career had fallen into two parts. From 1808 until 1836 he had served in the Navy, proving himself to be an officer not only of exceptional administrative ability but also one of outstanding courage. He had been made a member of the Jockey Club in 1821, and turf historians have noted that the first sentence of 'warning off Newmarket Heath' ever to be inflicted occurred at the first meeting which he ever attended. He was in many ways a typical sailor, bluff and outspoken, and often dictatorial in his manner, but he was a man of rigid principle and a vigorous opponent of racing's many disreputable practices and of the countless rogues who infested Newmarket Heath. Once he had left the Navy, he devoted the whole of his considerable powers of organisation to the administration of turf affairs and revealed himself as the most skilled handicapper of his age. The debt which English racing still owes to him is a notable one, and it was fortunate indeed that the greatest crisis in the national sport occurred at a time when Admiral Rous and Lord George Bentinck were becoming the champions of racing integrity.

But although Admiral Rous was the enemy of cheating, he was never an opponent of betting. This he considered an essential part of racing, and he saw no evil in it unless its influence resulted in corruption. He believed that gentlemen of wealth and standing should be allowed to bet as heavily as they wished. At the same time he had become gravely alarmed by the manner in which they were associating with those who were neither gentlemen nor men of integrity. It is only possible to include here a brief summary of his evidence before the Select Committee, but part of it, at least, should be given verbatim:

Lord Palmerston: Do you wish to give it as your opinion that there is no mischief in gaming, unless it is fraudulently conducted?

Rous: I think that in respect to society commercially, the great harm happens to clerks; but I think that with respect to a rich man it does not signify whether he loses his money as long as the money is distributed among the public. What should I care what a rich man does with his own? ... The poor should be protected, but I would let a rich man ruin himself if he pleases.

Lord Palmerston: Would you draw a distinction between a common gaming house, and such as it is supposed Crockford's was?

Rous: I should draw the greatest distinction; for the members of Crockford's are persons of a certain station, and, therefore, it signifies very little to the working people, and the prosperity of the country, whether those men are ruined.

Mr Escott: Are you aware that many men of large property have lost a great deal of money at Crockford's?

Rous: I have not known anything the last ten years at Crockford's. I thought it prudent to take my name out of Crockford's the year I got married.

Mr Escott: Have you heard that persons of station in the country have lost large sums of money there, larger than they have been able to pay?

Rous: I have heard of them losing larger sums than they liked to pay, but not more than they could pay.

Mr Escott: Do you think it a great evil that persons of station in the country should abridge their funds by playing at hazard, and make up their minds to lose money when it was not convenient to pay?

Rous: So far as regards my opinion: I wish Crockford's had been burned down many years ago.

Captain Berkeley: Is it a greater evil going to Crockford's and playing publicly, or sitting down to private play?

Rous: I think they are both evils. Both lead to your certain destruction.

Captain Berkeley: Do you not think that the great gambling there is now on the Turf does injury to horse-racing?

Rous: From my general knowledge, I do not think that one-tenth of the money is betted now on horse-racing that there was twenty years ago, except on the Derby and St Leger.

Captain Berkeley: Do you think that heavy betting does injury to horse-racing?

Rous: I think that the heavy betting many years ago did no injury to horse-racing, but did injury to individuals.

Thus Admiral Rous was expressing a view which was widely held at the time – namely that the idle rich were entitled to lose their money gambling, or in any other way they fancied, and had only themselves to blame for their foolishness if they did so. But the poor man, who could not afford to lose and therefore could not afford to gamble, ought to be protected from temptation. The fact that such legislation would result in a different law for the rich and for the poor, and could therefore only cause resentment against the privileges enjoyed by the upper classes, did not seem to strike either the Admiral or the majority of his listeners, so these anomalies in the gaming laws continued for more than a century, when the rich man could bet on credit with his bookmaker but the poor man was breaking the law when betting 'off the course' with ready money.

William Crockford was called before the committee, and most of his evidence was guarded, to say the least. He was old and he was sick, and he had no intention at this late stage in his life of incriminating himself in any way; fear of the police had always been one of the dominating emotions of his career. He was praised at the time for the way in which he seemed to be shielding members of Crockford's Club, but in this he was probably largely prompted by the desire to shield himself. For the most part his attitude when questioned was reserved and evasive. He adopted the role of a faithful servant who had no intention of saying anything damaging about his previous employers.

When asked his occupation, he replied that he had none; but was concerned 'in mines and other things'. Even after he had been advised that the committee had powers to grant exemptions in respect of any offences committed by witnesses and revealed by them in their testimony, he still continued to hedge. When he gave up his proprietorship of the club, he said, it had been by a purely private and unofficial arrangement; it was taken over by gentlemen who made their own arrangements and who paid him rent in respect of the building. The money due to him was received by his son, and he did not know who paid it. His son had no connection whatsoever with the club, and knew nothing whatever about the business carried on there. Crockford denied ever having being the owner of a house or hotel in St James's Street, and he refused to describe his occupation before his club opened, observing petulantly, 'Am I to give a history of my life? I should rather decline it. I do not come here to state my private business and character, I must decline it.'

He was then questioned closely about his attitude to sharp practice on the turf, notably when a horse was known secretly to certain people to be lame or amiss. His answer was that 'everybody bets with his eyes open, and if they know a horse to be lame they bet against him, and why should the owner be excluded from the privilege which other persons have?'

He was then questioned on the subject of those who defaulted over their gambling debts, and who were generally known as 'Levanters'. Asked if he had ever had anything to do with 'Levanters' he refused to answer. When asked if it was not true that there had been extensive gambling at the club, he replied, 'There may have been so. But I do not feel myself at liberty to answer that question – to divulge the pursuits of private gentlemen.'

He also refused to be drawn over any question involving the amount of money lost by members of Crockford's Club when gambling. When it was put to him that a great many young men had lost sums of £10,000, £20,000 or even £50,000, he replied, 'I cannot say that I know it.' Asked if he knew of any person who had sustained serious losses at games of chance, he answered that he did not know what was meant by a serious loss. He had never known, he said, of anyone losing as much as £100,000. He could not even recall anyone losing as much as £50,000. He further declined to reveal anything which took place in his own club house.

The question of bad debts, and the practice of defaulting over money owed as the result of gambling in gaming houses, was repeatedly raised – and as repeatedly evaded. Thus when he was asked whether he considered that a gentleman was committed in honour to paying a debt incurred at hazard as one incurred on the turf, he replied, 'Most certainly'. But when he was asked whether a loser at hazard would be considered to be acting dishonourably if he sought to recover money lost by resorting to the law, he replied with indignation that such a person would be acting most dishonourably and added, 'I should take all the pains I could to avoid such a man.'

Thus spoke the witness now resident in Carlton House Terrace as he piously defended the honour of the turf and of the gentlemen gamblers of England. The hunter who had killed all the game in the reserve was declaring that it had all been sportingly achieved, that not a snare had been laid nor a trap set and that no one had ever shot a sitting bird. Perhaps at the time he may even have believed it himself.

But it is doubtful if the committee believed it. They were men of the world and they knew how 'deep' the gambling at Crockford's had been and could become. They must also have been personally acquainted with many noblemen who had lost heavily, and who had in some cases been left destitute by their losses at hazard and cards.

On the other hand, they may well have been influenced by the evidence given by Admiral Rous, so clearly a disinterested witness, when he spoke of the honour which existed amongst the noblemen and gentlemen of the turf. His actual words had been:

I am a confederate in the stable with the Duke of Bedford, the Duke of Beaufort, Lord Spencer, Lord Albemarle, and Captain Spencer; and I am quite satisfied that if any man were to propose to any of these gentlemen to commit an action, or to make any bet with others in a way which might be considered a dishonourable transaction, he would be turned out of the room. In my opinion men of the highest integrity and the highest honour, are members of the Turf.

But alas for the gallant Admiral and those manly words, so stoutly and sincerely spoken. Although he believed them at the beginning of 1844, and may well have convinced many of his listeners of their truth, the whole façade of integrity on the turf was soon to be exposed by the events which so quickly followed in the early days of the summer, when the race for the Derby was to be made memorable for the most calculated acts of roguery and deception that had ever been practised on a racecourse.

Whatever the committee may have believed about the honesty of racing as they sat listening to the evidence given before them at this inquiry, their whole attitude must have been altered a few months later after the Derby had been run. The horses and their riders who swept past the winning post at Epsom that Wednesday afternoon in May carried away with them the whole racing world of William Crockford – and the new broom of Victorianism was then called upon to cleanse the turf.

It did not become pure overnight, but it was never allowed to sink to such depths again. The disgust which the Queen expressed over the whole degrading affair was echoed in the minds of her subjects. If this was the so-called sport of kings, then Victorianism could only be its enemy.

Before describing this fateful Derby of 1844 in detail, it is necessary to outline the events which led up to it.

In 1843 William Crockford had been given new life by the news reaching him throughout the summer of the progress of his two-year-old chestnut colt, Ratan, who was trained for him by Joe Rogers at Newmarket. The colt, ridden by the trainer's son, Sam Rogers, had run in the New Stakes at Ascot – always a good guide to the classic races of the following year – and had beaten the even-money favourite, Assay, very easily by three lengths. Lord George Bentinck had gambled heavily on Assay that afternoon, and he saw nothing to alter his opinion that she was an exceptional filly. The inference thereafter was clear. If she *was* exceptional, and yet had been soundly beaten, then the horse that had beaten her must be outstanding. He sought out John Gully and asked him to name a price against Ratan winning the next year's Derby, and from then on, throughout the summer, he snapped up any good odds that were on offer against Crockford's colt.

Joe Rogers, Ratan's trainer, was of the same opinion as Lord George; and he advised Crockford to follow Lord George's example and to start backing Ratan to win the Derby of 1844.

Meanwhile Ratan continued to improve. In the autumn of 1843 he won the Criterion Stakes at Newmarket without being extended, and once again Crockford and Lord George at once obtained the best odds available over the colt for the following year's Derby; both, too, continued to back Ratan throughout the winter. It is always galling for an owner to see others backing heavily on his own horse, but this was something Crockford himself had often done in the past, and he respected Lord George's judgement.

At the Craven Meeting at Newmarket in the spring of 1844 Ratan was brought out again, was backed down to 'odds on' and beat the opposition with ease. Clearly he had wintered well, and now the Derby seemed at his mercy unless there was another colt of exceptional promise in the field.

There was. And it was owned by his enemy, John Gully.

This, then, was to be the show-down; the final reckoning, for although Gully was still in good health, Crockford was not. He knew that it might be years before he could ever hope to possess another such colt as Ratan, and yet his own days were numbered. The climax to his lifelong rivalry with Gully had been reached, and the final battle would be fought out between them over the Derby course.

Gully's colt was called The Ugly Buck. It was trained by old John Day at Danebury and owned by him in partnership with Gully. The racing spies whose duty it was to keep heavy backers such as Crockford and Lord George informed reported that The Ugly Buck was strongly fancied at Danebury; but the test would come when the colt ran in the first of the season's classic races, The Two Thousand Guineas at Newmarket, as a prelude to running at Epsom.

Ratan was not entered for this Newmarket classic. If The Ugly Buck won, as it seemed certain that he would, how might one judge just how good he might be?

The key to this problem would be the showing made against

The Ugly Buck by one of his opponents, Devil-to-Pay. This colt was owned by Lord George Bentinck, who would thus be in a position to gauge The Ugly Buck's potential. But Devil-to-Pay was to be ridden by Ratan's jockey, Sam Rogers, so he, too, would have a shrewd idea of the strength of the Danebury candidate after The Two Thousand Guineas had been decided. It was one of those intriguing situations so beloved by students of racing form.

At Newmarket, on the day of The Two Thousand Guineas, The Ugly Buck was almost unbackable at 7/2 *on*, whilst Devil-to-Pay was not even quoted in the betting. The race quickly developed into a match between the two, and in a driving finish The Ugly Buck, ridden by John Day junior, won by a neck, with the remainder of the field trailing. After this it seems probable that *all* the interested parties: Crockford and his trainer, old Joe Rogers; Gully and his trainer, old John Day; the two jockeys concerned, young Day and young Rogers; and finally Lord George Bentinck himself, came to the same conclusion. Ratan would probably beat The Ugly Buck at Epsom. This piece of intelligence gave everyone concerned much food for thought – and especially John Gully.

In the St Leger of 1824, money had talked louder than words when the chances of Jerry had been ignored by the Ring despite his good form. The inference then was that Jerry would be not allowed to show it. Now a similar situation began to develop. Gully and the Danebury Confederacy began to pour money on to The Ugly Buck, although they had good reason to believe that Ratan had the beating of him. The answer to this puzzle, for those who had the astuteness to see it, was that Ratan was not going to be allowed to win – and it was John Gully who was going to make certain that he did not.

The Derby was to be run on Wednesday, 22 May, and the betting in the weeks preceding it suggested that it would be a two-horse race, with only The Ugly Buck and Ratan concerned in the finish. Both Crockford and Lord George Bentinck continued to place heavy commissions on Ratan, yet The Ugly Buck remained a firm favourite at about 5/2 whilst Ratan was freely on offer at 3/1 or more.

It is surprising that Lord George Bentinck and Crockford did not at once see the red light more clearly. Perhaps they did, but Bentinck, who was something of an amateur detective, was receiving too many contradictory reports and picking up too many contradictory clues to accept it, whilst William Crockford, old, sick and worried, and now confined to his bed in Carlton House Terrace, could not get about to make the inquiries he might have wished. Instead he lay in his bed and fretted, becoming ever weaker as he became more apprehensive. He realised that something was afoot – and that John Gully was behind it. It was an alarming situation.

He sent for his trainer, Joe Rogers, and cross-questioned him repeatedly. The trainer assured him that Ratan had never been better. The closest guard was being kept upon him, and only Roger's son, young Sam, and the head lad of the stable were allowed anywhere near the colt's box. There was nothing for the owner to worry about. William Crockford sank back exhausted on his pillows and closed his eyes. But he continued to worry a great deal.

Lord George also began to worry, but he did more about it. His investment on Ratan was a big one, and he also had a marked dislike of being cheated. If the Danebury Confederacy thought that they could put one over on him, they must be taught a lesson. He redoubled his investigations and increased the number of his informants. Shadowy figures stopped him in the street and whispered in his ear; and dirty scraps of paper were pushed surreptitiously into his hands.

Lord George made it his business to find out what was happening, and he succeeded. Ratan was to be ridden at Epsom by the jockey who had partnered him throughout the previous season – the trainer's son, Sam Rogers; and the whisper came through to Lord George that Sam Rogers had been talking to Gully, and that Sam Rogers was now backing The Ugly Buck.

Lord George was prepared to act in secret whilst making his inquiries, but once he had reached what he believed to be a just conclusion, it was in his nature to bring the matter out into the open and to make his attack in public. Having secretly obtained Sam Roger's betting book, with certain non-committal entries in it, he called a public meeting of all those interested in the Derby betting outside the Spread Eagle Inn at Epsom, and standing majestically on the steps of the Inn, he called upon John Gully to answer certain questions. It was a high-handed act, the act of a man who was both autocratic and resolute; Gully had little option but to submit to this cross-questioning.

Is it true, Lord George demanded of Gully, that you have laid Sam Rogers £300 to £25 against The Ugly Buck, although such a price has never been available to the public? (The implication was obvious – that Gully was making it well worth Sam Roger's while to see that The Ugly Buck won.) Gully agreed that this was true. Is it also true, he was then asked, that Rogers has other bets on The Ugly Buck with you, but that no price is quoted over these transactions? To this question, Gully again nodded in agreement.

But Lord George was still only fencing, after the manner of a barrister seeking to extract a damaging admission from the witness in the box. It was his next question on which the interrogation really turned.

'Are these *all* the bets you have with Rogers, Mr Gully?'

'If you have any more in my name, my lord, and will specify them, I shall be better able to answer you.'

A clever barrister might well have phrased the question differently, and provoked a more definite reply. What Lord George Bentinck was trying to establish was by far the most damaging piece of evidence of all: it was that Gully had persuaded Sam Rogers to lay him £10,000 to £1,000 *against* Ratan. This meant that Rogers would profit considerably if The Ugly Buck won, and would still win £1,000 providing only that Ratan did *not* win. In other words the astute Gully was taking out a form of insurance against Sam Rogers indulging in a double-dodge by winning on Ratan after all, for he would then have to pay out £10,000.

But this Lord George could not prove; and it was a transaction which Gully would certainly never admit to having made. The interrogation then ended, with Lord George turning haughtily on his back, leaving 'Honest John' to gaze ruminatively up at the sky, and the crowd that surrounded him to gaze as ruminatively at their boots and to make what they liked of all that had been said and implied.

It is certainly not surprising that after all this there were many men who viewed Ratan's chances in the coming race with rapidly diminishing enthusiasm.

Lord George was to a certain extent talking 'through his pocket'; and he was certainly prejudiced in his attitude to the Danebury stable. Until the autumn of 1841, his own fine string of racehorses had been trained by old John Day at Danebury – and trained so successfully that in the turf parlance of the day he found himself 'literally walking on gold laid out by himself'. But the Danebury methods, brilliant though they undoubtedly were, had yet so close an affinity with double-dodging that a man of Lord George's integrity and sportsmanship could not tolerate them. He had therefore removed his string suddenly and peremptorily, and taken them to the Duke of Richmond's estate at Goodwood, leaving old John in no doubt at all of why this arbitrary change had been made. From that day on it had been the desire of the Danebury stable to beat a Bentinck horse with one of theirs, and thus prove how unwise he had been. There was certainly no love lost between the two racing establishments.

During all this altercation, William Crockford remained in the background doing nothing; but his hatred of Gully, and his frustration at what was going on, must have caused him acute distress and must have further damaged his already failing health.

So much was being talked about Gully's activities and the obvious implications behind them, that little attention was being paid to the other runners in the Derby, the betting only concerned the two main contenders, The Ugly Buck and Ratan, with 10/1 and 12/1 offered bar two. The Derby of 1844 was seen as a two-horse race, and nobody was seriously concerned with the chances of such as Colonel Peel's pair, Ionian and Orlando, Mr Wood's Running Rein, Leander owned by the Lichtwald brothers, and – least of all – Lord George Bentinck's Croton Oil.

It never occurred to the average punter therefore that in the shelter of this most convenient smoke-screen which was being put up around The Ugly Buck and Ratan, other devotees of dope, fraud and the double-dodge might also be actively at work with their plans for turning this Derby of 1844 to their advantage. Only Lord George Bentinck remained deeply suspicious of all that was going on, and he saw to it that his intelligence service was made to work with increased intensity to probe the many mysteries which existed. But even he felt that if further roguery *was* being planned, it would be discouraged by the vigour with which he was seeking to uncover it.

The Derby is only open to 3-year-old colts or fillies. No horse of any other age is qualified to run in any of the classic races of the English turf. Now a 3-year-old racehorse is still immature, and is therefore at a physical disadvantage against older horses. To match a 3-year-old against a 4-year-old is more or less equivalent to matching a schoolboy against a fully grown man. This is not to say that a brilliant schoolboy may not beat a fully grown man, or that a brilliant 3-year-old may not beat a horse of 4 or 5; but simply on the question of physique and muscular development, the elder of the two must always hold a considerable advantage.

Quite early on in the history of the classic races therefore it occurred to the 'artful dodgers' of racing that if the facts of a horse's birth could be falsified, it might sometimes be possible to present a 4-year-old as a 3-year-old, with the consequent great advantage in development. However this was a very difficult thing to achieve, especially with a horse belonging to a well-known owner and trained by a well-known trainer, for both would be warned off the turf immediately if such a fraud were discovered. Still it was just possible that an owner and trainer of exceptional cunning, and about whom little was known, might succeed in staging such a coup (and indeed Gully and Ridsdale had always been suspected of this trickery with St Giles).

Amongst the runners for the 1844 Derby were two horses whose owners and trainers fell into just such a category of cunning allied to carefully preserved obscurity. One of these horses was Leander, which was owned and trained by two shady German brothers named Lichtwald, who were ostensibly engaged in the business of exporting horses to the Continent. The other was a horse called Running Rein, a bay by The Saddler out of Mab, who had been bred by a Malton chemist by the name of Cobb, foaled in 1841 and purchased as a foal by a notorious small-time gambler known variously as Abraham Levi Goodman or Goodman Levy, a man deeply sunk in all the iniquities of the turf. In the November of 1843, some 6 months before the Derby, Goodman had handed over this horse to a Mr Alexander Wood, a corn merchant of Epsom, in lieu of money which was owing for corn. Running Rein, if it *was* Running Rein, was a 3-year-old, fully qualified to run in the Derby at Epsom.

But the point which intrigued a few of the more astute gamblers of the turf, and which had certainly not failed to impress itself on the ever-alert Lord George Bentinck, was that there seemed some reason to doubt whether the horse which Mr Wood had taken in all good faith in settlement for his corn debt and which he believed to be Running Rein might not in fact be something else; and that during the two years in which it had been under the care of Goodman or Goodman Levy – years in which it had been transferred from first one stable to another with such bewildering rapidity that it had scarcely had time enough to settle down in its box before being transferred again – it had become 'mixed up' with another horse, by the name of Maccabeus, by Gladiator out of Capsicum.

Maccabeus had been bred by Sir C. Ibbotson and had been foaled in 1840, and had been bought by Goodman, or Goodman Levy, at the Doncaster Races of 1841, whereafter it had undergone a similar nomadic existence to Running Rein, being switched so rapidly and so frequently from one stable to another that it must have become almost as confused as Running Rein. Mr Goodman, in short, was playing a sort of two-card trick with his two animals, shuffling them so frequently and dealing them so adroitly that no one was ever quite sure which was which. He was thus in a position to 'ring the changes' and by taking advantage of a similarity in colour and build between the two, he was able to substitute one for the other.

The suspicions of the racing world were first aroused at Newmarket in 1843, when Running Rein had been entered for a 2-year-old race which he had won easily. He looked then to be too big and strongly developed for a 2-year-old, and the Duke of

Rutland, who had owned the horse which had finished second
to him had at once objected. Goodman had backed Running Rein
substantially, bringing its price down from 10's to 3's, and his
behaviour and demeanour throughout the afternoon had been
highly suspect. Bets owing to him were paid under protest, and
the racing world waited expectantly for the Stewards' Enquiry
which resulted.

Everything turned on the evidence to be given by a stable-lad
in the employment of Mr C.R.Cobb, the Malton chemist who
bred the *real* Running Rein, for the lad was certain to know on
the instant whether or not this was the colt whom he had helped
to bring into the world and whom he had helped to rear. The
boy was brought to Newmarket under the closest supervision
and allowed to see no one before he gave his evidence to the
Stewards of the Jockey Club. But first he was taken by Lord
Stradbroke to the stable where the horse was stabled, told to
examine the animal carefully and to pronounce whether or not
this was indeed Running Rein or some other animal.

The lad – whose name has long since been forgotten – was no
fool. Looking Lord Stradbroke straight in the eye he announced
that the horse that stood before them was Running Rein. And the
Stewards had no other course open to them but to award the
race to Goodman.

Even so, Goodman continued to be viewed with considerable
suspicion, and it was still being openly said in the weeks before
the Derby of 1844 that Running Rein was not Running Rein at
all, but Maccabeus, and that he was not qualified to run in the
race. This did not prevent the horse from being quoted in the
betting, when heavy wagers were made about him, particularly
by Goodman, who backed the horse repeatedly at odds varying
between 20/1 and 10/1.

What, one may well ask, were the bookmakers doing about all
this? What was the reaction of the Stewards? How did the other
owners of runners in the Derby view this extraordinary situation,
whereby there seemed a chance that they might be robbed of the
greatest prize on the turf by an animal that was not even qualified
to run?

The astonishing thing was that very little was done at all. By turf law, if an objection was lodged *before* the running of the race, the onus would be on the Stewards of the Jockey Club to discover the truth; but if it were not lodged until *after* the race, then the onus would be on the person lodging the objection, and it would be his task to prove that fraudulence had taken place, and this he would presumably have to do in a court of law.

In fact some steps were taken by the interested parties before the race, but they proved ineffectual. The impression one is given is that the authorities – that is to say, the Stewards of the Jockey Club – were reluctant to lay themselves open to another rebuff such as they had already received. Their attitude was to allow the horse to run, and to hope that he would lose. Only in the event of his winning would they be required to take any further action.

But what of the bookmakers, and the heavy bettors? Goodman, of course, found himself in a strong position. He had backed his horse at a good price, and was now able to cover himself. If, as seemed probable, Ratan, the second favourite, was going to be 'taken care of', then that only left The Ugly Buck as a serious rival. The rest of the field clearly did not amount to much.

The Ring, meanwhile, who probably knew everything, had decided that if Running Rein lost, they would win handsomely over the Goodman bets; and if the horse won, they could refuse to pay, or at least hold back payment until after the official inquiry, in which case they hoped that Goodman would be exposed. Their opinion, which subsequent events proved to be the right one, was that Goodman was a small-time crook who had got away with it once, and was now imagining that he would get away with it again. He had staged a minor coup at Newmarket the previous season, and was now attempting to stage a major one in the Derby at Epsom – which was altogether a very different proposition.

Meanwhile the brothers Lichtwald were pursuing their own secret operations with their Derby runner, Leander, and their Oaks runner, Julia, *both* of which were open to the suspicion of being 4-year-olds. Leander was being trained at Ashstead, not far from Epsom, by old John Forth, whose chief claim to fame in racing – apart from his association with Leander – is that he rode the Derby winner of 1829 when aged 60, and this is still a record. He had also trained the Derby winner of 1840, named Little Wonder, whom it had been his custom to describe as 'an early foal', by which he implied that the colt had been born early in 1837, although there were those who interpreted this as meaning that in reality it had been born in 1836, so that it, too, may have been a 4-year-old when it won the Derby.

However, as Leander came from one of the smaller stables, and had not been backed for very large amounts, the Ring were not unduly concerned with his chances. The big money was on Ratan and The Ugly Buck, and with these two out of the way, a big profit by the Ring would be made on the race no matter who won.

And what of the ordinary backer? The man-in-the-street or – as in this case – the man on Epsom Downs, wagering his much-needed shillings and even sovereigns? What of him? Well, he remained the eternal simpleton, who had been born into the world to be exploited. So perhaps Admiral Rous was right. It was the poor who needed the State's protection.

It so happened that the Police Commissioners, acting on the same belief, were at this moment coming to the conclusion that there was altogether too much roguery at Epsom races, and that whereas they could not control what happened in the Derby, this being the province of the Stewards of the Jockey Club, they could at least control what went on in the sideshows which formed a part of the traditional Epsom scene.

These booths and sideshows had already become a public scandal. Epsom on Derby Day had by now taken the place of the old-time fairs which had been such a feature of London life at the beginning of the 18th century, when the May Fair held in the area just north of Piccadilly had become the scene of so much roistering, violence and immorality that it had become necessary to suppress it. Being broad-minded men on the whole, and accustomed to the ways of the Cockney when enjoying himself, the police were not opposed to the drinking tents where the racegoers could become paralytically drunk; nor even to the tents which, outwardly, were appealing only to their aesthetic senses, by offering them artistic *tableaux vivants*, whilst in fact providing them with a strip-tease display and the full amenities of a brothel during the hours of racing. But as the result of the new attitude to the gaming laws, and Parliament's decision to restrict gambling, the police were now determined to stamp out the menace of the gambling tents where cards, roulette and hazard could be played, and where the thimble men and the rest of the sleight-of-hand fraternity could practise their tricks upon the gullible public without fear of the law.

The Epsom Derby Meeting of 1844 opened on Tuesday, 21 May, and it was on the eve of the Derby itself, which was to be run on the Wednesday, that the Police Commissioners issued a surprise ultimatum. All gambling booths were forbidden, and anyone found operating such a booth, or participating in the play, would be summarily arrested. Moreover, in order that this ban on gambling should be enforced, it was announced that 500 extra constables would be drafted into the area on Derby Day.

The owners of the gambling booths were not struck dumb by this announcement, for they were nothing if not vocal. Instead they went into earnest conclave. Should they defy the police – now so substantially increased in numbers – or should they stage a more formal protest, by sending a 'memorial' to Sir James Graham, the Home Secretary, protesting against this high-handed curtailment of their traditional liberties?

The thought of the 500 additional constables tilted the balance in favour of legalised action, and the 'memorial' was painstakingly composed and dispatched to the House of Commons, although with little hope of success, for Sir James was well known to be a man of autocratic and unconciliatory attitude.

Derby Day, Wednesday 22 May, dawned neither fine nor clear. On the contrary, it opened cold and depressing, with rain in the air. However, the weather relented during the early morning, and by the time the huge throng of racegoers was beginning to prepare for its exodus from London – by coach, cart, wagon and the new railway service, now in its seventh year – by the time these would-be racegoers had in fact been faced with the decision as to whether they should set out at all, the skies had cleared and the weather had grown quite reasonably warm. Everyone was delighted, except for the gambling booth owners who were left, both figuratively and indeed quite literally, to sulk like Achilles in their tents.

But there was one prominent personality who did not order his carriage to be ready at eleven, and whose box in the Grand Stand had not been prepared to receive him.

This was William Crockford, sick and tired and old. His wife, Sarah, had forbidden any suggestion that he should make the long and dusty journey to Epsom, and in truth he had shown no desire to go. His heart – if indeed he ever possessed such a thing – was with his colt, Ratan, but he had neither the energy nor the courage to watch him run. For if Ratan won, and the ambition of a life-time were achieved, the excitement might prove too great for an old man to bear. And if he lost, and the ambition of a lifetime vanished for ever, then the disappointment might prove equally unbearable. All that William Crockford could do was to sit hunched-up in his chair in the window of his house in Carlton House Terrace and wait for the messenger to arrive with the result of the race.

Ratan! The colt could be the instrument of his revenge on a Society whom he had robbed, but which had always despised him. Ratan could make the name of Crockford immortal in the annals of the turf.

And what, one is left to wonder, was going in the minds of the others who were so deeply involved in this drama of racing which was to be played within a few hours on Epsom Downs? What was passing through the mind of John Gully as he thumbed through his betting book and considered his profit-and-loss account on the great race? What were the thoughts of old John Day, that master trainer who knew that he had brought The Ugly Buck to his peak? And what were the hopes and fears in minds of the jockeys riding in the race – young John Day, Sam Rogers and all the rest – whose split-second decisions during the running could win or lose a fortune for their masters, and who were so committed to villainy that they could not now turn back.

In the jockeys' changing room before the race, and in the Grand Stand where the owners and trainers were assembling, some sidelong glances must have been thrown, some unspoken queries made.

The jockey boys, Newmarket's crew,
Who know a little thing – or two ...

So many people on that fine May afternoon at Epsom knew a
little thing or two. But those who live in a world of double-
dodging must for ever be on the look-out for those engaged on
the double-double-dodge. There was so much at stake. So much
to win, and so much to lose. And if things went wrong, as they
so easily might, there were so many tracks to be hastily covered
up, and so many excuses to be prepared in order to explain away
the unforeseen occurrence.

And no doubt Admiral Rous, that upright and truly honest
English gentleman, when he came to look down upon the scene,
must have thought with pride of the great traditions that the
Derby had brought into being, and the even greater traditions –
of honesty and honour and fair dealing – which the noblemen
who lent their patronage to English racing lived by and so
earnestly believed in.

Lord George Bentinck must also have looked down upon that
scene, but with less elevated thoughts – *his* mind teeming with all
the secrets that had been committed to it and his brain turning
over the problems of just how far the Danebury Confederacy
would dare to go, and what was in store for Ratan.

One might have supposed that with such huge sums involved
in the betting, and with such prestige and glory to be attained by
horse, rider and jockey alike, every care would have been
taken of the course itself, and that it would have been brought
to the best possible condition so that the going at least could not
be blamed for any fiasco that might occur.

Nothing could have been further from the actual state of
affairs, for the state of the Epsom course for this Derby of 1844
was terrible. It could scarcely have been worse, or more dangerous.
The Times, reporting on the state of the going on the morning of
the race, summed the matter up with clarity when it said:

What used to be called turf can hardly be called so now. The stunted
vegetation and the aridity of the soil have produced a rusty, russet tint,
the livery of dust, and the ground is as hard, without being as even, as
wood pavement.

The writer concluded with the comment that it was to be hoped that the following day's report on the Derby would not have to refer to broken limbs and fatal accidents.

Yet this was the course on which the world's greatest horse-race was about to be run, and the setting for one of the biggest betting events of the century.

The betting before the race followed the pattern of the previous days. At White's, on the Monday night, so *The Times* reported, a noble lord had offered £90,000 to £30,000 against The Ugly Buck but had found no takers. On the Tuesday the course betting had for a time so favoured Ratan that he had been made a temporary favourite at 9/4, but renewed weight of money for The Ugly Buck (or perhaps second thoughts on that curious scene between Lord George Bentinck and John Gully outside the Spread Eagle Inn) had brought Gully's colt back to favouritism on the day, with 5/2 against him freely offered and as freely taken, Ratan laid to less money at 3/1, and a small but steady flow for Running Rein at 10/1. Backing of Leander by the Lichtwald brothers made it firm at 14/1, and Colonel Peel's pair, Ionian and Orlando, were on offer at around 15/1 to 20/1, the general opinion being that Ionian had the better credentials of the two. The rest of the field, which totalled 29 in all, were given very little chance and were only nibbled at in the market.

The new official mood of discipline, already evidenced by the Commissioners of Police with their ban on all gambling booths, was now made further apparent in Sir Gilbert Heathcote's warning of the jockeys before they left the weighing-room on the penalties which would be imposed for any sort of foul riding or other malpractice. The little, wizened-faced men with their sharp and shifty eyes no doubt listened to him with an outward show of respectfulness, nodding their heads as each point was made. There was to be no anticipation of the dropping of the starting flag, said Sir Gilbert, no jostling for places, no shouted abuse and no calculated interference during the running of the race. In the same way does the referee in a boxing match address the fighters who are about to inflict every conceivable form of skullduggery on each other in the coming encounter, and express the pious hope that it will be a good, clean contest.

The crowd on the Downs was now enormous, and the spectators who jostled round the starter witnessed only two false starts before the field was sent on its way at exactly 3 o'clock.

Leander was taken at once to the front by his jockey, Bell, who made the early running, either because his mount was going well or because he was frightened of the jostling that was bound to occur rounding Tattenham Corner, when the prospect of the sharp turn and the foul riding of the other jockeys gave him good cause for alarm. So off he went in front, with the field charging along behind him and the hooves of the horses thundering out on the rock-hard going.

During its long history the Derby course has been altered on several occasions, but certain features have remained constant, above all the sharp left-hand downward sweep round Tattenham Corner into the straight. At all times difficult and even dangerous to negotiate, this turn becomes far more so when the field is a large one and has become bunched, with the riders fighting for a good position. And when the going is dry and slippery, as it was on this occasion, the dangers are considerably increased. In 1844 these hazards were rendered still worse by the fact that the old course was still in use (it was not first altered until 1847) and the bend at Tattenham Corner was much sharper than it is today. On such a day, and under such conditions, it could well become a death-trap.

Leander reached the corner first, but with the field closing rapidly on him, and he was then seen to stagger – whether because he was cannoned into from behind or simply because his legs crumpled beneath him has never been clearly established. But his off-hind leg fractured suddenly between the hock and the fetlock with a sound like a pistol-shot, and the poor animal stumbled miserably to a halt, but without collapsing.

The field swept on past him, the jockeys screaming abuse at each other, lashing out at each other with their whips and crossing each other's paths, with some mercilessly driving their mounts forward and others already beginning to take the 'pull' which caution demanded if their horse was to be kept out of the first three, for crooked riding tactics can easily be covered up in the mêlée but are not so easy to camouflage when the field is strung out in the straight.

Once a Derby field has reached the straight, the pattern of the race becomes apparent. Now Running Rein was taken to the front and at once given his head, so that there could be no doubt about *his* jockey's intentions. The Ugly Buck was in touch, but was young John Day riding with quite the determination that was to be expected? Meanwhile Colonel Peel's pair, Orlando and Ionian, were being driven up to challenge, with Orlando going the better of the two; and the 20/1 chance, Bay Momus, was there with a chance but looked to be fading.

And Ratan? What of Ratan and Sam Rogers, unmistakable in Crockford's colours of white with red cap? Ratan, as everyone on the course could see, was 'dead meat'. The jockey's whip was flailing and his efforts appeared to be intense, but the horse was labouring painfully, struggling ineffectively to keep his place and in fact dropping behind with every stride he took. And the book-makers smiled, for one thing at least was obvious. Ratan had truly been 'taken care of'. It was quite certain that he could not win.

Their smiles grew broader as the last two furlongs were reached. Running Rein, still cutting out a tremendous pace, now held a commanding lead, and only Orlando and Ionian were left to challenge him. Orlando finished the stronger, and did in fact get within three-quarters of a length of the leader without ever looking like passing him, leaving Ionian struggling on 2 lengths behind. The Ugly Buck came in a bad 5th; Ratan an even worse 7th. But the outcome had been apparent to all long before the judge's chair had been reached.

Now in very truth the cat was amongst the pigeons. A suspect horse had won, and the Ring howled their disapproval and re-fused to pay out over the winner, whilst the backers crowded round and the confusion grew ever greater. In the Grand Stand, the Stewards met hastily to decide on their course of action, whilst Admiral Rous gazed on the scene in bewildered disgust and Lord Bentinck thundered his denunciations abroad. Rogues, crooks and robbers! Ratan nobbled, The Ugly Buck nowhere, and the race won by a horse that was almost certainly not eligible to run!

On Derby Day, after the great race has been run, there is usually one person who commands the centre of the stage; one person whom everyone is cheering and who makes his way to the un-saddling enclosure whilst his back resounds from the many hands that thump it enthusiastically in approbation. This is the owner of the winner. But where, on this occasion, was the owner of Running Rein – the self-effacing Mr Alexander Wood, the corn-merchant from Epsom, who had taken the horse in lieu of payment of an outstanding bill? The shout went up 'Where is Mr Wood?' But he was nowhere to be seen, and the horse was walked into the unsaddling enclosure unaccompanied.

Where *was* Mr Wood? Now the news reached the Stewards that the excitement and the tumult of this great occasion had proved too much for Mr Wood. He had left a message to say that he had gone home to bed.

No doubt he was wise to do so, for once the implications of the race had fully dawned upon all those concerned the storm broke with a vengeance. Colonel Peel, urged on by Lord George Bentinck, immediately lodged an objection, claiming the stakes and the race. The Stewards agreed to the withholding of the stakes from Wood, pending further inquiries, and the betting ring was thus thrown into the utmost confusion.

But if the hubbub on the course was bad enough, it was soon to be eclipsed by that which broke out at Tattersall's Subscription Rooms at Hyde Park Corner on the following Tuesday, when the big punters who had backed Running Rein tried to draw their money and failed, and so did those who had backed Orlando. And all over the country the lotteries and sweepstakes which had been held by tradition were thrown into utter confusion.

The Derby of 1844 had been run and the Epsom meeting was over, and yet no one yet knew who was the winner. Indeed the only betting that took place was on whether or not Running Rein would keep the race, and odds of 2/1 *on* were quoted that he would. The backers, in other words, were supporting Goodman against the formidable combination of Orlando's owner, Colonel Peel, Lord George Bentinck and Admiral Rous when the race came finally to be run all over again in a court of law, which was clearly the only way in which it could be decided.

But there was one certain loser, and that was Ratan's owner, William Crockford. When they had brought him the news, and the description which they gave him of the race confirmed his suspicions, so that he knew that his great horse had been beaten by either foul riding or dope, or by both, the unhealthy and enfeebled body collapsed under the shock. He died three days later, on Saturday, 25 May 1844, bitter, broken and overwhelmed by self-pity.

Only one small comfort had been given to him. Ratan had lost, but at least The Ugly Buck had not won. Indeed they hinted to him that even the pride of the Danebury stable seemed also to have been nobbled. And at this piece of intelligence he was able to give a feeble smile. He and John Gully had been the two biggest bookmakers of their day, and the double-dodgers had now brought both of them down together!

His last words were 'I have been "done". That was not Ratan's right running.'

In the inquests which were held all over England, but above all at Newmarket, where the experts were assembled, it was generally felt that in order to make doubly sure, Ratan had not only been nobbled before the race but his jockey had also been bribed to pull the colt during it, just in case the dope given to him was not proving fully effective. The infamous 'Crutch' Robinson, one of the worst of the 'legs', whose speciality had always been to field against favourites, openly maintained that Ratan had been 'got at' by a shadowy figure named Hargreaves who operated on the outskirts of the Danebury contingent, and that Hargreaves had gained access to Ratan's stable on the night before the Derby and had administered poison – probably arsenic – to the unfortunate animal.

Hargreaves, a sly, mysterious figure whose shadow was to fall across more than one Derby in the years to come, remains the mystery man of the Ratan affair. Of all the many crooks on the turf at this time, he was the most despicable, but all that posterity seems to know of him was that he was 'a lucky, screaming gentleman with a large face and pink eyes' and that he came from Manchester. He certainly made a fortune out of the Derby of 1844, although of course he would never reveal how he had done so, but it is quite possible that he accepted a large bribe from the Danebury backers of The Ugly Buck, and having poisoned Ratan, he then turned his attention to The Ugly Buck and nobbled it as well, just for good measure, thus revealing himself as a past-master in the art of the double-dodge.

The curious thing about all this is that although both William Crockford and his trainer, Joe Rogers, must have known that something was in the wind, and must have suspected that John Gully and his confederates were out to get at Ratan, they do not seem to have taken adequate precautions to prevent this. Even the incident outside the Spread Eagle Inn, when Lord George Bentinck had openly accused John Gully of trying to bribe Ratan's jockey, the trainer's son, young Sam Rogers, failed to put them on their guard. Probably William Crockford was too ill to take any active steps, and Joe Rogers could not and would not believe that his son was in any way implicated with the Danebury stable. Not that young Sam was a model son, by any means, for he was neither averse to keeping bad company, nor to having a bet. But the old man believed that the boy was honest at heart and that he would never stoop so low as to betray his own father; and perhaps old Joe was able to convince William Crockford that this was so.

Yet William Crockford was without sentiment, and more suspicious than most. He should have been ready to mistrust anyone, and certainly young Sam. It is true that on the night before the race the guards who were always on duty outside Ratan's box had been doubled, and that the horse and his jockey had been locked inside, and had slept in adjoining stalls. In the light of subsequent allegations, this may well have been unwise, but there was never any suggestion later that Sam Rogers had interfered with Ratan, but only that he had 'pulled' him during the race.

'When the key was turned on Ratan he was in glorious health,' wrote Thormanby in his book, *Sporting Stories*, 'with a skin like satin and muscles of steel. When he showed on the downs the next morning his coat was standing like quills upon the fretful porcupine, his eyes were dilated, and he shivered like a man with the ague.'

This account of Ratan's condition before the race is probably exaggerated, for if he had been in quite such a bad condition this would have been reflected in the market, and he would not have started second favourite. But his running in the race was certainly far too bad to be his true form. Admittedly he was struck into, and given a very rough passage, and this may have been sufficient to deprive him of all chance of winning.

One of the shrewdest comments made after the race was that Orlando had always represented the best bet because his jockey, Nat Flatman, was one of the few jockeys riding in that Derby who was above suspicion; and he was certainly one whom Colonel Peel trusted implicitly.

The result of the Derby remained undecided, but there was no doubt about the fact that William Crockford was dead. He may well have had a sense of foreboding, for his will was only drawn up and signed a short time before the Derby was run. (The exact date, curiously enough, is unknown, for the space left blank in the phrase 'dated this   day of May 1844' had not been filled in, a most surprising oversight on the part of the two witnesses to the document, his doctor, James Johnson, and his daughter, Elizabeth Crockford.)

The will itself was surprisingly brief, considering that a sum of nearly three-quarters of a million pounds was involved, and its terms were concise. Everything was left to his wife, Sarah Frances, 'trusting her to do what is right', which was certainly more than she had ever been able to do with him during his lifetime. From what little is known of her she seems to have been a good wife and mother, and a refining influence on him if not a restraining one. The fact that she was kept so much in the background may well have resulted in her knowing comparatively little of his activities and his unscrupulousness on the turf. Her duty had been to stay at home and to look after the children; and to soothe her husband when his gambling luck deserted him or his business ventures collapsed. If, as the writer of the Crockford biography in *Bentley's Miscellany* suggested, she had at one time been the governess employed by a lady of wealth whom the young Crockford had seduced, it is unlikely that she was ever a woman of aggressive nature, her take-over bid for her mistresses lover having no doubt been engineered in a discreet and reticent manner. But there it is – we know almost nothing about her.

There may well have been another factor beside the defeat of Ratan which may have contributed to Crockford's decline in health during the last few weeks of his life. On 20 May, at the beginning of the Epsom week, the Committee of the House of Commons had issued their *Report on Gaming*, in which they made a number of recommendations that could only prove damaging to the continuance of gambling as it had been carried on until that time. Amongst these recommendations was one which had suggested that the police should be empowered to enter any house after they had received a declaration by two householders that it was being run as a gaming house. Shortly before the Derby, the police had staged a raid on a gaming house at 34, St James's Street, and the son of the proprietor had become so alarmed that he had tried to escape over the roof, had fallen into a courtyard and been killed. Throughout May these police raids had been stepped up, and some 73 people had been arrested for gaming and subsequently fined. The banning of all gambling booths on Epsom Downs during the Derby meeting was the culmination of this drive towards the enforcement of the gambling laws and the punishment of those who transgressed them; and it may have been that even Crockford felt cause for alarm.

Inevitably the death of William Crockford produced at once a number of stories concerning the time and manner of his decease, the most curious of which – and one which has since been built up into a Crockford legend – was that he died *before* the Derby, and that his dead body was then propped up in a window of Crockford's Club, where the passers-by along St James's Street might see it, and thus believe that he was still alive, for by the rules of racing and betting then in existence a horse whose owner died before a race had to be scratched (this was not altered until comparatively recently) while death also rendered all bets void.

This curious legend was widely believed at the time, and many turf historians still give it credence, partly because such a well-known authority as the famous barrister, Sergeant Ballantine, always maintained that it was true. The legend was perpetuated in verses that were written to commemorate the incident, under the title of 'A Chronicle of Crockford's':

> The Derby is lost, and the Derby is won;
> The race of all Races has come and is gone;
> So homeward each whirls, whether loser and sad,
> Or winner of 'flimsies' with countenance glad:
>
> When in ROME a grand Triumph enlivened the Road
> That leads to the Victor's Imperial abode,
> 'Via Sacra' they called it; so multitudes greet
> The Winners who climb up St James' holy Street.
>
> 'Thou art mortal!' still whispers a voice in each ear:
> Some have paid for life's whistle uncommonly dear;
> As at CROCKFORD'S they glance, 'twixt a sigh and a frown
> Some remember won money's not always one's own.
>
> On the eve of the DERBY a whisper had spread;
> A ridiculous rumour that 'CROCKY' was dead;
> A tale that had faded ere brightened the looks
> Of the 'Jeunesse dorée' who were deep in his books.
>
> There he sits, in a window, as four-year-old fresh;
> Rather paler than usual, but still in the flesh;
> With NUGEE'S best surtout; and a faultless cravat;
> Some old friends he salutes; to some touches his hat.
>
> No choice but to pay; all the winners are known:
> To the usurer's dovecot the 'flimsies' have flown;
> And the payers ne'er knew, till a twelvemonth had sped,
> That the man in the window was 'CROCKY', but – dead.

There can be no truth behind this legend whatsoever. Crockfords death took place a whole three days after the race, and he died of a Derby favourite's failure.

8

THE AFTERMATH
The New Victorianism and the Turf

> Grafton's Duke has sunk to rest,
> Light of other days . . .
> Crockford with his white cravat,
> Thornhill and his grays . . .

The lines are a Newmarket elegy, written in memory of the year of 1844, which saw the death of those whose names it mentions. Crockford, had he ever known that they might be written, would have felt flattered that he should one day find himself listed in such company, for George Henry Fitzroy, 4th Duke of Grafton, had been one of the great gentlemen of the turf, as had Squire Thornhill of Riddlesworth in Norfolk. Both had been landowners of the old school, autocratic but kindly, dogmatic and yet understanding, men who had won the respect and the love of those who served them. Both had won the Derby: Thornhill in 1818 with Sam, and two years later with Sailor, and the Duke of Grafton once only, in 1815, when his bay colt, Whisker, had triumphed by just about the distance which his name suggested. Both, too, had been 'Newmarket men', and the Duke's successes in the Two Thousand and the Thousand Guineas have never since been surpassed.

Both were men of honour, which was more than William Crockford had ever been, but William's name was included with them because he, too, had been 'a Newmarket man' all his life. The fascination that this small country town has had for so many racing men is something that is not easy to explain. The wind blows cold across the Heath, and the ghosts of Newmarket haunt these mournful wastes, from those of the ancient Romans to that of Fred Archer; and Death itself, the pale rider on his great white steed, may be glimpsed there on a moonlit night.

Of this year of 1844, it may well be said that it was not so much the end of an era as the beginning. The very heavy betting which had characterised the turf and the gambling clubs of St James's Street in the first two decades of the century was already on the wane, as Admiral Rous had emphasised in his evidence to the Select Committee of the House of Commons. There was more betting, it is true, but the size of the bets had decreased. Roguery, too, was on the wane, and the events of the Derby of 1844 had brought out this evil into the open.

Still, this Derby made it clear to all that the wholesale dishonesty which the result had exposed could not be allowed to continue. It was not merely a matter of the young Queen and her consort both denouncing the wild and irresponsible ways of the upper classes and the unashamed manner in which they mixed with the riff-raff of the racecourse; nor was it just a matter of Parliament grown suddenly exasperated with the manner in which the gaming laws were being flouted. It was the barefaced criminality of it all that shocked the public. Here was revealed a sport riddled with corruption – with bribery, poisoning and falsification of the identity of horses for the unashamed purpose of making vast sums of money out of racing! And it was not merely the bookmakers and the backers who were being defrauded; it was also the racing authorities themselves, who were being tricked into awarding the greatest prizes of the turf to criminals who had no right to them whatever.

The pious declarations by English sportsmen now had little meaning. The turf was *not* an honourable institution. It was a cesspit of infamy.

Since no official inquiry had taken place *before* the Derby into the antecedents of Running Rein and Leander (the Stewards had done no more than acknowledge the objections lodged against each before the race, and promise an investigation after the race if either should win), the whole matter had finally to be decided in a court of law.

This reluctance of the Stewards to take any action before the race reveals their temerity and lack of authority. Moreover a point which they seemed to have altogether overlooked was that *only the second can object to the winner*. Thus, had Running Rein finished first and Leander second, no objection would have been made; for the owners of the second would then have been just as guilty as the owner of the winner and the last thing they would have done would have been to object and thus bring a hornet's nest around their own ears as well. Also it is conceivable that had some impoverished owner's horse come second, it would have only been necessary for Goodman to bribe him in order to keep his mouth shut. Goodman himself was said to have won about £50,000 on the race, so he would have been happy to do it.

Colonel Jonathan Peel, owner of the second horse, Orlando, and of the third, Ionian, was not fully convinced of the merits of his case, even though he did lodge an objection and claimed the stakes as soon as the race had been run. He was younger brother to Sir Robert Peel, the Prime Minister, and he may well have felt a certain reluctance to become involved in what was clearly going to become one of the major scandals of the decade. It was Lord George Bentinck and Admiral Rous, pushing him from behind, who really forced him to go through with his legal action. It is true that Rous had been one of those who had advised the Stewards of Epsom *not* to make formal investigation before the Derby, but he no doubt had his reasons for this. Either he thought that neither Goodman nor the Lichtwald brothers would dare to win the race; or he felt that nothing would be achieved by banning their horses from competing. But once Running Rein had won, it was the Admiral, breathing fire and brimstone in a manner which he had not even displayed in his days on the quarter-deck, who charged into the attack in company with Lord George Bentinck. Both were equally determined to expose the wrongdoers, for both were looked up to as leaders of the turf and its foremost reformers.

It was Lord George Bentinck however who proved himself to be something more than just a devout protector of turf morality. He now became its chief criminal investigator as well, and set to work with an assiduity and perspicacity which even Sherlock Holmes could have applauded.

Indeed his methods of inquiry had more than a touch of Baker Street about them. Running Rein was a 'ringer'. Of that he was certain. And it seemed highly probable that in reality he was the 4-year-old named Maccabeus. Now in order to ring the changes, Goodman would have to purchase dyes suitable for either human or animal hair. Goodman was crafty but not so crafty that he might not have proved careless in his buying of such dyes. They would need to be of the highest quality, and 'fast', so that they would not be affected by either rain or perspiration. They would therefore need to be bought from a reliable chemist's shop; from a barber's shop; or more probably still from an expensive ladies' hairdressing saloon.

Lord George Bentinck armed himself with a map of London and drew a circle on it round Foley Place, just north of Oxford Street, where Goodman had his stables, and where the 'ringing' must almost certainly have taken place. He then visited every chemist's shop in the district. But he drew a blank.

In no way discouraged, he started his travels again, but this time he visited all the barbers' shops and ladies' hairdressing saloons. Finally he discovered a woman serving behind the counter at Rossi's in Regent Street, who remembered selling a large quantity of dye to a gentleman whom she was able to describe, particularly so as he had collected a second jar for which he had omitted to pay. The owner of the shop, Mr Rossi himself, also remembered the man well, and so Lord George took him in a cab to a nearby tavern frequented by Goodman; and when Goodman came out, Rossi was able to identify him.

It has already been remarked that Goodman had made the mistake, so common amongst successful small-time criminals, of thinking he could pit his wits with equal success against experts. He was now to learn his lesson. But although he was the prime mover behind the whole deception, it was the unfortunate Mr Wood, who throughout seems to have been little more than a pawn in the game, who remained the official owner of the horse and on whose shoulders all further action therefore rested. The Stewards of the Jockey Club had not officially disqualified Running Rein. All they had done, at the instigation of Colonel Peel, had been to withhold the stakes, so that Wood could only get his money by bringing a civil action against them. This he was forced to do. The defendant was Colonel Peel, both as instigator of the move to prevent payment and as the representative of the Jockey Club.

The case of Wood versus Peel was heard in the Court of Exchequer and opened before Mr Baron Alderson, himself an expert on racing matters, and a special jury on Monday, 1 July 1844, the issue on which the jury were to give their verdict being, 'Whether a certain horse called Running Rein was a colt foaled in the year 1841, whose sire was The Saddler and dam Mab'.

Alexander Cockburn, the great advocate of his day, who later became Lord Chief Justice, appeared on behalf of the plaintiff, Wood. Sir Frederick Thesiger, of almost equal legal stature, and afterwards Lord Chancellor, appeared for Colonel Peel.

There was a great deal of money involved, which was why such big guns had been assembled; and it was not long before the battle was joined. Sir Frederick Thesiger, acting on the information supplied to him by Lord George Bentinck, outlined the full story of how the two horses, Maccabeus and Running Rein, had been constantly moved from one stable to another by Goodman. Thus everything turned on Goodman – and on the horse. But Goodman was sheltering in comparative safety behind Wood, who was the official owner of Running Rein; and the horse itself could not be found.

Cockburn wanted to call Goodman, but was not permitted to do so. Instead therefore he vented his wrath upon Lord George Bentinck, whom he accused – quite rightly but with excessive bitterness – of being the real promoter of the litigation and of acting the dual role of detective and attorney, cross-questioning witnesses in the former part and browbeating them in both. Lord George was not called as a witness and could not therefore defend himself in court, but he was not the sort of man to take this high-handed treatment quietly, and he demanded that he be interrogated. Cockburn objected to this, and his objection was upheld by the Judge.

But the Judge was more interested in the horse. 'Produce the horse – produce the horse!' he ordered, but this was something no one could do, for the horse had disappeared. The unfortunate Wood, for whom one has some sympathy since he clearly had no very clear idea of all that was going on, gave evidence that on the day before the Judge had indicated that he would wish to see the horse, Goodman had removed it from Wood's care and both of them had then vanished.

It has been noted that the betting, on the opening of the case, was 2/1 *on* Running Rein keeping the race. But by the end of the first day, with neither Goodman nor the horse anywhere to be found, the market underwent a not altogether surprising change, with 10/1 *against* Running Rein freely offered but nowhere taken.

Here it is possible to interpolate one of those intriguing little footnotes which can make the compilation of turf history so rewarding. Earlier that summer a certain Captain Osborn found himself heavily in debt and faced with ruin. His only hope of rescuing himself from this predicament was by betting, and he chose Orlando in the Derby as the means of his salvation. He backed it with every penny that he could raise, and then saw it beaten into second place at Epsom by Running Rein. He became convinced there was little hope of the result being reversed, and decided to shoot himself, but just before the trial started a crumpled piece of paper was thrust into his hand in the street. On it was written the information that Running Rein was indeed 'a ringer' and the advice that he should find whatever money he could still lay his hands upon and continue to back Orlando. On making inquiries he found that the writer was a tout whom he had once befriended, and so he took the odds on offer against Orlando before the case started.

On the second day of the hearing there was still no Goodman and no horse. 'It is a clear case of horse-stealing,' thundered the Judge. 'I can only say if I try them I will transport them for life.'

The inference was obvious, and Cockburn threw up the case and withdrew all the imputations which he had made against Lord George Bentinck. Baron Alderson, in his address to the jury, observed that the case had filled him with disgust. An atrocious fraud had been exposed, which had revealed the evils that could develop when gentlemen associated with those of far lower rank than themselves. He concluded with the observation that if gentlemen condescended to race with blackguards they must also condescend to be cheated by them.

The jury gave their verdict for Colonel Peel, and the Derby

of 1844 was officially awarded to Orlando, who finished second in the race but goes down in its annals as the winner. Goodman fled to Boulogne and died there in poverty. As for Running Rein, it was said that he underwent yet another change of marking and appeared a year later under the name of Zanoni amongst the entries for the Chester Cup. But he was not allowed to run, and ended his days on a farm in Northamptonshire, where it is said that his ghost still haunts the lanes along which he trod, pulling a cart in ignominy, with his head held low in shame.

But the Derby scandal of 1844 was not yet ended, and two further questions still remained to be answered. Was Leander, who was owned by the Lichtwald brothers and who broke his leg at Tattenham Corner, a 4-year-old as well? And to what extent was Ratan's failure due to the foul riding of his jockey, Sam Rogers?

There are numerous stories still being told of what happened to Leander. The official account, which appeared in the Racing Calendar of 1844, states that 'the horse broke his leg in running, and was shot the same afternoon. His lower jaw was taken off before he was buried, and shown to Mr Field on the Saturday morning following, when he gave his opinion that it was the jaw of a 4-year-old horse. Late on Friday night or early on Saturday morning, the remains of Leander were dug up, and submitted to Mr Bartlett, Junior, a vetinerary surgeon at Dorking, who pronounced it to be the head and upper jaw of a 4-year-old horse. An investigation subsequently took place before the Jockey Club ... and Messrs Lichtwald were declared for ever disqualified ...'

Friends of old John Forth maintained that he was astonished to learn of all this, for he had genuinely believed that Leander was only a 3-year-old. But another contemporary account relates that after a rowdy party at John Scott's home, which was also near the course, some revellers seized lanterns and shovels and stealthily visited the spot where Leander had been buried and dug up the corpse. The lower jaw was missing, but the upper jaw was still attached to the skull. It was removed, taken back, boiled and also submitted for expert examination, when the same pronouncement was made. Leander was certainly not a 3-year-old.

In view of John Forth's record, and the fact that his Derby winner of 1840, Little Wonder, was also in all probability a 4-year-old, his protestations of innocence and the story of his amazement when told the truth about Leander's age ring somewhat false. But there the matter rested. The Jockey Club expressed their own view by warning the Lichtwald brothers for ever off Newmarket Heath, and they retired to live in Germany, where – so it was said – they openly sneered at the English experts for ever having thought that Leander might be a 4-year-old as it should have been quite obvious to them that he was in fact a 5-year-old.

As for Julia, their filly which ran on the Friday in the Oaks, she finished down the field, after an objection had been lodged against her before the start of the race, and on the same grounds: that she was a 4-year-old. The mind boggles at the thought of both classic races at Epsom being won by 4-year-olds in the same year!

Thus Colonel Peel was left to count his winnings over the Derby and to collect his stake money. He may well be considered a lucky man, for he owed much to the efforts of Lord George Bentinck, without whose persuasion he would never have fought the case.

In fact he was a lucky man in every respect. He was born and bred to be a soldier, and yet he never quite caught up with whatever wars there were about, having gained his first commission as second lieutenant in the Rifle Brigade on 15 June 1815, which was just three days before the Battle of Waterloo, and by the time the formalities of joining his regiment had been completed, the war was all over. The next major affray was the Crimean War, by which time he was a General and too old for foreign service, although he tried to join the army before Sebastopol. But he was an excellent military administrator and finally became Minister for War. He never won the Derby again. But his gratitude to Lord George Bentinck he expressed in his friendship with him throughout their lives, and to his jockey, Nat Flatman, the honest man amongst so many rogues, he showed exceptional generosity, making him a present of £5,000, which was a very large sum for a jockey to receive in those days.

The question of Sam Roger's involvement in the affair still remained to be decided. How far had Ratan's failure been due to interference in the running, how far to being doped, and how far to deliberate restraint from the saddle? Both Lord George Bentinck and Admiral Rous held the view that not until this issue had been settled could the Derby scandal of 1844 be said to be ended. In this matter, of course, Lord George Bentinck did have a vested interest, for he would have won a very large sum in bets if Ratan had won. But he was not a vindictive man – only one to whom the integrity of the turf was a matter of great concern.

The legal inquiry into the Derby running was held within a few weeks but the inquiry into the riding of the jockeys in the race – and notably of Sam Rogers on Ratan – was not held by the Stewards of the Jockey Club until the October Meeting at Newmarket. It is difficult to see why there was such a long delay, which left Sam Rogers under a cloud and only served to keep the unsavoury memory of the Derby alive in every racegoer's mind.

With Lord George Bentinck still acting as sleuth in the matter, Rogers must have spent an unhappy summer, for he had a wholesome respect for Lord George's secret sources of information. Rogers had never been able to learn how Lord George had discovered about his betting transactions with Gully in the first place, before ever the Derby had been run, and it was Rogers' confusion and embarrassment when first confronted about these bets which had really put Lord George on the scent, and had led to the scene with Gully before the Spread Eagle at Epsom. Lord George's chief commissioner, of course, was Harry Hill, the bookmaker, and Hill was a crony of Gully's. But would Gully ever have told Hill what he was up to, and would Hill ever have passed this information on to Lord George? The ramifications of this Derby of 1844 are endless; and the turf historian who sets out to explore them finds himself delving into many obscure corners, for this was certainly the twilight world of the double-dodge.

The outcome of the inquiry, when it was finally staged, was

that Sam Rogers was found guilty and warned off Newmarket Heath, which was equivalent to a total exclusion from all English racing for life.

It says something for Lord George's magnanimity that he was instrumental in getting this sentence reviewed by the Jockey Club three years later; and since Lord George was by then the Senior Steward, Sam Rogers was allowed to return to the turf. The Stewards, in giving their judgement, expressed their hope 'that the punishment these delinquents have received may be a warning to them which they will never forget, and that their conduct hereafter may justify the leniency now extended to them' which was the Jockey Club's way of saying that they were all heartily sick of the Derby scandal of 1844, and were devoutly hoping that such things as occurred at Epsom on that afternoon in May, 1844, would never occur again.

Perhaps their hope was fulfilled. By 1848 after Rogers had scored a brilliant victory in the Cesarewitch, Lord George's trainer, John Kent, in his biography of his much revered master, was able to make the pious observation that 'all recollection of Ratan's year, and of other transgressions, was obliterated from the public mind'.

The public memory is notoriously short. By the autumn of 1848, William Crockford had been in his grave for more than four years, whilst Gully had won the Derby of 1846 with Pyrrhus the First, although the 'legs' had previously done for him again in the Derby of 1845, when his much-fancied runner, Old England, had unquestionably been 'got at', and the menacing shadow of Hargreaves, that sinister figure from Manchester, had once again been cast across the path of a fancied Derby runner.

But here again, we need shed no tears for 'Honest John'. Those who live by the sword also perish by it, and those whose purpose in life is to cheat others are often in the end cheated themselves. John Gully lived on until 1862, becoming ever more honoured and respected in the north of England, and ever richer as well. He married twice, and had in all 24 children. In this he was ostensibly representative of the new Victorianism, which stood for middle-class respectability, a large family, the sanctity of the home, regular attendance at Church on Sunday, and growing prosperity. But he happily coupled it with sharp practice, double-dealing and ruthlessness restricted to business only, and was careful to cloak it with the outward garment of pious righteousness.

William Crockford, to a lesser extent, had followed the same pattern in life and in death, dying in the utmost respectability and in a mansion of impressive size, and leaving behind him a devoted and sorrowing widow and 14 devoted and sorrowing children, all of whom were most handsomely provided for, and all of whom had received the advantages of a liberal education; for according to Crockford's biographer in *Bentley's Miscellany*, writing not long after his death, 'Some are entered of learned and liberal professions, others are engaged in trade, but all employed in honourable and lucrative pursuits. One son is handsomely endowed in the Church, and three others are carrying on the business of wine merchants in St James's Street. Of the female portion of the family, one is married to an eminent medical practitioner. The widow of Mr Crockford is a lady of refined manners and amiable disposition, and much and deservingly respected by those who have the pleasure of her acquaintance. To her extreme care and attention in the exercise of such qualities, Mr Crockford owed not only the enjoyment of great domestic comfort, but the correction of much of his early coarse and un-educated manner, and the removal of habits ill-suited to his after associations.'

Thus the sins of the father were not visited on the children, but rather the income from around three-quarters of a million pounds.

The closing stages of the Crockford saga ends, therefore, as it began, in a cloud of obscurity. Mrs Crockford, who must always have found herself a little overwhelmed by the grandeur of her surroundings in Carlton House Terrace and by the noble breeding of her neighbours there, sold the house to Henry Granville, the Earl of Arundel and Surrey, who became the 14th Duke of Norfolk some ten years later. He subsequently passed it on to William Ewart Gladstone, who invested the building with the ultimate aura of respectability, and even held cabinet meetings there during his premiership, in a room which had once been much favoured by William Crockford.

Tempora mutantur, nos et mutamur in illis: which, in this context, can be roughly translated as, 'The times change, and even Carlton House Terrace may change with them.'

After quitting Carlton House Terrace, Mrs Crockford turned her attention to that white elephant of St James's Street, the Crockford Bazaar, reconstructed it, divided it into two storeys and converted it into Chambers. Having done which she withdrew from the fashionable scene altogether and lived out the remainder of her days in comfort on her husband's fortune.

She revealed no sentimental attachment to his birthplace, the bulk shop at Temple Bar, which he had still owned at his death and to which he had refused any alterations to be made during his life-time. It was pulled down in 1846, being then one of the last of its kind in London. The old Temple Bar itself was removed in 1878 and re-erected in private grounds at Theobalds Park, Cheshunt; and the site of the bulk shop is now occupied by the Law Courts, at the entrance to Fleet Street. The monument known as 'The Griffin' marks the site of the Temple Bar.

Thus William Gladstone, that pillar of the parliamentary establishment, came to occupy the mansion where Crockford died, and the manufactory of British Justice came to be erected on the spot where William Crockford had been born. In all this there may be a moral; but if there is, the reader is invited to draw it for himself.

It is doubtful if either Mrs Crockford or the family – or indeed William Crockford himself – were much interested in the future of Crockford's Club once he had washed his hands of it. The Committee tried to struggle on after his departure, but they were fighting a losing battle. The end came on the last day of 1845. A friend of Tommy Duncombe, now the chief exponent of radical views in the House of Commons, wrote to him on Christmas Eve of 1845 with the news that the Club was to be closed on the 1st of January. 'It appears there is no intention to form another club out of it. In fact, it is such a motley set that there would be great difficulty to do so.'

The interior was re-decorated in 1849 and was then opened

for the Military, Naval and County Service, but was closed again two years later. It then degenerated into a cheap dining-house, named 'The Wellington'. The sight of the once famous Club, shorn of all its former glory and become instead a refuge for the destitute, brought a lump to the throat of Captain Gronow as he passed by it many years later.

How are the mighty fallen! Irish buckeens, spring captains, 'welchers' from Newmarket, and suspicious-looking foreigners, may be seen swaggering, after dinner, through the marble halls and up that gorgeous staircase where once the chivalry of England loved to congregate; and those who remember Crockford's in all its glory, cast, as they pass, a look of unavailing regret at its dingy walls, with many a sigh to the memory of the pleasant days they passed there, and the gay companions and noble gentlemen who have long since gone to their last home.

This fall from grace was terminated when it became the home of the Devonshire Club, who still occupy the building at the top of St James's Street, a stone's throw from Piccadilly. Ben Wyatt's rather severe but elegant Georgian frontage has been overlaid with some late 19th-century ornamentations; but the exterior still remains basically as it was when Crockford's Club was opened in 1828.

Of Crockford relics in the Club there are very few; a gaming-table, some chairs, an etching by R. Seymour – but little else, save for the cellars, reputed to have been designed by Crockford for the dual purpose of serving as a cockpit and as a secret exit or hiding-place in case of trouble.

As for the title of 'Crockford's Club', this remained in abeyance from 1844 until 1928, when it was formed again and existed for some time as a bridge club. The Betting and Gaming Act of 1960 provided an opportunity for something of the original club's gambling traditions to be revived, and Crockford's Club is now today to be found in Carlton House Terrace – but at No. 16 and not in William's old house at No. 11.

The atmosphere is luxurious, but who can say whether some late 20th-century chronicler, writing his reminiscences of the fashionable London scene after the manner of Captain Gronow, may be inspired to make reference to 'the clear, ringing voice' of a player such as that agreeable reprobate, Tom Duncombe, as he cheerfully calls a seven, or of noting 'the powerful hand' of some modern Sefton in throwing for a ten.

The age of Crockford ended with their passing, but at least they had one honourable tradition to pass on to the gamblers who have followed their example through the passing years – 'the gentlemanly bearing and calm and unmoved demeanour, under losses or gains, of all the men of that generation'.

BIBLIOGRAPHY

There is a surfeit of material which covers the background to the Crockford era, but the foreground is harder to fill in, so that the picture is complete in some respects and incomplete in others. Crockford's childhood and private life, as has already been observed in the *Foreword*, remains shadowy. But there are numerous contemporary descriptions of him in the role of bookmaker, backer, racehorse owner and club proprietor. Histories of London itself, and histories of the London clubs, contain frequent references to Crockford's Club in St James's Street.

The most informative work on William Crockford and his club is *Crockford's*, by A. L. Humphreys, which was published by Hutchinson in 1953. In this the author set out to collect all the available material about the building of the Club in 1827, its opening in 1828 and the personalities who were to be encountered there during its golden era. It contains numerous extracts from the principle contemporary sources, including verse by Luttrell and others; and descriptions of the Club and its members given by Captain Gronow in his *Reminiscences*; in the Greville Diary; and in the Creevey Papers. It also contains a list of the principal members of the Club, with their nicknames, and a list of the Crockford characters who have appeared in fiction. It is a very detailed work, although it only numbers some two hundred pages. It contains a long list of the chief authorities which should be consulted by those doing research into the Crockford era, and since these are the authorities which I have consulted myself, I shall only deal with them briefly in this bibliography, and suggest that anyone who intends to carry out any extensive investigations into Crockford's life should first obtain a copy of A. L. Humphreys' book. I am happy to acknowledge my debt to him.

No full-length biography of William Crockford ever appears to have been written. The longest assessment of him is that which appeared in *Bentley's Miscellany* in the year after his death, but even this does not run to much more than 25 pages. In 1951 The Falcon Press published a novel by Connery Chappell called *Two Pleasures for Your Choosing* which gives an informative account of William Crockford's life, although fictional characters are also introduced. In his Author's Note at the end of this book, Mr Chappell also lists the sources of his information, which inevitably duplicate the list given by A. L. Humphreys.

The history of gambling is described in detail by Alan Wykes in *Gambling*, which was published in 1964 by Aldus Books. For the mathematicians, and those who like to view gambling as an intellectual exercise rather than a human failing, *Focus on Gambling*, by E. Lenox Figgis, published by Arthur Barker in 1951, will prove informative, and Lancelot Hogben's *Mathematics in the Making* (Macdonald, 1960) has a chapter on the history of gambling and the theory of probability. The classic work on the subject of gambling and gamblers is, of course, *The Gamblers*, which was written by Andrew Steinmetz in 1870 in two volumes. This is full of anecdotes about gamblers and their ways, and contains some interesting information about Crockford and his Club. Historians such as Trevelyan have plenty to say about the gambling disease which proved so injurious to 18th-century Society, and I would refer my readers, as I have already referred them in *Old Q*, to Trevelyan's *The Early History of Charles James Fox*, in which he has much to say about the manner in which impressionable young men were led astray and ruined. The psychological angle, particularly in so far as it concerns the effects of a matriarchal society on the male ego, is discussed by Gordon Rattray Taylor in *The Angel-Makers, A Study in the Psychological origins of historical change, 1750–1850*, which was published by Heinemann in 1958. Finally, in the realm of fiction, there is much to be learnt about the lust for gambling in Dostoevsky's novel, *The Gambler*, for the author was himself a compulsive gambler.

In my earlier chapters I discuss Crockford's London, and deal at length with the two worlds which he occupied – the world of Temple Bar, Fleet Street and the Strand, which was the world of his childhood and the formative years; and the world of St James's Street and fashionable Society, which was the world which he later succeeded in invading. The number of books which have been written about both are legion, and there is no point in burdening the reader with a lengthy catalogue. I will therefore only mention the books on which I have relied.

Topographically, Hugh Phillips' *Mid-Georgian London* is my basic work of reference, but those who require even greater detail about the history of London should consult *The Survey of London* produced by the Greater London Council at County Hall, Westminster – a work of many volumes that is still incomplete. *The 18th Century in London*, by Beresford Chancellor (Batsford, 1920) is another book to which I constantly refer, and so also is Reginald Colby's *Mayfair* (Country Life, 1966). Boswell's *London Journal, 1762–1763*, gives all the local gossip of Fleet Street and the Strand in the period just preceding Crockford's birth; and then, of course, there are the basic works on London life, London slums and the misery suffered by London's poor throughout the centuries – Mayhew's *Characters* and Mayhew's *London's Underworld*, Taine's *Notes on England*, E. Royston Pike's *Human Documents of the Industrial Revolution in Britain* and *Human Documents of the Victorian Golden Age*, R. J. Mitchell and M. D. R. Leys' *A History of London Life*, Griffith's *Chronicle of Newgate*, Bloch's *Sexual Life in England, Past and Present*, and the novels of Dickens. To this list I would also add, as of particular interest, W. C. Sydney's *England and the English in the 18th Century*, published in 1891.

Those who wish to get the 'feel' of London life in the Crockford era, especially in so far as it affected the young sporting bloods of the period, should read Pierce Egan's contemporary description of it: *Life in London; or, The Day and Night Scenes of Jerry Hawthorn, Esq., and his elegant friend, Corinthian Tom, accompanied by Bob Logic, Oxonian, in their Rambles and Sprees through the Metropolis*. Also the sequel, *Real Life in London*, with its many illustrations by R. and G. Cruickshank, W. Heath and H. Alken, Dighton, Brooke, Rowlandson and others, some of which have been produced in *Hell and Hazard*. I would also recommend *Rogue's Progress*, edited by John L. Bradley and published in 1966 by Longman's, which is the autobiography of Renton Nicholson, a notorious confidence trickster of the period who has some interesting things to say about Crockford and his club. A more general survey of this area is provided by Beresford Chancellor's *Life in Regency and Early Victorian Times* which was published by Batsford in 1926.

Descriptions of William Crockford, Crockford's Club and the Crockford set in general appear frequently in the works of the 19th-century novelists. These are recorded in detail in A. L. Humphreys' book, already referred to, and it is only necessary to list here Disraeli's *Sybil, Coningsby, Endymion, Vivian Grey* and *Henrietta Temple;* Thackeray's *Pendennis;* Bulwer Lytton's *Paul Clifford;* Harrison Ainsworth's *Crichton;* Henry Luttrell's *Crockford House* and *Crockford's or Life in the West*.

Numerous books have been written on the history of London's clubs, and Crockford's Club is mentioned in the majority of them. Its former premises are now occupied by the Devonshire Club, the history of which was written in 1919 by H. T. Waddy in a book called *The Devonshire Club and Crockford's*. Reference should also be made to Beresford Chancellor's *Memoirs of St James's Street* (Grant Richards 1922) and Ralph Nevill's *London Clubs* (Chatto and Windus, 1911). Benjamin Wyatt, the architect of the Club, is referred to in most of the histories of English architecture, and his family life is described by Anthony Dale in his biography, *James Wyatt* (Blackwell, 1956).

All the major histories of the turf refer to both William Crockford and John Gully, and John Gully is, of course, referred to at equal length in all the leading histories of English pugilism. Pierce Egan's *Boxiana* tells the story of John Gully's exploits in the ring, and Thormanby's *Kings of the Turf* has a chapter on Gully, and also one on Lord George Bentinck and on Admiral Rous. Both Crockford and Gully are to be encountered in Frank Siltzer's *Newmarket* and J. S. Fletcher's *History of the St Leger Stakes*.

The Derby of 1844 figures prominently in all histories of the Derby, of which the best-known are the recently published *The Derby Stakes* by Roger Mortimer, and *The History and Romance of the Derby*, by E. Moorhouse. The Derby scandal of 1844, and the legal wrangle which followed it, are described in T. H. Bird's *Admiral Rous and the English Turf* and John Kent's *Racing Life of Lord George Cavendish Bentinck*. My admiration for Lord George and my suspicions about the character of John Gully are echoed in William Day's *Reminiscences of the Turf*. The basic facts about the running of this Derby of 1844 are given in *The Racing Calendar of 1844*, which also outlines the litigation which followed the witholding of the stake money from the winning owners. It was something of a *cause célèbre*, and is also often to be encountered in law books and in biographies of the prominent legal figures who took part in the case.

Index